D.L. NELSON & J.Z. WILLIAMS
18881   MORA KAI LN. #21
HUNTINGTON BEACH, CA 92646

GOD IS RED

GOD IS RED

A Native View of Religion

Second Edition

VINE DELORIA, JR.

NORTH AMERICAN PRESS
A Division of Fulcrum Publishing
Golden, Colorado

Library of Congress Cataloging-in-Publication Data

Deloria, Vine.
    God is red : a native view of religion / Vine Deloria, Jr.
— 2nd ed.
       p.   cm.
    Includes bibliographical references and index.
    ISBN 1-55591-904-9 :
    1. Christianity—Controversial literature. 2. Indians—Religion and mythology. I. Title.
BL2776.D44   1993
299'.7--dc20   92-32065
                                                 CIP

Printed in the United States of America

0 9 8 7 6 5 4 3 2 1

North American Press
a division of Fulcrum Publishing
350 Indiana Street, Suite 350
Golden, Colorado 80401-5093

Contents

53102

INTRODUCTION

When I was a boy I often accompanied my father on trips to the different Sioux reservations in South Dakota. During these trips he would point out various features of the landscape and tell me the names and stories associated with them. Regrettably, I can only remember a few of the places today, but indelibly imprinted on my mind was the fact that the Sioux people cherished their lands and treated them as if they were people who shared a common history with humans. In 1972 when I was writing the first version of this book, I sought to emphasize the role that spaces and places play in our human religious perceptions.

From the invasion and occupation of Alcatraz in 1969 to the occupation at Wounded Knee in 1973, I felt that the various Indian protests had a much deeper meaning than simply securing additional lands for reservations. At the bottom of everything, I believed then and continue to believe, is a religious view of the world that seeks to locate our species within the fabric of life that constitutes the natural world, the land and all its various forms of life. As long as Indians exist there will be conflict between the tribes and any group that carelessly despoils the land and the life it supports. At the deepest philosophical level our universe must have as a structure a set of relationships in which all entities participate. Within the physical world this universal structure can best be understood as a recognition of the sacredness of places.

I have been very pleased to see the outpouring of books and articles attempting to deal with sacred spaces and places by Indian and non-Indian writers in the two decades since *God Is Red* was first published. It will take a continuing protest from an increasingly large chorus to reprogram the psychology of American society so that we will not irreversibly destroy the land we live on. Today our society is still at a primitive aesthetic stage of appreciating the personality of our lands, but we have the potential to move beyond mere aesthetics and come to some deep religious realizations of the role of sacred places in human life.

Feeling that a sufficiently significant number of people are now alerted to the ecological meltdown that we face, in this revised edition of the book I have felt free to raise additional questions about our species and our ultimate fate. It seems to me that our history on earth is far different than what we have been taught to believe. I suggest in this revised edition that we have on this planet two kinds of people—natural peoples and the hybrid peoples. The natural peoples represent an ancient tradition that has always sought harmony with the environment. Hybrid peoples are the product of what I refer to in chapter 9 as ancient genetic engineering that irrevocably changed the way these people view our planet. I can think of no other good reason why the peoples from the Near East—the peoples from the Hebrew, Islamic, and Christian religious traditions—first adopted the trappings of civilization and then forced a peculiar view of the natural world on succeeding generations. The planet, in their view, is not our natural home and is, in fact, ours for total exploitation. We are today reaching the "nth" term in this sequence of exploitation and face ecological disasters of such complete planetary scope as to surpass our wildest imagination.

Only a radical reversal of our attitudes toward nature can help us. While it is comforting to see the nations of the world meet and begin to deal with our environmental catastrophe, we may even now be too late to change the conditions we have created. It is extremely disturbing to see so many Americans wanting to clear cut the ancient forests, overgraze the remaining grasslands, and use the precious water of the continents for frivolous consumptive purposes. How many shopping malls and parking lots do we really need? In the

United States we stand but a few dry years from ecological disasters that we cannot begin to fathom. Yet we see our government busy authorizing the destruction of the remaining wetlands on the continent so that a few developers can squeeze yet a few more dollars from a complacent public.

We are now in the process of celebrating the 500th anniversary of the discovery of the New World and the attitudes that marked the original discovery remain entrenched. In two recent decisions the U.S. Supreme Court has all but prohibited the practice of Indian traditional religions (*Lyng*, 1988 and *Smith*, 1990) and opened Indian lands to coalitions of developers, mining interests, and other exploiters. All this exploitation unwittingly aided by the Christian churches, which have no understanding of the nature of the creation, now presses traditional people to the wall. It gives me no comfort to have predicted religious confrontation two decades ago only to see it now in its most virulent form. Nor do I look forward to paying the penalties that Mother Earth must now levy against us in order for Her to survive.

In traveling around the country I now see revivals of ancient ceremonies in many tribes as if the people had been warned of the catastrophes that await us. It is time for the people to gather and perform their old ceremonies and make a final effort to renew the earth and its peoples—hoofed, winged, and others. Because many of these ceremonies are performed on behalf of the earth, all humans, and the other forms of life, it seems incomprehensible that they would be prohibited. But the prohibitions and the failure of the government to protect these traditions only highlights the nature of the conflict. Clearly the struggle is between a religious view of life and the secularization that science and industry have brought.

It remains for us to learn once again that we are a part of nature, not a transcendant species with no responsibilities to the natural world. As we face the twenty-first century, the next decade will be the testing ground for this proposition. We may well become one of the few species in this vast universe that has permanently ruined our home. Future explorers from other planets will walk this earthly wasteland and marvel at our stupidity and wonder why we could not accept the reality of our own finitude.

Vine Deloria, Jr.

CHAPTER 1

THE INDIAN MOVEMENT

Until 1890 American Indians played a critically important role in American domestic affairs, symbolizing the vast wilderness and frontier that Americans wished to tame. From the 1890s until the 1960s Indians were truly the "Vanishing Americans" and most people believed that the tribes had largely been exterminated. There were token Indians present at Columbus Day and Thanksgiving celebrations and some Indian women sitting at the Santa Fe railroad stations selling pottery, but for most Americans Indians had ceased to exist.

It is difficult to describe just how America began to embrace Indians again in recent years. When the Indian protests began in the 1960s, white Americans learned that in the remote canyons of the West, the swamplands of the Great Lakes, and the southeastern United States were seemingly thousands upon thousands of Indians. Perhaps their first response was a sense of outrage and shock. Where were these angry Indians coming from and what was their gripe? They soon discovered that Indians had enjoyed treaty rights for nearly a century. They learned that as resources had been gobbled up by urban America they were now in conflict with American Indians over the remaining natural resources of the continent, the best of which were in Indian hands.

The initial tendency of many whites was simply to demand that these resources also be taken and that Indians be moved into the mainstream of white society thereby removing their legal rights to these lands. Needless to say, these same officials did not demand that African Americans and Chicanos or Hispanic Americans be given the same rights as whites; they were not sitting on oil, water, and mineral resources. White America only agitated to take away whatever rights Indians still had. Always this pressure was disguised under the argument that all people, being citizens, should enjoy the same basic rights. Thus where Indians had preserved hunting and fishing rights, the right to self-government, tax exemptions on land, the power to zone reservation lands, the cry was to bring about equality. At the county and town level, where Indians did not have employment, housing, equal criminal justice, and social equality, there was no corresponding effort to provide these things that allegedly all Americans enjoyed.

In the 1860s conditions were terrible for American Indians. The California Indians, for example, had been systematically neglected by generations of state and federal bureaucrats. In the 1850s the federal government had signed a series of treaties with the bands and communities of Indians in California. These treaties gave the Indians clearly defined reservations in certain areas of the state, primarily in places not wanted by the whites or at that time inaccessible to them. But as gold fever grew in intensity, and mining technology grew more sophisticated, arriving settlers began to prowl the length and breadth of the state looking for gold. The miners' objections to the federal effort to preserve the Indian ancestral lands were loud and violent.

The miners embarked on a program of systematic genocide against the Indians of California, going so far as to have Sunday "shoots" in which bands of whites would attack Indian villages killing as many people as they could. Tribes were massacred to prevent them from holding their lands intact and out of reach of the gold-crazed miners. Political pressure was intense in Washington, D.C., and the California Indian treaties were never ratified by the U.S. Senate. Instead they were conveniently buried in the Senate archives, where they remained as classified documents for a half century. By the 1960s most whites in California were not aware of the treatment of the indigenous peoples and had not the faintest idea that they had made treaties with clearly defined boundaries.[1] State and government officials were not so innocent, however.

During the Great Depression the Bureau of Indian Affairs (BIA) was given orders to find lands for the many homeless California Indians who now lived in tiny pockets of poverty on the outskirts of cities in the extreme southern and mountainous northern parts of the state. Agriculture was having a difficult time of it during the Depression and so the program was used to assist wealthy white landowners, primarily ranchers and farmers, instead of the Indians. Lands classified as "submarginal"—lands that the Department of Agriculture believed could not support a family farm or ranch—were purchased from the whites to prevent their bankruptcy and given to the Indians. Some Indians did move to these lands and the BIA organized them as tribal governments under the 1934 Indian Reorganization Act. Then, they were largely abandoned by the federal government because the populations of most of these new reservations were so small that national programs could not reach them.

During World War II a large number of Indians came to the west coast to work in war industries, and after the war they were shunted aside as returning white veterans were given back their jobs. In the 1950s, in order to get Indians off their reservations so that the lands could be sold and the tribal existence terminated, the BIA began a massive "relocation" program that placed thousands of Indians in low-paying jobs in the urban areas of California, primarily Los Angeles, San Francisco-Oakland, and San Jose. By the 1960s this mixture of original California Indians and newly migrated Southwestern and Plains Indians formed a community to assert their Indian identity. Thus, the first stirrings of what became known as the Indian movement began.

In almost every other part of the nation, Indians were treated with disgust and disdain by the whites of their region. South Dakota, the beautiful land of Kevin Costner's *Dances with Wolves*, was littered with signs reading "No Dogs and No Indians Allowed." Oklahoma systematically oppressed Indians while on festive occasions its politicians laid claim to Cherokee, Chickasaw, and Choctaw bloodlines from a mythical princess who had saved a wandering white man who startlingly resembled Gary Cooper. If Oklahoma Indians realized the repressive conditions under which they lived, many simply accepted that Indians' fortunes were supposed to be harder than whites because Indians were stupid. However, most of the Oklahoma tribes maintained their own societies and ceremonies belying the myth of inferiority that kept them in social and economic bondage.

Most Eastern Indians (with the exception of the Six Nations whose cultural survival was chronicled by Edmund Wilson in his best-selling book *Apologies tc the Iroquois*) simply did not admit to an Indian identity to avoid being singled out for discriminatory treatment. They kept most of their traditions to themselves and were highly suspicious of outsiders. But their history was beyond dispute in most instances. The Tunicas of Louisiana, for example, could trace their political lineage back to the days of French occupation of the Mississippi Valley; the Passamaquoddys and Penobscots of Maine still possessed a letter from George Washington that he sent at the beginning of the Revolutionary War asking them to *please* side with the colonists.

In the Southwest most of the tribes were just beginning to discover the invading white urban society around them. On the Navajo, Papago, and Apache reservations the majority of people were full-bloods, spoke their own languages and practiced traditional religions. A surprising number had only seen one or two whites in their lives, usually the local BIA agent or schoolteacher. In the Pacific Northwest the Indians struggled with fish and game agencies to preserve their treaty fishing rights. Washington state was systematically breaking the six treaties signed with the Indians between 1854 and 1855. These agencies claimed that it was necessary to curb Indian fishing for conservation purposes at the same time they allowed commercial and sports fishermen to take almost all the annual salmon run. The Great Lakes Indians were living on barren reservations doing odd jobs for local whites. Their lands had been stripped of prime timber during the 1890s when the "timber ring" had worked with the BIA to strip the Indian forests on the pretext that removing the trees would enable Indians to become farmers.

In 1964 and 1965 there were some "fish-ins" in Washington state along the Nisqually River, one featuring Marlon Brando and Dick

Gregory. It was clear to careful observers that Indian country was about to explode, but the first significant protest occurred in Canada in 1968 when Canadian officials demanded that the Mohawks pay tolls to use a bridge and pay customs on goods brought back from the United States. On December 18, 1968, the Mohawks led by militant Kahn-Tineta Horn, a former actress and model, blockaded the Cornwall Bridge claiming Canada had violated the Jay Treaty of 1794. They were arrested and tried in March 1969, but the prosecutor levied wild charges and the Indians were acquitted. The incident, widely reported in *Akwesasne Notes*, a national Indian newspaper, inspired Indians all across the United States to take a closer look at protests.[2]

Pressure continued to build. The next major eruption occurred in Gallup, New Mexico, in August 1969. Gallup is a study in contrasts. It proudly brags that it is the Indian capital of the world. The town is almost totally dependent on its Indian trade. Yet, it systematically brutalizes its Indian population and excludes them from participation in most civic events. The National Indian Youth Council, some of whose members had been active in the fish-ins, protested the holding of the Gallup Ceremonial in the summer of 1967 by passing out mimeographed leaflets denouncing the festival. The leaflet was titled "When Our Grandfathers Had Guns" and refuted the happy image of smiling Indian pottery vendors that the Chamber of Commerce wished to perpetuate. It also protested that the ceremonial was largely controlled by non-Indians who gave minimal support to the Indian participants in the festival. This protest shocked the older Indians who had placidly accepted life in Gallup and felt confused about the fuss the young people were making. From the Indian standpoint the protest was a tremendous success because it was the younger generation that had taken a positive aggressive step in resolving local problems of discrimination.

The Pacific Northwest had its share of problems. The Quinault tribe had been pleading with non-Indians to refrain from littering its beaches but to no avail. Owning 29 miles of the last good stretch of beach in the area, the tribe wanted to protect its resource, but non-Indian tourists wandered over the area removing large quantities of driftwood and stealing or destroying Indian fishing nets. In 1969 the tribe closed the beaches to the public. White response was quick in coming; petitions were sent to the governor asking him to institute legal proceedings against the tribe. Then Attorney General Slade Gorton (now U.S. Senator) said he didn't think the tribe had the "unchallenged right to exclusive control of the beaches." He was ready to go to federal court to defend the right of non-Indians to litter and destroy, but the beaches remained closed.

These actions dealt primarily with local problems. They inspired Indians across the continent to defend their rights, but what was needed was some national symbol, a rallying point, that could launch a national movement. At the end of October 1969 a large convention of urban Indian groups met in San Francisco to discuss their problems. The night after the convention dispersed the Indian Center caught fire and burned completely, a singularly tragic event for the Indian population in the Bay Area because social service programs and pow-wows were run out of the center for more than two decades. They were suddenly without a meeting place. Looking across the Bay at Alcatraz with its massive buildings sitting empty, the Indians knew they had found their national cause.

Securing Alcatraz for Indian use was an old goal of the Bay area community. After the prison had been closed in 1964, Allen Cottier, Dick MacKenzie, and Adam Nordwall, three Indians living in the area, had landed on the island and claimed it under the 1868 Sioux treaty, but there had been no effort to occupy the island. On November 9, 1969, a small contingent of Indians landed on the island and spent several exciting hours being chased by the security guards. They were taken off the island the next morning. Not the least bit discouraged, they regrouped and ten days later landed two hundredpeople and secured the prison. Calling themselves the "Indians of All Tribes," they issued a proclamation asking for title to the island so it could be used for a spiritual center, university, and social service center. They compared Alcatraz to most Indian reservations: no water, no good housing, land unfit for cultivation, no employment; in short, a prison. Although the composition of the group continued to change, Indians occupied the island for about a year and a half. By then other developments had taken the spotlight. During their tenure, however, they were visited by movie stars, appeared on the Merv Griffin talk show, and had a boat donated to them by the Credence Clearwater Revival rock group.

Indians in the Seattle area adopted the cognomen Indians of All Tribes and invaded Fort Lawton on the northwest corner of the city of Seattle during the winter of 1970. Jane Fonda, who had come to Seattle to protest the Vietnam War, participated in the invasion and helped to bring TV publicity to the protest. Rejecting the idea of claiming the fort under the 1868 Sioux treaty, the Seattle Indians used an old federal statute that allowed the use of abandoned federal military posts as Indian schools. Negotiating aggressively the Seattle Indians were able to secure a long term lease on some of the land and then built the Daybreak Star Center which is still a major part of the social services available to the Puget Sound Indian Community.

Invasions now seemed to come from every direction. The Six Nations landed protestors on Stanley Island that formed part of the St. Regis Mohawk reserve. The island extended a short distance into the St. Lawrence River and had been leased by the government in 1900 to an American citizen for the magnificent sum of $6 a year. Lots on the island were worth upwards of $20,000 for use for summer cottages. Involved in this protest was the question of whether or not the Six Nations were joint conquerors of Canada during the French and Indian War and therefore coowners of the Dominion. Therefore, the protest had a practical and a historical/ideological dimension both.

The summer of 1970 saw a full national Indian movement in action, protests happening in the most unexpected places and with irrefutable historic claims made by individual tribes. There was no sense of national coordination and the issues appeared to be a conglomerate of local complaints, which taken together could be resolved only with great difficulty. It was apparent, however, that beneath all of these local protests there was the important issue of restoring the old ways and raising the question of people and their right to a homeland; for Indians this meant a return to the ceremonial use of lands.

In June 1970 the Pitt River Indians tried to reclaim their ancestral lands from the Pacific Gas and Electric Company. Led by Richard Oakes and Mickey Gemmill, who had been active at Alcatraz, a task force of Indians occupied lands near Big Bend, California. The

Indians fully intended to reinstitute traditional religious life because the lands were near Mount Shasta, the center of their ceremonial life. Although arrested and charged with trespass, they were acquitted because no one wanted to bring up the treatment under the 1850s California treaties and the manner in which the California Indians were all lumped together in the California land claim.

In another urban center, the Chicago Indians established an Indian village as a protest against housing discrimination in that city pointing out that they had been forced into the cities because their lands had been taken by the government in the Menominee Termination and allotment of the small Wisconsin forest reservations. This protest was very important because it linked urban Indians and the old policies of the government, particularly those that forced Indians to leave their lands in rural areas. In an ideological structure, the Chicago protest finally put together easily articulated complaints against historic and existing BIA policies.

The movement had its humorous moments. The Indians of Milwaukee spread the rumor that they were going to invade the Milwaukee Yacht Club so they could have "Red Sons in the Sail Set," but it was rumor and nothing more.

At the encouragement of some of the aggressive Lutheran pastors working with Indians, AIM occupied a dormitory at Augustana Lutheran College in Sioux Falls, South Dakota, during a conference of the National Council of Churches in late summer to protest against the churches' lethargy in assisting Indians. The pastors wrote up a list of "unnegotiable demands" that they passed through a back window to the protestors so that the Indians learned why it was they had been protesting. Negotiations resulted in the establishment of community development funds and a Lutheran national council of Indians to supervise spending it.

In the Pacific Northwest the Indian fishing rights cause was a continuing problem, originating with the treaties by which the whites gained title to lands in Washington, Oregon, and Idaho. In 1854 and 1855 Isaac Stevens negotiated a series of treaties that guaranteed Indians the right to fish in their traditional sites. As soon as whites discovered the income in fishing they began to push Indians aside. Numerous Supreme Court cases clearly supported the Indian rights, but each succeeding state government found a way to quibble about the interpretation of the language in the treaties resulting in Indian arrests and attempts to get the federal courts to override the treaty provisions. Particularly annoying were the Nisquallies and Puyallups who now clung to the river banks making a living by fishing. They had lost most of their lands to whites through the forced sale of their allotments. In a continuing and escalating series of fishing rights confrontations just after Labor Day 1970, a fishing camp was set up near Tacoma, Washington. The Indians, primarily from the Nisqually and Puyallup tribes, were busy fishing and making preparations to take the fish back to their homes.

Almost three hundred Tacoma city police, state game wardens, and state police silently surrounded the camp. They trained telescopic rifles on the adult males who could be easily seen from the bushes in which the police force was hidden. Then the raid began.

Tear gas was thrown into the camp and the Indian fishermen and women were rushed and brutally beaten. As many as six policemen grabbed little Allison Bridges, a slip of a girl weighing less than 100 pounds and standing just above 5 feet tall, threw her to the ground and handcuffed her. People in the camp were arrested for disorderly conduct although the disorder was police inspired. The camp was leveled, the Indians' cars were impounded and taken to Tacoma where they were virtually destroyed while in police custody. Dick Cavett allowed me to show pictures of the attack on the Indian camp on his national television show resulting in a great public outcry against the actions of the police. As a result of the pressure, the federal government filed suit against the state of Washington and eventually won a ruling that entitled Indians of the state to receive an allocation of half the fish in the state.

When the trials of the Indian fishermen began it turned out that the arrests were illegal because neither the city of Tacoma nor Washington state had jurisdiction over the lands where the fishing camp was located. The question of jurisdiction continued to plague everyone and the Puyallup tribe began to negotiate with the city of Tacoma and the federal government to clarify jurisdiction. Finally in the late 1980s a settlement was worked out in which the tribe received over $150 million and additional land in exchange for modifying its reservation boundaries. The combination of the two developments, the winning of the fishing rights case and the settlement of the Puyallup boundary put sufficient pressure on the state of Washington that it sought to create better relations with the tribes. In 1990 it established a form of tribe-state compact with mutual recognition of each other's political status. Today the state is seen as the most progressive of the western states in its relations with Indians.

As 1971 opened it became apparent that the issue of grave robbing had not yet been satisfactorily resolved. Some whites had taken to heart the pleas and logic of some of the Indian protests and an interest in and awareness of Indian issues was rising dramatically across the nation. But most whites still did not know how to relate to living Indians. Their education had taught them that almost all the Indians were dead, so they promptly began to search for dead Indians. The results were confusing and devastating. In early June an Indian skeleton was uncovered on Cemetery Road near Lowville, New York. It was promptly taken in by the Lewis County Historical Society as an artifact. Mohawk chief Sakokwenonk asked for the skeleton back. "Many times people of the sciences do not respect the dead, and instead of making matters right, cause further difficulties by taking the bones into their own houses and place of work, storing them there, or bothering them further," he wrote to Arthur Einhorn curator of the Lewis County Historical Society.

Einhorn was sensitive to the Mohawk argument and used his influence to get the skeleton returned. The Mohawks took the bones to their reservation and conducted the proper burial ceremonies. In Minnesota budding anthropologists and archaeologists were not so enlightened.

In mid-June 1971, forty-five students from the Minneapolis area, sponsored by the Twin Cities Institute for Talented Youth, went to Welch, Minnesota, to begin a six-week project in excavating the site of an Indian village. The motivation for the students' fieldwork was puzzling. Apparently they may have been led to believe that digging up Indian remains was a form of showing respect. The students dug for about five weeks, carefully collecting materials and classifying them as "artifacts." The Indians of Minnesota were outraged by the excavations. They believed that the dead should be left alone. AIM, led by Clyde Bellecourte, invaded the site one evening. They took shovels away from the students, filled in the trenches, burned the excavation notes, and offered to compensate the students for property losses. They did not, however, want any further digging. They did not believe their ancestors had buried their dead for the express purpose of providing summer adventures.

The archaeologists directing the dig could not understand the viewpoint of the AIM members. Les Peterson, a Minnesota Historical Society member who had headed the excavation, declared "five weeks of work down the drain," indicating that the moral question of disturbing the dead eluded him. The students also failed to comprehend the problem. One student who had been planning a career in archaeology said the incident made her lose respect for Indians. Another student was in tears as she tried to explain how carefully the students had treated the materials they uncovered. Another student explained that they "were trying to preserve Indian culture, not destroy it."

None of the whites could understand that they were not helping living Indians preserve their culture by digging up the remains of a village that had existed in the 1500s. Daniel Dalton, assistant AIM program director, said that if the situation were reversed and Indians were digging up the site of a white colonial settlement, all hell would have broken loose. The general attitude of the whites, however, was that they were the true spiritual descendants of the original Indians and that the contemporary Indians were foreigners who had no right to complain about their activities. Everyone in Minnesota took sides in the dispute. Few non-Indians understood the Indian objections. Because Minnesota was at that time trying to levy an additional tax on Indian reserves, it was apparent that the only Indians worth preserving were dead ones.

Minnesota was a hotbed of compassion, however, in comparison to its neighbor Iowa. In early June 1971 the state highway department began a new road project about 2 1/2 miles from Glenwood, Iowa. Work progressed until one day a bulldozer uncovered an unmarked cemetery. It was quite old, the bodies were only about 6 inches beneath the topsoil. Ernest Barker, a long-time inhabitant of the area who lived in nearby Pacific Junction, estimated that the cemetery was at least a century old because he thought his grandmother and three of her children had been buried there in 1867.

As the roadwork continued, bits of tombstones and the bodies of twenty-seven people were uncovered. One of the bodies was buried with several hundred glass beads, some brass finger rings, and metal earrings. This body was tentatively identified as the remains of an Indian girl, although there was absolutely no way that any positive identification could be confirmed. No such artifacts were discovered with the bodies under the other tombstones. The remains of the other twenty-six bodies were reverently taken to the Glenwood Cemetery and reburied. The remains believed to be an Indian girl had another destination. State Archaeologist Marshall McKusick demanded that the bones be sent to him under the provisions of an Iowa law that entrusted him with articles of historical importance.

Running Moccasins, an Indian woman concerned about discrimination, demanded that the bones, considered those of an Indian girl, be given proper burial after she discovered that they had been taken to Iowa City for a museum exhibit. She called McKusick's office several times, but he refused to answer her calls. When asked about his stand on the matter McKusick replied, "I don't want that woman to think in any way that if she raises a fuss, I'll give her a couple of boxes of bones." Running Moccasins appealed to Governor Robert Ray who suddenly became too busy to see her and allowed his aides to turn her pleas aside.

McKusick remained formally committed to his stand claiming, "I just can't go giving remains to private individuals. It sounds nice to say just give them back to the Indians so that the girl can be reburied, but I have to follow the Code of Iowa." Later McKusick said that it would take a court order for him to release the remains to the tribe to which the girl belonged. Apparently he was unable to discover the tribes to which the twenty-six white bodies had belonged. Rather than place all the bones down at Iowa City, he took only the Indian remains to his museum, allowing the bones of the whites, which under the Code of Iowa were of no historical significance, to be reburied at the Glenwood Cemetery. The ironic part of this controversy is that there was no proof other than the jewelry that the skeleton was that of an Indian. It might just as well have been that of Ernest Barker's grandmother because whites had glass beads and brass finger rings also. But the fact that it *might have been* an Indian skeleton meant discriminatory treatment.

By early fall 1971, Indians were on the defensive all over the country, trying to prevent the looting of their burial grounds. Whites were just as determined to preserve Indian culture on their terms even if they had to dig up every Indian skeleton on the continent. Near Pedricktown, New York, the Abnaki Archaeological Society continued its excavation of an old Abnaki village site, uncovering its ninth body in less than a year. A story about Abnaki in early September in *The Philadelphia Inquirer*, optimistically related that the digs would reveal a cross section of Indian life and not just burial patterns. It would have been nice if the settlers in the region had learned something from the Abnaki when they were contemporaries so that the dig would not have been necessary.

In neighboring Pennsylvania, the looting of Indian graves became a community function. The archaeology section of the William Penn Memorial Museum in Harrisburg uncovered three Susquehannock villages near Paxton. Four graves containing two infants and two adults were exposed. In an interview with the *Paxton Herald* Ira F. Smith III, expedition leader, declared the West Branch Project an "overwhelming success" not only from the scientific standpoint but also from the human interest it generated. He applauded volunteer participation from local residents who usually fail to comprehend the purpose of field explorations and seem to resent such a presence in their locality.

There was great historic irony in these tender excavations to learn about the Susquehannock Indians. On December 14 and 27, 1764, a local group known now as the Paxton Boys massacred two villages of Christian Indians, accusing them of aiding the tribes on the frontier in sporadic attacks on the settlements. After the two massacres the Paxton Boys marched in Philadelphia, where some 500 Christian Indians had been taken by the Moravians for safety, and announced to Governor John Penn that they were going to kill every Indian in Pennsylvania. Benjamin Franklin helped to turn aside this slaughter. So, little over two hundred years later, the great-grandsons of the Paxton Boys were at it again.

In Illinois the Field Museum of Natural History was not to be left behind in the race to uncover Indian skeletons. Anthropology students, digging under museum auspices, unearthed the remains of nine Indians buried under a motorcycle path in a forest preserve. The museum made its find public with glowing reports that the bodies were those of Miami Indians of the late seventeenth century. Since the Miamis used to live in Indiana before they were forced to move to Oklahoma, the museum made plans to ship the remains to Indiana University for display. But the Chicago Indians arrived at the museum to confront Dr. Donald Collier, museum curator. Mattehew War Bonnet, leader of the Indian delegation, demanded that the bones be given to the group for a ceremonial burial in a Winnebago burial ground in Wisconsin.

The museum agreed and the Indians took the bones to Wisconsin Dells and held a burial ceremony. The museum paid for the evening ceremonial fire, hired a medicine man to perform the ceremonies, and provided gifts to be given at the ceremonies. The museum wryly noted that, despite providing financial support for the Indians, it did not want to be considered a "soft touch," indicating that this was a one-time arrangement. But the Field Museum was headed in the right direction. Later in 1989 and 1990 its representatives participated in an Indian/museum dialog that led to national legislation repatriating human skeletal remains to the tribes. Reports were that Field has played a major role in bringing the museum community to see the Indian point of view.

The final, bizarre, and perhaps fitting touch to this summer of looting Indian graveyards was the invasion of a century-old Nez Percé burial ground near Clarkston, Washington. Thieves invaded the sacred grounds and drove rods into the ground to locate the coffins of the Indians. Then they dug up the graves to take any jewelry that might have been buried with the bodies. The Indian skulls were stolen, many of them severed from the rest of the body, and sold in an underground market in California where they brought as much as $20 dollars apiece. A white dentist paid an exorbitant price for the skull of Chief Joseph, beloved leader of the Nez Percé.

The grave robbing can be seen in another, more profound, and very disturbing light. Carl Jung, Swiss psychologist, suggested that we have a collective unconscious that lies behind, under, and in support of our conscious ego/personality. In his *Wotan* essays[3] Jung related how he was able to predict the rise of National Socialism by analyzing the dreams of young Germans shortly after World War I. He suggested that at times an idea, or archetype, might sweep into the consciousness of many individuals who were otherwise not known to each other nor related in any way, and inspire or motivate them to perform simultaneously certain actions that they did not really understand. If the propensity of whites during the summer of 1971 to grasp some bit of authenticity by locating, excavating, and embracing Indian skeletal remains can be interpreted as a frantic attempt to discard their own physical, cultural, and spiritual heritage, then the collective psyche of white America was indeed in deep trouble.

The outburst of grave robbing seemed to end abruptly after 1971, and the nation began to see sporadic killings of Indians. Early in 1972 five white men captured Raymond Yellow Thunder, a fifty-one-year old Sioux from the Pine Ridge reservation in Gordon, Nebraska. They severely beat him, stripped him of his clothes below the waist, and pushed him into an American Legion hall where a dance was in progress. Yellow Thunder thus became the grotesque amusement of white veterans his own age who had fought in World War II and Korea to protect American rights and liberties, including Yellow Thunder's rights and liberties. But the whites had no concept of these same rights applied to Indians. Yellow Thunder later died from his abuse.[4]

AIM was furious over the Yellow Thunder incident and called on the Nebraska Human Rights Commission to do something. When it refused to consider the complaint, AIM sent out a call for protestors and more than two thousand Indians swarmed into Gordon demanding justice. Federal authorities, who usually investigate civil rights crimes, decided they had no jurisdiction even though federal law requires the Justice Department to protect Indians. After much confusion, stalling, and passing the buck from one level of government to another, the whites responsible for this tragedy were charged on lesser counts and tried in Alliance, Nebraska, a town almost as notoriously anti-Indian as Gordon.

Within weeks of the Yellow Thunder episode Indians were killed in California and Arizona under suspicious circumstances. Russell Means, an Oglala Sioux and one of the leading AIM officers, urged a march on Washington to demand a federal law that would make it a crime to kill an Indian if it had to be as an amendment to the Endangered Species Act.

On a lonely piece of land in California, Richard Oakes, leader of the Alcatraz movement, was slain by Michael Morgan, a guard at a YMCA camp. Morgan claimed that Oakes had appeared from behind a clump of trees and had come menacingly toward him. However, there were no weapons found on or near Oakes at the time of the shooting. According to Indian witnesses, Oakes had gone to the camp to inquire about a young Indian boy who had had trouble with Morgan earlier in the week. Morgan was charged with involuntary manslaughter and set free on a $5,000 bail.[5]

By early October 1972 plans were well under way to form a caravan to march on Washington and demand a new Indian policy while there were still enough Indians alive to make it feasible. Cars filled with Indians left the West Coast, visiting as many reservations as possible on their drive eastward. The march became formally designated as the "Trail of Broken Treaties" because many of the complaints dealt with treaty violations. A major meeting was held in Minneapolis where the Indians sought to clarify their objectives prior to reaching Washington. The famous Twenty Points were constructed here, a list of reforms the people wanted to see initiated.

The march reached Washington, D.C., on the Friday before the national elections and immediately got into trouble. Advance men, headed by Robert Burnette, a Rosebud Sioux, had not made any provisions for housing and feeding the people. There was no place for the six-hundred-member contingent to stay. The leaders met with Commissioner Louis Bruce in the BIA headquarters. On November 2, as they were beginning to leave the BIA building, a scuffle broke out between the younger Indians and federal building guards. Fearing mass arrest and police brutality the Indians seized the building and began a wild weekend in which office furniture and BIA files were destroyed.

Operating behind the scenes, the White House was able to get the Indians to agree to vacate the building with the promise of a $66,000 grant (or bribe) to cover travel expenses. After a week of occupation before they left the Bureau, and the day before the election, some of the people moved a large number of files from the Bureau as "hostages" and hid them in obscure parts of the country, driving panel trucks filled with federal files from fifteen to eighteen hours to get far enough from Washington to make their escape complete. Later Hank Adams, one of the leaders of the caravan and one of the outstanding proponents of fishing rights in the Pacific Northwest, would try to secure possession of the documents and be arrested along with Les Whitten, an aide to Washington columnist Jack Anderson, who was doing a story on the occupation. The two men were held in jail while the FBI changed the arrest warrants made out for Jack Anderson, who they had hoped to arrest instead of Les Whitten.

According to the *Washington Post*, the occupation had done more damage to a federal building than had the British burning of the White House in the War of 1812.[6] Strangely, the public was in favor of the Indians; several congressmen noted that their mail was running nearly eight to one in favor of not prosecuting the activists. A few weeks after the occupation some tribal chairmen known to be favorably inclined toward the government were given a tour of the building to see the destruction. While they condemned the occupation, they also pointed out that the obscene slogans painted on the walls had fresh paint, indicating that parts of the scenario had been staged for their benefit.

The Indians went home. Many AIM members announced their intention to go to Pine Ridge and hold a victory celebration. But the government was ready for them. Funds had been given to Dickie Wilson, tribal chairman of the government at Pine Ridge, to increase its police force. Wilson hired a rough gang of reservation and bordertown toughs as his police. This special police force was soon harassing Wilson's political opponents claiming they were AIM members. Through December and January tensions quickly escalated at Pine Ridge. When efforts to impeach Wilson failed through procedural trickery, the situation reached the flashpoint for violence.

Then Wesley Bad Heart Bull, an Oglala Sioux, was killed in a bar in Buffalo Gap, South Dakota. When local police seemed hesitant about indicting his killer, an immediate storm of protest rose in western South Dakota, and a crowd of Indians went to the county seat in Custer to protest the police inactivity. Local and state police incited a riot during which a small Chamber of Commerce building was burned. The Indians then returned to Pine Ridge and the county attorneys began writing up charges against the identifiable leaders of the group.

Believing they had to make some kind of stand against the treatment they were receiving, in February 1973, a large contingent of Sioux Indians and their supporters marched in and occupied Wounded Knee, South Dakota, a small settlement consisting primarily of a trading post, a church, and a few houses. The move was a public relations coup. Most of the reading public were familiar with the massacre of Sioux Indians at Wounded Knee just after Christmas 1890 as a result of Dee Brown's popular bestseller, *Bury My Heart at Wounded Knee*. No one wanted a replay of that tragedy. The local tribal police, nicknamed the "Goon Squad," quickly surrounded the village and a standoff ensued.

The next two months were both tragic and comic. Rumor had it that Lehman Brightman, an Indian activist from the West Coast, had one thousand "dog soldiers" at Rapid City who were marching to the reservation to relieve the siege. Ralph Abernathy offered to intercede with President Nixon on behalf of the occupants of the village. Marlon Brando sent Sasheen Little Feather to reject his Oscar and chastise the Hollywood community for its detrimental portrayal of Indians. The occupation was on national television almost every night, and one evening people saw network crews helping to slaughter local cattle to feed the people. Many people assumed that the Indians did not know how to butcher. In reality this was a ploy so that the Indians were not seen butchering someone else's cattle in case they would be charged with rustling once the occupation was over.

Sporadic efforts to settle the dispute marked the two-month occupation. The White House played an active role in these efforts. Indeed, many people suspected that the incident was kept on the front pages so that the Watergate scandal, which was just breaking open, would not get national attention. In early May the Indians surrendered on the promise that the White House would send out a delegation to discuss the violations of the 1868 Sioux treaty. In June representatives of the president did come to the reservation and hold talks with the traditional chiefs, but nothing came of the discussions. In January 1974 AIM leadership trials began in St. Paul. The Indians had an outstanding defense team headed by William Kunstler, but the government had planted an undercover agent Douglas Durham as an AIM security officer. Everything the

Indians did to plan their defense was known immediately to the government.

The trial of Russell Means and Dennis Banks, two of the most vocal and charismatic Indian leaders, occupied headlines most of 1974. Although the government had a vast amount of incriminating evidence, it could not resist the temptation to make its case airtight. Consequently federal officials altered evidence and suborned witnesses to such a degree that Judge Nichols declared a mistrial. A high point of the trial was the testimony of the local Twin Cities FBI supervisor that he did not sign most of his correspondence, including Christmas cards, that he sent Judge Nichols. Consequently he did not recognize his signature on some of the sheets of tainted evidence.

The Wounded Knee trials pretty much checkmated the Indian movement. Most of the leadership were spending their time in court or preparing to defend themselves; it was impossible for them to take part in protests. But Wounded Knee had been such a media spectacular that no protest could have had any greater impact. For purposes that were never made clear FBI officers surrounded a home west of Pine Ridge in June 1975. The Indians, frightened by the presence of federal agents, fought back. Two FBI men were slain, Jack Coler and Ronald Williams. How these deaths came about is still vague. Peter Matthiessen presents a reasonable sequence in his book, *In the Spirit of Crazy Horse*. But many questions remain. The agents' bodies had multiple wounds, but the evidence indicates that the Indians fled the scene of the killing rather quickly. This has led people to speculate if the FBI itself did not mutilate the bodies in order to enhance sympathy for the federal position. Several Indians were accused of the killings. Leonard Peltier was convicted of them. Matthiessen outlines the many discrepancies and flagrant illegalities practiced by the federal government in order to get Peltier's conviction. However, all efforts to get Peltier a new trial have failed, and he remains a prisoner in a federal penitentiary.

Two measurable results came from the Wounded Knee occupation. In the summer of 1974, South Dakota senator James Abourezk introduced the American Indian Policy Review Commission Resolution and Congress authorized a two-year study of the conditions of Indians.[7] Unfortunately, the commission's work was subdivided among eleven task forces, organized by topics, and almost every Indian politician of note was placed on one of these task forces. In 1978, when the report was released, BIA employees were asked to write the final draft because there was so much material that the commission staff was overwhelmed. Thus the perennial enemies of Indians became the people who articulated what their problems were.

In the years following the Abourezk commission, several small pieces of legislation were passed by Congress including the American Indian Religious Freedom Resolution, which was considered critical to the protection of traditionals who continued the ceremonial and ritual life of the tribes. The Indian Child Welfare Act (1978) was also part of this reform legislation as well as an effort to upgrade reservation community colleges. Perhaps just as important was the tendency in Congress to work out settlements of long-standing problems and solve them by passing "settlement" acts that avoided prolonged and contentious litigation. Settlement involves handling a problem (i.e., water rights quantification, identification of land claims areas, or solution of a disputed boundary) by having the parties involved present a possible solution acceptable to all parties for consideration and passage by Congress as a statute thereby avoiding a federal or state court case.

The second result of the Indian activist movement was the tremendous surge of interest in traditional religions and customs. At the BIA occupation and again during the Wounded Knee confrontation, medicine men had been prominent in performing ceremonies for the activists. Leonard Crow Dog served some time in a federal prison for his prominence in the protests of the 1970s. Frank Fools Crow, a leader of the traditional people at Pine Ridge, was the leading spokesperson during the meeting with White House officials in the summer of 1973.

Years after Wounded Knee, Russell Means was asked what the beneficial results were, considering all the killings and violence that had infested the Pine Ridge reservation during 1973 and for years afterward. He told a little story of watching three little Indian boys playing. The two more aggressive boys chose to be Means and Banks. They pointed at the third boy and said, "You have to be Dickie Wilson."

The third boy went home crying. He was ashamed to even pretend to be a traitor to his own people. Somehow, through all of the protests and symbolic gestures, a different sense of Indian identity was born.

Notes

1. Jennings Wise covered the burial of the California treaties in his *Red Man in the New World* (Macmillan, 1971), which I updated. Aubrey Grossman, attorney for the Pitt River people, did a monograph on the treatment of the California Indians and in recent years additional materials have been published dealing with the California treaties.

2. *Akwesasne Notes*, the national newspaper published by the Mohawk people at Rooseveltown, New York, featured a series of articles and newspaper clippings on the Cornwall bridge incident during 1969 and 1970. Most libraries have copies of *Notes* for this period on microfilm of the issues covering the incident. I have briefly sketched the sequence of actions here by summarizing the various articles published in *Akwesasne Notes*.

3. Carl Jung, "Wotan," in *Civilization in Transit, Collected Works*, vol. 10 (New York: Pantheon Books, 1953–1979), 179–93.

4. The incident was well covered by the American Indian Press Association and later by writers who attempted to intepret the background of the Wounded Knee occupation. Peter Matthiessen's book, *In the Spirit of Crazy Horse* (New York: Viking Press, 1983), integrates the Raymond Yellow Thunder incident with Wounded Knee II very well.

5. Here again the accounts in *Akwesasne Notes* for 1972 Summer issue are most helpful in providing information on the Oakes killing.

6. The *Washington Post* had several articles suggesting this comparison, and I have adapted it. The articles ran approximately a week after the Indians left the BIA headquarters the second week in November.

7. Copies of the report can be obtained by writing the Senate Select Committee on Indian Affairs, Washington, D.C.

CHAPTER 2

THE INDIANS OF
THE AMERICAN IMAGINATION

Until the occupation of Wounded Knee, American Indians were stereotyped in literature and by the media. They were either a villainous warlike group that lurked in the darkness thirsting for the blood of innocent settlers or the calm, wise, dignified elder sitting on the mesa dispensing his wisdom in poetic aphorisms. Strangely, the malevolent image can be attributed to the movie carica-ture while the benign image comes from anthologies, pageants, and the fervent wish by non-Indians to establish some personal sense of Jungian authentication.

As the Civil Rights movement began to be eclipsed by antiwar protests, and Martin Luther King, Jr., linked Vietnam with American domestic problems, the public began to turn to other minori-ties for the reassurance that they were, in spite of themselves, good guys. American Indians were a natural choice for public attention: their protests had so far taken place in remote areas of the country, they wanted to be left alone, they would not be purchasing homes in one's neighborhood, and they were a very colorful part of America's past isolated from modern problems. With a growing interest in America's history and the heightened visibility of American Indians in 1967, the publishing industry made a deliberate effort to feature Indian books. A year later Stan Steiner's *The New Indians* described the recent exploits of younger Indians "leading the way" in the 1960s.

Many of the Indians appearing in Steiner's book were sought out by publishers and contracts were given out freely. The publication of *Custer Died for Your Sins* helped focus the anger of young Indians on specific targets such as the anthropologists, the BIA, and the Christian churches. A year later *Bury My Heart at Wounded Knee* by Dee Brown, a well-written accounting of the Indian wars, presented another dimension of the American Indian experience to the reading public.

These books stand out in the literature about the American Indian because the rest of the field is so easily classified and deals primarily with a fantasy image of Indians, the kind of Indians that many groups of Americans would like to believe exist. The Indians occupying Wounded Knee knew they could benefit from the publicity that the book had already achieved. Insofar as they believed that the existing literature on Indians would provide people with additional background to help explain their struggles, they were sorely disappointed. A review of the literature available on American Indians during the years when the activist movement was so predominant indicates the tremendous conceptual barrier they were facing.

With the exception of N. Scott Momaday's Pulitzer Prize-winning novel *House Made of Dawn*, and Hal Borland's *When the Legends Die, Stay Away, Joe*, there have been few successful novels about modern Indian life. *Little Big Man*, Thomas Berger's very successful novel of the old West, covers Indian life and culture obliquely, and its time period could hardly be said to relate to contemporary Indian life. Many novels have not even had the success of *Little Big Man*. In attempting to present, in fictional format, Indian life as it was experienced in the last century, most novels have fallen into a "go-in-peace-my-son" style, with the credibility of the plot dependent on the lonely white trapper, gunfighter, or missionary who comes across the Indian princess. The parallel between the unexpected and fortunate event in the Horatio Alger stories that catapults the hard-working hero to fame and the fortunate "salvation" event that makes the Indian tribe accept the white hero in the Indian novel is no mistake. It is virtually impossible to change cultures or economic status without what would appear to be an almost supernatural intervention.

Where other fields of literature have so successfully enabled people to empathize with conditions and cultural variances, novels about Indians have been notably bereft of the ability to invoke sympathy. Rather they have been dependent on an escapist attitude for their popularity. As a consequence the Indian activist movement could not make contact with a group of informed, sympathetic readers for there were none. There is no emotional unconscious that Indians and non-Indians share that can be tapped on behalf of American Indians, insofar as they are people, like other people. Their sufferings are historic and communal; this is the lesson that America has learned from its literature on Indians.

The communal nature of Indian personal existence is further supported by the presence of a large body of literature on the histories of the respective tribes. For generations it has been traditional that all historical literature on Indians be a recital of tribal histories from the pre-Discovery culture through the first encounter with the whites to about the year 1890. At that point the tribe seems to fade gently into history, with its famous war chief riding down the canyon into the sunset. Individuals appear within this history only to the extent that they appear to personalize the fortunes of the tribe. A mythical Hiawatha, a saddened Chief Joseph, a scowling Sitting Bull, a sullen Geronimo; all symbolize not living people but the historic fate of a nation overwhelmed by the inevitability of history.

Some of the earliest Indian protests challenged this image of Indians and the numerous false stereotypes projected by this type of literature. Sincere but uninformed whites honestly asked Indians during the height of the activist movement if we still lived in tents, if we were allowed to leave the reservations, and other relevant questions, indicating that for a substantial number of Americans, we were still shooting at the Union Pacific on our days off. On one memorable evening as a guest of the Bill Barker show in Denver, I was asked by a radio listener how the Indians celebrated Christmas before the coming of the whites. Bill and I broke out laughing and he had to punch in a commercial so I could compose myself before trying to answer this silly question. There were constant protests directed to whites writing books on tribes to include something about modern Indians in their books. The result of this protest was that several writers of books on Indians added a final chapter in which a quick sketch of the contemporary condition of the tribe was reviewed.

As late as 1964 many publishers thought (1) Indians could not write books, and (2) any book written by an Indian would be "biased" in favor of Indians.[1] Whenever the subject of Indians writing their own books arose, even the friendliest of non-Indians stated that a great many Indians had written books and that we should be content with what they had left. The trail of books written by Indians is significant if considered as the recorded feelings of a race once extant, but insignificant if it is meant to communicate modern social and legal problems that have created and intensified poverty conditions among a segment of the American population.

It was disconcerting to realize that many people felt that the old books on Indians were sufficient to inform the modern American public about the nature of Indian life and to give sufficient information about Indians to make an intelligent choice as to how best to support Indian goals and aspirations. One historian wrote that there are already a sufficient number of books by Indians, and that books chronicling contemporary outrages should not be published because they stir up bad feelings between Indians and whites.[2] He recommended *Sun Chief* (the autobiography of a Hopi, published in 1942), The *Son of Old Man Hat* (the autobiography of a Navajo, published in 1938), and Black Hawk's autobiography (published in 1833). Could these books have correctly informed the reader on the struggle of the Navajo and Hopi against Peabody Coal Company at Black Mesa or explained the protest at the Gallup ceremonial?

This fundamental gulf between the available information about Indians and information that Indians wanted communicated about particular and pressing problems came to dominate Indian concerns. For that reason the activists made maximum use of television and greatly simplified the issues that concerned them. When the National Indian Youth Council was coming into existence and young Indians were attempting to get sympathetic non-Indians to listen to their story, a non-Indian law professor replied that he was very interested in the plight of Indians and had recently read *Ishi in Two Worlds* (a story about the last member of a California Indian tribe, who spent his final days as a mascot of a California museum in the first decade of this century). As a result, Indians, particularly young, educated Indians in their twenties who wanted to do something about conditions, were very frustrated.

The tension being experienced by young Indians, the awareness that something was dreadfully wrong, was recorded in Steiner's *The New Indians*. In this book Steiner reviewed the developments within Indian country since World War II. He pointed out that the tremendous sums the federal government had spent for Indian education were beginning to produce results. Rather than a quiet group of civil servants, however, the younger Indians had become political theorists, activists, and cultural revivalists. Steiner warned of the impending landslide of concern, which was bound to manifest itself in continuing protests against federal policies that had never taken into account the nature of Indian society or the historic feeling of betrayal that the Indian community has held throughout the twentieth century.

However, the reading public, the literary critics, and many of the people directly concerned with the problems of modern Indians were attracted to two other books also published in 1968. Alvin Josephy published *The Indian Heritage of America*, and Peter Farb published the book with the long title, *Man's Rise to Civilization as Shown by the Indians of North America from Primeval Times to the Coming of the Industrial State*. Both books were best-sellers and popular book-club selections. Josephy devoted all of 20 pages in a 365-page book to the period from 1890 to 1968, failing to cite any contemporary Indian political leader at all and mentioning the National Indian Youth Council once in passing.

Farb did a brilliant analysis of prehistoric Indian cultures, covered items that had not previously been on any anthropological agenda, and cleverly wove together almost all of the relevant information on Indian cultural traditions into a 332-page book. His work was considered by reviewers as a major step forward in understanding the American Indians. He did not, however, mention the Indian Reorganization Act of 1934, which has formed the basis for communal survival in the postwar world. He did not mention the Indian Claims

Commission of 1946, which attempted to redress the injustices of land confiscation through relitigation of land claims. Farb frankly stated that he would leave such a job to another. How he came to figure that he had taken Indians up to the modern industrial state, however, is another question, since his book appears chronologically to stop shortly after the Dawes Act of 1887.[3]

The incongruity of the impact of the three books became more apparent with the addition of other facts. Josephy and Farb were among the inner circle of consultants upon whom then-Secretary of the Interior Stewart Udall relied for his knowledge regarding the formation of policy for American Indians. Steiner was regarded as a itinerant relic of the Jack Kerouac school of wanderers, a person who could not conceivably possess any information on Indians that would be relevant to the formation of policy. In 1968 the inherent schizophrenia of the Indian image split and finally divided into modern Indians and the Indians of America—those ghostly figures that America loved and cherished.

In the next four years it seemed as if every book on modern Indians was promptly buried by a book on the "real" Indians of yesteryear. The public overwhelmingly turned to *Bury My Heart at Wounded Knee* and *The Memoirs of Chief Red Fox* to avoid the accusations made by modern Indians in *The Tortured Americans* and *Custer Died for Your Sins*. The *Red Fox* book alone sold more copies than the two modern books. It was later revealed to be a reprinting of an older book that "Chief Red Fox" had simply copied.[4] Each takeover of government property only served to spur further sales of Brown's review of the wars in the 1860s. While the Indian reading public was in tune with *The New Indians*, *The Tortured Americans*, *The Unjust Society* by Harold Cardinal, a Canadian Indian, and other books written by contemporary Indians on modern problems, the reading non-Indian public began frantically searching for additional books on the Indians of the last century.

The result of this intense, non-Indian interest was the publication of a series of books that were little more than cut-and-paste jobs, the anthologies. *Touch the Earth* by T. C. McLuhan and *I Have Spoken* by Virginia Armstrong consisted of a series of excerpts of the speeches by famous chiefs with a few short quotations from living

Indians to give the book a timely flavor. McLuhan inserted a number of sentimental sepia pictures of old chiefs riding along the crest of canyon to add further maudlin emotions to an already overemotional book. The public took McLuhan to heart, and *Touch the Earth* also hit the book clubs. There were also dozens of other anthologies printed following the success of these books but they simply recycled some 150 quotations between new covers. They added nothing new about contemporary Indians and events. Unfortunately this kind of book still continues to be produced with equally dismal results.

In addition to the sentimental anthologies, a number of books were rushed into print and hopefully to judgment; they were little more than editing jobs on reports to government agencies. Among them was *American Indians and Federal Aid* by Alan Sorkin, a study done by the Brookings Institution under a grant from the Donner Foundation. The book featured numerous tables demonstrating Indian poverty but was devoid of any mention of the forces then moving in Indian affairs that sought to combat poverty and racism. *Big Brother's Indian Programs with Reservations* by Sar Levitan and Barbara Hetrick, a study funded by the Ford Foundation, was published shortly after Sorkin's book. It was distinguishable from Sorkin's book chiefly through its use of photographs as if there really were Indians alive today, its big words, and its utter lack of knowledge about hiring Indians.

In the fall of 1972 there were no less than seventy-five books on American Indians released. Most staggered into print, received few reviews, and collapsed. It was plain that the initial phase of interest in Indians was over. Then, just before Election Day, the Trail of Broken Treaties arrived in the nation's capital, ready to do battle with the Nixon administration. In little over a week the Administration, the tribal leaders, and a great segment of the American public sat stunned as the Indian activists completed their destruction of the Bureau collected some $66,000 in travel money from the federal government, and set off to terrorize the headquarters of some tribes and BIA field offices. Somehow American Indians had arrived in the twentieth century.

In order to understand why this particular event occurred, we must try to understand the reception that modern Indians received when they have tried to communicate their immediate problems to an uncomprehending society. When a comparison is made between events of the Civil Rights movement and the activities of the Indian movement one thing stands out in clear relief: Americans simply refuse to give up their longstanding conceptions of what an Indian is. It was this fact more than any other that inhibited any solution of the Indian problems and projected the impossibility of their solution anytime in the future. People simply could not connect what they believed Indians to be with what they were seeing on their television sets.

Let us pretend that the black community received the same reception in the Civil Rights struggle that the American Indian community received when its movement was attracting public attention.in its struggle.

It is 1954, and the Supreme Court has just handed down its famous case, *Brown v. Topeka Board of Education*; the Civil Rights movement is beginning to get under way. Soon there is a crisis in Montgomery, Alabama, and Dr. Martin Luther King, Jr., begins to emerge as a credible leader of the Civil Rights forces.

At a news conference King is asked about the days on the old plantation. He attempts to speak on the bus boycott, but the news media rejects his efforts. It wants to hear about Uncle Tom, the famous black of literature. The news conference ends with the newsmen thoroughly convinced that King is merely a troublemaker, that everything is fine down on the old plantation, and that everything will be all right if the blacks simply continue to compose spirituals. Sympathetic supporters stand in the background dressed in slave costumes cheering him on.

Two books are published recounting the blessed days of slavery on the one hand and the cultural achievements of the tribes of black Africa in the 1300s on the other. They are almost immediate successes on the best-seller lists. The American public now worries about the Muslims confronting the primitive tribes of the interior of the African continent and changing their culture. Mohammed becomes a public villain. In a desperate effort to raise the issue of Civil

Rights in American society, Martin Luther King, Jr., writes *Stride Toward Freedom*. Outside of a few people who seem to intuit that things are not well down South, King's ideas are ignored. Two new black writers, James Baldwin and LeRoi Jones, publish books that have a sporadic, perfunctory reception, and they are ignored.

The movement continues to grow with television coverage and feature-length descriptions of the poverty conditions of the black community, prefaced by quotations from Booker T. Washington and George Washington Carver to the effect that blacks should remain separate until earning the right to participate in American society. The Freedom Rides begin, sparking a series of anthologies of Negro spirituals about traveling to the promised land. *A Negro Travel Book*, showing the great migrations in Africa in the 1300s, becomes a best-seller. Boy Scout groups drop their camping activities and begin to perform minstrel shows complete with authentic black dialog.

Finally the movement grows intense as plans are made for a march on Washington. People rush here and there, preparing for the march; the activists down in the Deep South are in trouble. Some have been killed for attempting to register voters. On the literary front, however, things are different. A new book, *Bury My Heart at Jamestown*, has rocketed to the top of the best-seller list. More than 20,000 copies a week are being purchased. People reading the book vow never again to buy and sell slaves. Sympathy for the slaves is running at a fever pitch, while Martin Luther King, Jr., is downgraded because "he doesn't speak for all the Negroes."

As the march gets under way, television finds a new hero. Field Hand Boggs, an elderly black who claims to be 101 years old and a nephew of Nat Turner, is discovered almost simultaneously by *The New York Times* and the "Oprah Winfrey Show." Field Hand Boggs has copied 13,000 words from *Uncle Tom's Cabin* by Harriet Beecher Stowe and is passing it off as his "notebooks" laboriously compiled over a century of struggle. Field Hand Boggs becomes the number one folk hero of America, and he recounts for thrilled television audiences his glimpse of Abraham Lincoln and General Grant sitting on the White House lawn the day that he gained his freedom. The march is conducted in virtual isolation.

As the Civil Rights movement proceeds, the literature shifts its emphasis; old government and foundation reports complete with charts and graphs are trotted out with fancy dust jackets that make them appear to be the latest battle communiqués from Atlanta. Anthologies of spirituals become very popular, and those that are interspiced with faded photographs of slaves working in the cotton fields prove the most popular. Introductions to these anthologies sternly inform us that we must come to understand the great contributions made by slaves to our contemporary culture, "More than ever," one commentary reads, "the modern world needs the soothing strains of 'Sweet Chariot' to assure us that all is well."

And finally Watts. As the section of Los Angeles burns, people resolve to do better. Government officials ask for full prosecution of the rebels, all the while handing out $100 bills to the rioters and advising them to go back to Virginia and South Carolina and sin no more. A task force is created of officials of various government departments to study the federal relationship to Civil Rights problems and to report back its findings no later than six months after it authorization.

In the summer of 1967, spontaneously in all parts of the country, professional and amateur archaeologists invade black graveyards. They disinter skeletons, label them, and send them to the city museums for display. Down South people rush to isolated slave graveyards with bulldozers, hoping to find some artifacts of that time when it was possible to own a human being. The National Park System locates sites where the underground railroad once ran and sets them aside for tourists, charging a minimal fee. Anthropologists rush to the defense of the looter explaining that it is necessary for anthropologists to have the bones of blacks because they derive immense scientific knowledge from them, but they refuse to publish any reports of this precious information.

What seems ludicrous in the black situation as recounted here is precisely what happened in the American Indian situation without anyone cracking a smile. For example, at the height of the Civil Rights struggle, would anyone have seriously entertained the idea that a 101-year-old man with a tenuous claim to black blood or heritage would truly represent the struggles of the black community? Certainly no intelligent critic would be taken in by such a hoax (fraud is rarely used when discussing minority groups).[5] Yet it not only happened to American Indians, but a substantial portion of the public yearned for it to happen.

What we dealt with for the major portion of a decade was not American Indians, but the American conception of what Indians should be. While Brown's *Bury My Heart at Wounded Knee* was selling nearly twenty thousand copies a week, the three hundred state game wardens and Tacoma city police were vandalizing the Indian fishing camp and threatening the lives of Indian women and children at Frank's Landing on the Nisqually River. It is said that people read and write history to learn from the mistakes of the past, but this could certainly not apply to histories of the American Indian, if it applies to history at all.

As Raymond Yellow Thunder was being beaten to death, Americans were busy ordering *Touch the Earth* from their book clubs as an indication of their sympathy for American Indians. As the grave robbers were breaking into Chief Joseph's grave, the literary public was reading his famous surrender speech in a dozen or more anthologies of Indian speeches and bemoaning the fact that oratory such as Joseph's is not used anymore.

The most remarkable body of literature in the years preceding the emergence of the Indian movement was the beginnings of a serious literature on Indian religions. Ruth Underhill's *Red Man's Religion* presented a quick survey of the various religious beliefs of the tribes, but it was phrased in traditional anthropological concepts and had the expert-lecturing-to-novice point of view. While it provided information, the subject could just as well have been the pottery styles of long-vanished peoples. Anthony F.C. Wallace examined the religion of Handsome Lake in *The Death and Rebirth of the Senecas*. It was a respectable effort but again plagued with the detachment of a historical point of view that gave no sense of urgency to the religious feelings then stirring in the younger generation of Indians.

Father Peter Powell completed his great two-volume work, *Sweet Medicine* explaining tribal religion in a serious vein. Powell's work, particularly his style of exposition, was based primarily on conversations with reservation people and reflected their language. An Anglican priest who operated St. Augustine's Indian Center in Chicago, Powell viewed all religious expressions as sacred and consequently treated the Cheyenne tradition with respect. His book did not take the superficial approach of listing the quaint beliefs of the Cheyennes as if the reader and the author were beyond such superstitions. *Sweet Medicine* impressed Indians with the validity of their own traditions.

The two most popular books dealing with Indian religion were *Black Elk Speaks* by John Neihardt and *The Sacred Pipe* by Joseph Epes Brown. Some universities had already installed American Indian studies programs by the early 1970s and almost every course included the two Black Elk books as required reading. Consequently they formed a kind of sacred national Indian religious canon by themselves. The Sioux teachings were phrased in a universal manner. Because they had close relationships in theological concepts with the beliefs of other tribes, many Indian young people who had grown up in the cities and who now formed the backbone of the activist wing of Indian affairs, believed them to be an accurate statement about Indian religions.[6]

As Indian country was tensing for the eventual showdown in the fall of 1972, two major books on Indian religion were published. One was *Lame Deer, Seeker of Visions* by John (Fire) Lame Deer and Richard Erdoes, an autobiography of a Sioux holy man. The book revealed a great deal about the general conditions of reservation life and had an immediate clientele among the very people who had decided to march on Washington. It also had a saucy style typical of the well-experienced Sioux elder making cynical but incisive comments on human behavior. Readers accustomed to the pious rigidity of Protestant tracts on the devotional life were shocked at Lame Deer's casual approach to such taboo subjects as death, sex, growing old, and religion. Yet from the pages of the book shone a wisdom found in few devotional materials.

The second book, *Seven Arrows* by Hyemeyohsts Storm, was even more controversial. *Seven Arrows* was unique because it tried to make a contemporary religious statement using traditional stories, mythologies, and symbols of the Cheyenne people. In a sense it modernized and simplified some of the ideas articulated by Powell in *Sweet Medicine*. People expecting to find a record of ancient Cheyenne rituals and ceremonies were stunned to see garish quasi-psychedelic shields, modernistic representations of culture heros, and the advocacy of the so-called "medicine wheel" that was supposed to enable a person to adjust their lives in order to solve pressing personal problems.

Seven Arrows had an incredible impact on young non-Indians. Accustomed to simplistic teachings from their own churches they found the key to an exotic religion that they had been led to believe was very complicated. Younger Indians living in isolated urban areas away from the reservation ceremonials also liked the book and believed that it was a true representation of their own tribal religions even though it was written for the 1960s. *Seven Arrows* provided a linkage between the emerging groups of non-Indians who were adopting non-Western religious traditions and the Indians who were asserting or relearning their own religious traditions. While it helped to create a groundswell of support for the Indian occupations of federal buildings, it also brought the subject of tribal religions into the marketplace of ideas for the increasing number of people looking for a personal religion and new kinds of religious experiences.

Several years before Storm's book a "cult" following for Indian religion had already been created by a series of books written by Carlos Castaneda, beginning with *The Teachings of Don Juan* and *A Separate Reality*, and a succession of clever titles. In this series of narratives Castaneda purported to have spent several years as an apprentice to a Yaqui medicine man Don Juan who lived in the Sonoran deserts and other obscure places in Mexico. Castaneda had learned very quickly all the secrets of the shaman's trade until the current book sales began to wane and he would pick up the narrative and reveal even further sophistications about making reality in your own mind. The Don Juan books were just what young whites needed to bolster their shattering personal identities, and the books were immensely popular.[7]

Movies did not keep pace with the Indian image during these years. The movie Indian was a thinly disguised young white who wished to have both the simplicity of nature and the modern involvement with social and political issues. The most popular movie alleged to deal with Indians was *Billy Jack,* a mixed-blood Indian and a war veteran who was an expert in the martial arts. He demonstrated his commitment to peace by breaking people's limbs in a spectacular fashion. One scene showed Billy Jack dancing in an abandoned Pueblo ruin and allowing a rattlesnake to bite him as he danced purporting to be some kind of ceremony that enabled him to be a brother to the snakes. The scene was pure Lutheran theology since Billy Jack's faith was supposed to make him immune to snake poison. Sequels to this movie did not do as well. The phenomenon was a passing fad but an extremely important one because it informed young non-Indians that their goals and the Indian goals were identical, that through mastering Indian religious ceremonials they could become invincible and heroic.

Tell Them Willie Boy Is Here, starring Robert Redford and Katharine Ross, chronicled an earlier incident in this century in which a sheriff's posse pursued a young California Indian. The movie had a ring of authenticity regarding both the reservation and the historical period. Because it did not show the Indian using magical tricks or being particularly religious, *Willie Boy* did not attract the great crowds that attended *Billy Jack,* and few people connected the conditions of Indians on California reservations with the demands of the protestors in Washington.

If we compare at the image of Indians projected in literature and somewhat in film with that of the Indians who marched on Washington one thing stands out clearly—underneath all of the symbols and ideologies is a religious context and religious motivation. But there was no way to communicate the complexities of this worldview to non-Indians and there was no way that Indians could articulate how this religious perspective could resolve existing problems. Two entirely different views of the world, of human beings, and of human history were about to clash and there was not a single bridge over which the exchange of ideas and sentiments could take place. Moving from the BIA occupation through the Wounded Knee occupation, the trials and the investigations by the American Indian Policy Review Commission, one of the first pieces of legislation passed to resolve Indian problems was the American Indian Religious Freedom Resolution (1978). So there could be no doubt that religion played a critical, if unarticulated, role in the Indian movement.

Two entirely different developments characterize the period from 1972 to 1990. First, Indians in their respective tribes began a serious revival of their religious traditions. Ceremonies that had long been discarded or suppressed were once again performed. Traditional people were sought out for their knowledge of ceremonies and customs. Young Indians all over the country felt it imperative to experience a vision quest, and some groups even reinstituted a version of the ghost dance. The movement even intruded upon the congregations of Christian Indians as Indian priests and ministers sought to combine the teachings and practices of both religions. Some traditional ceremonies were even carried out in Protestant churches so that it became difficult to tell whether one was going to attend a hymn-singing or a healing ceremony when people gathered.

The reasoning behind this integration of two religious traditions is interesting because it goes to both the nature of religion and the nature of cultural identity for answers. Christian Indian priests and ministers felt no sense of guilt in conducting traditional ceremonies because they felt that the ceremonies were as much Indian cultural expressions as religious acts. Additionally, with the argument that there was but one deity, the difference in religions was merely one of choice and expression. Hence a universal sense of religious feeling replaced what had been rather precise formulations of religious beliefs. Some Indians expressed the thought that every culture was in effect an "old testament" with the "new testament" topping them off and making sense of all earlier cultural reaching toward God.

The churches eagerly embraced this new movement for the most part. Their congregations had been declining drastically for years as reservation residents gained more mobility and small settlements on the reservations could no longer support churches and chapels that had been founded during the 1880s and 1890s, a period of impressive conversions. Much nonsense occurred during this period. Episcopal bishops, already looking silly in ecclesiastical costumes standing on the South Dakota prairies looked absurd when this dress was topped off with awkward fitting war bonnets. Indian Christians and traditionals alike were offended when masses were held coincident with the sun dance in spite of the arguments given for merging the two traditions.

Christianity among Indians has fared rather badly during recent years. When placed next to traditional religions, it has very little to say about responsibilities to family and community; most Christians deal simply with the church as if it were the deity. Indian symbolism is not symbolic in the same way that Christian symbolism is; therefore, mixing liturgical objects has become anathema to many Indians. Indian cultural traditions provided an easy explanation for certain kinds of religious acts whereas Christian religious acts depended primarily upon the acceptance of Western culture. It was this cultural and historical perspective that Indians rejected. The result we see today is the rapid movement away from secularism and Christianity toward a more serious traditional religious life.

The second development that emerged following the cresting of the Indian movement was the intense interest in tribal religions by non-Indians and the seemingly wholesale adoption of some of their beliefs and practices by significant segments of white society. The medicine wheel was the symbol most easily adopted by whites through workshops, conferences, and gatherings. The seven directions to which the Plains Indians pray with the pipe became a means of orienting people to the natural world so that the pipe and some semblance of Indian ceremonies were also taken over. Whites then began making and using drums and feather fans for their own use in ceremonies they were holding. The first wave of appropriation, therefore, was simply the symbolic costumes that non-Indians believed would place them closer to nature.

As the demand for authenticity increased so did the fees paid to real Indians to hold ceremonies. Sun Bear, a Chippewa from Minnesota, created his own tribe, the Bear tribe, and found a way to bring non-Indians into his own version of Indian ceremonial life. Eventually he expanded and had an advertisement in *Shaman's Drum*, a magazine devoted to educating the thousands of young whites who wished to be Indians—and shamans. The ad featured a nice picture of Sun Bear with the caption, "Sun Bear needs spiritual warriors." This ad exemplified the motivation of non-Indians—they wanted some kind of power so they could deal with their own culture and be successful.

A variety of Indian medicine men and purported medicine men moved into white society where there were easy pickings. Whites would pay hundreds of dollars for the privilege of sitting on the ground, having corn flour thrown in their faces, and being told that the earth was round and all things lived in circles. The next step was performing sweat lodges for non-Indians. Another step was to cut out the best-looking blonde for a "special ceremony" in which she would play Mother Earth while the medicine man, or whoever had conned the blonde, would be Father Sky. They would couple to preserve the life on the planet. In short, the arena between cultures became a scene of intense exploitation.

Added to this confusion was the elevation of whites once again to be the primary exponents of Indian religion and culture. This phenomenon was triggered unexpectedly by Ruth Beebe Hill in a badly written novel entitled *Hanta Yo*. Hill purported to "know" the Dakota language before missionaries had written it down and therefore ruined it. She claimed to have written a 1,500-page book in this language, translated it from an early English dictionary in order to get authentic English sentence structure, and published it. Her informant was a strange Santee Indian named Chucksa Yuha. Otherwise known as Lorenzo Blackmith, his personal history and claim to ancient knowledge was refuted by investigators at every turn. Hill's major thesis was that she alone knew the truth about the original Dakota/Lakota Indians, that their descendants were pale imitations, and that the original resembled nothing less than Ayn Rand's *Fountainhead*, rugged individuals who bowed to nothing including the deity.

Hanta Yo, according to its editor, was thrown over the transom (in other words, came in unsolicited), read avidly, and seen immediately as a classic—the first time anyone had rendered an accurate version of traditional Sioux life. Without delay it was announced that the book was an Indian *Roots* and that David Wolper, who had produced the original *Roots*, had somehow acquired the television rights to the work. Indians protested vigorously and slowed down production of the television movie. A group at Pine Ridge, however, could not resist the money being offered by Wolper and endorsed the film. It was finally shown under the title *Mystic Warrior* and thankfully disappeared.

Ruth Beebe Hill had proved a very important point. As interested as whites were in Indian culture and religion, they preferred to learn from non-Indians who posed as experts in the field. Thus, the books on Indian religion written by Thomas Mails, complete with very good drawings of Indians and sacred objects, and the books by Richard Erdoes, confidant to a group of traditional people on the Rosebud Sioux Reservation in South Dakota, did a brisk sale and continued to be popular. These books were within the scope of respectable offerings because so much of their material was taken directly from existing literature and was sullied only by their own occasional personal interpretations of events and activities.

Beginning in the late 1970s and continuing through present time, the literature on American Indians includes not only books on Indian religion written by non-Indians but also anthologies and treatises on ecology allegedly using Indian principles. One example of this fantasy literature are books by Lynn Andrews, a talented show business performer. Andrews has demonstrated that it is possible to say almost anything and have it believed providing it is packaged correctly; at that job she is without peer.

Andrews' first offering was *Medicine Woman* in which she purported to have been an apprentice to a Canadian medicine woman named Agnes Whistling Elk. The narrative is thrilling because almost without pain or discomfort Andrews is given all the secrets that every white person has sought for centuries. We learn in the last chapters of the book that her mission is not to live among the Canadian Indians performing simple healing and condolence ceremonies like other medicine practitioners. Instead she is commissioned to go throughout the world revealing religious secrets of the Indians. Following *Medicine Woman* are an incredible number of books in which Andrews visits the outstanding medicine women in the world and is accepted immediately into secret societies that have been preserving the ancient knowledge for thousands of years.

The concept of proselytizing on an apostolic commission inspired some Indians to claim similar missions. Today an alleged shaman can explain his or her absence from the reservation or absence of Indian blood with the excuse that after being trained by elders, the individual has then been authorized and commanded to go among all peoples and preach the Indian gospel. It seems that this surplus of shamans could severely tax the credibility of these practitioners. How can there be so *many* medicine people who have been commissioned to hold ceremonies for non-Indians while their own people suffer without religious ministrations?

In what has been called the "New Age" circuit Indians have devised a clever answer to this question. They insist that they are "pipe carriers," an office that has rather hazy historical and cultural antecedents. No definition is ever given of the exact duties of the pipe carrier except that he or she can perform all the ceremonies that a shaman can perform without being called to account when nothing happens. This status was just what non-Indians need to avoid the accusation that they are practicing traditional ceremonies without any real knowledge or understanding of Indian ways. Now everyone from movie stars to gas station attendants has claimed to be an authorized pipe carrier. The belief is that one need only recite these magic words to turn aside all criticisms and skeptical expressions of the listeners.

In the 1990s, Indian religions are a hot item. It is the outward symbolic form that is most popular. Many people, Indian and non-Indian, have taken a few principles to heart, mostly those beliefs that require little in the way of changing one's lifestyle. Tribal religions have been trivialized beyond redemption by people sincerely wishing to learn about them. In isolated places on the reservations, however, a gathering of people is taking place and much of the substance of the old way of life is starting to emerge. Some keen observers predict that within a decade people serving on tribal councils will have to have a full traditional ceremonial life to get elected.

Notes

1. Stan Steiner, the writer who broke open opportunities for Indian writers with his The New Indians (New York: Harper & Row, 1967), told me in 1968 that he had recommended me to several publishers in 1965 and 1966, but the universal response was that I would be "biased" in favor of Indians and could not get a contract.

2. I presented these same ideas in *Natural History Magazine* in a book review of *Seven Arrows* by Hyemeyohsts Storm (Random House, 1970) and received a barely rational letter informing me of the greatness of the books listed in this paragraph. I have basically summarized the feelings of the letter writer in this paragraph.

3. Peter Farb was a keen observer of social realities but he was also perhaps the last writer of the 1960s to perpetuate the old "Indians are exotic and also children" attitude that had been characteristic of whites writing on Indians during the early decades of this century.

4. *The New York Times* did an investigation of Chief Red Fox and found that almost every fact he had presented did not check out. A significant number of people still believe that he was an Indian, although he was unable to name any relatives on the Sioux reservations (see *The New York Times* [March 10, 1972]: 1, 22).

In recent times there have been more frauds than real Indians writing books. In 1991 it was revealed that Forrest Carter, the author of *The Education of Little Tree* (Delacorte Press/E. Friede, 1976), was in fact a virulent racist who had devoted a good deal of his life to the Ku Klux Klan.

5. The problem of individuals alleging to have Indian blood has become exceedingly serious. Imposters regularly gain access to federal jobs claiming Indian preference and being upheld in their claims. New Age gurus claim to be medicine people of an "intertribal" nature, which is traditionally impossible because individuals had to belong to one tribe or another. Even in litigation on Indian rights it is not always possible to determine if the plaintiff is an Indian. *Bowen v. Roy*, a Supreme Court case involving an individual alleging to be an Abnaki Indian, was adversely decided against Indian rights and the allegations of claims to Indian religious traditions were problematical at best in this case.

6. Most of the books discussed in these paragraphs had some contact with reality and were done with some degree of scholarly concern. In the last decade there has been a deluge of nonsense as non-Indians, along with a few Indians such as Wallace Black Elk and Sun Bear, have developed a curious interpretation of Indian religion that includes crystals, medicine wheels, sweat lodges, prayer circles, and almost any other kind of adap-

tation of popular non-Indian group dynamics to Indian traditions. The deluge of books on tribal religions is simply an appropriation of external Indian symbols to meet the emotional demands of the age and has no relationship whatsoever to what traditional Indians did religiously even several decades ago.

7. People appeared to be divided on whether or not Castaneda had actually met any Indians, let alone studied under Don Juan. The consensus is that the religious experiences were either made up or came out of a sugar cube somewhere on the West Coast.

CHAPTER 3

THE RELIGIOUS CHALLENGE

Indian activists holding religious ceremonies in the BIA building concluding their stay by looting the building seems incongruous and ridiculous, unless we probe deeper into the nature of the relationship between Indians and whites. Indian activists accused of fomenting the destruction made a rather weak reply. What about the rape of the North American continent, the destruction of tribal cultures, the wasteful use of human beings, the deprivation of rights to a helpless minority? Do not these crimes make the destruction of a building pale in significance, they asked.

Do they?

In one sense the capture and destruction of the BIA headquarters was a historic anachronism. Watts burned in 1965, the urban areas seethed and burned following the death of Martin Luther King, Jr., in 1968. Was not the Indian occupation of a federal building in the nation's capital an event dreadfully out of time? Was not the sacking of the BIA headquarters and the occupation of Wounded Knee the final spasm of the rugged 1960s when any type of change was considered beneficial, and the institutions of society were considered not only obsolete but malignant? Perhaps it was the last hurrah of an era when people could thumb their noses at established authority without fear of painful reprisal. But the Indian incidents must also be seen within the context of the Indian experience in this nation's history and in that context the Indian movement raised an entirely different kind of question—that of religion rather than the equal enforcement of the law.

There certainly was an aspect in which the Indian protests were events of the 1960s, although occurring in 1972 and 1973. Since 1968 the major Christian denominations had been pouring funds into social movements of all kinds. They believed deeply in the militant interpretation of black power as continuous confrontations, and grants were made to organizations within the respective minority groups that they were sure would produce the desired protests. A group that snapped and snarled about its social problems stood a much better chance of receiving funds from the churches than did a group that calmly and carefully articulated a problem that they hoped to solve.

Church officials often gauged their relevancy in proportion to the violence of the groups they were funding. Any church not receiving its share of frothing-at-the-mouth demands for money felt isolated from the great events of the American social movement. Thus, it was that when AIM captured a dormitory at Augustana College in Sioux Falls and presented a set of demands carefully worked out by sympathetic Lutherans in secret sessions, the Lutheran churches eagerly embraced the Indian cause. While they had not been overly enthusiastic about helping the blacks during the Civil Rights movement, some church officials felt that they could get the same kind of action from the Indians without taking a position on a social movement that would antagonize their church members.

Many Lutherans were ecstatic when informed by Indians that they were guilty of America's sins against the Indians, and they embarked on a massive program of fund-raising to pay for their alleged sins. But they were not the only victims. Because the Presbyterians, Episcopalians, and Congregationalists all gleefully responded to the accusation that they had been responsible for nearly all of the problems of American Indians, they also decided that they could purchase indulgences for these sins by funding the Indian activists to do whatever they felt necessary to correct the situation. By early 1971 almost every major Christian church had set up crisis funds to buy off whichever Indian protesters they might arrange to have visit them. Confrontations escalated as each group sought to become more relevant than its competitors, and the path toward destruction was clearly visible to everyone. In a real sense Christian churches bought and paid for the Indian movement and its climactic destruction of the BIA headquarters as surely as if they had written out specific orders to sack the BIA on a contractual basis.

Not every Indian protest, however, was inspired by the financial rewards to be gained from the churches by playing the protest game. Many of the incidents were valid protests by a people who had suffered too much for too long. Even more, younger Indians had seen in the Civil Rights movement that the institutions of this country respond only when there is a threat to their property, or when disorder in their lives forces them to confront problems that have not been solved for generations. Yet the Civil Rights issue was peripheral at best when understood in the Indian context. The different tribal groups suffered discrimination and prejudice generally, but more specifically the broken treaties meant immediate hardship for the different communities. Could young Indians enter a Civil Rights movement and press for removal of discriminatory hiring practices while enjoying preference under federal law for employment in tribal programs based on treaties and agreements? Major institutional differences really did exist among American racial minorities.

Few Indians ever accepted the premises of the Civil Rights movement. If the tribal chairmen demanded the prosecution of the Indian militants following the departure from the destroyed BIA building, it was a weak response compared to tribal reactions on being asked to join in the Civil Rights movement and marches half a decade earlier. That the basic goals of the Civil Rights movement could not attract more than a handful of Indians at any one time should give pause to everyone. What was it that turned Indians off other than the fear that they might be identified with blacks as a minority group?

American history gives us a partial answer and allows us to raise certain questions that must be asked. The Civil Rights movement was probably the last full-scale effort to realize the avowed goals of the Christian religion. For more than a century, the American political system had proclaimed the brotherhood of man as seen politically in the concepts of equality of opportunity and justice equally administered under the law. Equality under the law, however, was a secularized and generalized interpretation of the Christian brotherhood of man—the universal appeal of individuals standing equally before God now seen as people standing equally before the law and secular institutions. While the National Association for the Advancement of Colored Persons (NAACP) Legal Defense and Education Fund fought a series of brilliant court battles leading up to the great Supreme Court decisions, in the background certainly lurked the great Christian message of the brotherhood of man. A majority of Americans rejected this secular version of brotherhood and sought to prevent its realization because of long-standing attitudes that people of color were necessarily inferior.

When the struggle in the South reached the point of open boycotts and nonviolent protests, it was the black Christian church leaders such as Martin Luther King, Jr., Ralph Abernathy, and Andrew Young who spearheaded the movement by translating Christian doctrines into political tools of resistance and eventually conquest. In large measure, the Civil Rights movement was a movement that found its ideology, strategy, and meaning in Christian religious doctrines. King's famous letter from jail in Birmingham was not addressed to the political leaders of the South or to liberals of the North, but to the Christian church leaders of the South, who were intent on reducing the Christian religion to a comforting and spineless recital of creeds.

There had to be a point in Western history at which the avowed beliefs of the Christian religion were placed on the agenda to discover if they could become a reality. Could Western Christianity practice the tenets that all people are created equal and that "thou shalt not kill"? The Civil Rights movement became the acid test in the field of domestic relations. Before the Civil Rights movement, however, one must look at the Nuremberg Trials as the moment of history in which Western Christianity achieved its greatest influence. In those trials the victorious Allied nations presumed to speak for all of civilization and judged the Nazi leaders not as losers but as those who had violated the basic tenets of civilized and religious existence. In setting themselves up as judges, the Western nations had first to overlook the atrocities of their Russian allies and secondly affirm before all societies that they themselves stood sinless before all and before history and were fit to judge.

After the Nuremberg Trials it became more or less inevitable that the Western nations would fall victim to the moral and intellectual weaknesses in their own societies. Could one really judge Nazi leaders when in one's own nation captured German prisoners of war received better treatment than the black soldiers who had captured them? No, the Civil Rights movement was inevitable once the Nuremberg Trials had taken place. The logic of national identity called for an effort to realize the reality of the Christian religion on a political basis. America had no choice but to embark eventually on a quest for post-Nuremberg meaning. That the Civil Rights movement began under the benign Eisenhower administration was an indication of the terrible conflicts in which America and its religious sensitivity would engage. If nothing else, Eisenhower personified the good citizen, the American Christian gentleman, the man to whom all good accrues because of his faithful adherence to the American credo. That Dwight D. Eisenhower was compelled by the logic of the law to order federal troops to Little Rock, Arkansas, over the protests of members of his party and the South to enforce a Supreme Court decree seems ironic yet appropriate for the unveiling of the American religious question and its resolution.

It was this terrible inconsistency that many Indians sensed as they approached the Civil Rights movement. In attempting to distinguish Indian issues from the concerns felt by the black community and understood by their white allies, many Indians began to discover their own culture. They began to trace out the reality of their own religious experiences and to distinguish between the technological superiority of the white man and his moral corruption and the falsity of his religious facade. It was during the Eisenhower years that some of the religious ceremonies of the tribes were first openly performed after many decades of suppression.

Through the 1960s the Civil Rights movement gained power and strength, calling millions of people to commitments that many had never considered making. One cannot but review the many martyrs of the Civil Rights movement, black and white, to understand the violence of the time and many religious people's depth of commitment. From the era came writers such as Malcolm Boyd and Harvey Cox, who in retrospect appear as valiant pioneers discerning a break in the ecclesiastical curtain, yet committed and powerless to break out of the deteriorating situation. Their books show a desperate effort to leapfrog American domestic theology and make it speak to the times that were unfolding. *The Secular City*, for example, tries to impress upon the mainstream religious community the fact that secularization has all but overtaken them in a tidal wave of change.

Perhaps the Civil Rights movement held too much promise of a better society. The fervor it inspired in people could not be maintained in the face of exhausting sacrifices for a few intangible accomplishments. Within it was the implicit promise that a better society was but a short distance into the future, and the reality of that society became a means of sustaining the broken heads and broken spirits of the movement. For many young people not in the social movements, the goal of discovering a reality to existence took a different track. The middle 1960s also saw in the rise of the drug culture an immediate release from the complexities of modern life. Timothy Leary's admonition to "drop out, turn on, and tune in" spoke of the *Take over* same stability of reality in the religious field as did King's dream of a just society, but it was predicated on the idea of individual isolation and a refusal to accept citizenship responsibilities. As the two movements began to intertwine, the formation of a "counterculture" was suggested as a means of explaining the apparent alienation between the two general modes of American existence.

King spoke out against Vietnam. Suddenly a new international dimension impinged upon the consciousness of America. True to his Christian ideals, King saw the pervading nature of racism and oppression that led directly from the Christian idea of history. That we were in Southeast Asia at all derived directly from our conception of ourselves as guardians of history against all movements that would upset the balance we had achieved by military and economic power alone. King saw that there could be no solution to domestic problems without a solution to international problems. And solving international problems meant giving up the Western interpretation of history and the role of Western nations in history.

Stokely Carmichael burst on the scene with his cry "Black Power," and the question of community integrity dominated concep-

tions of measuring social change. No longer was it possible to pass
Civil Rights laws. Now the political and economic stranglehold over
local communities had to be surrendered. The idea of forming a unified
and homogenous nation vanished as blacks demanded the right to
dissent culturally, and other groups, as if waiting for a signal, charged
into the breach in the ideology of integration. Christianity had been
built on the individual response to external events, as verified by
internal feelings of righteousness and satisfaction. A universal brotherhood of responsible citizens had been conceived in which, with every
person acting responsibly in the civil realm, no rupture of the social
fabric would occur. Now it was all gone. In its place stood the racial and
ethnic communities, demanding the right to national existence in a
melting-pot society where there was to be neither Jew nor Gentile.

Finally the ecologists arrived with predictions so chilling as
to frighten the strongest heart. At the present rate of deterioration, they
told us, mankind could expect only a generation before the species
would be finally extinguished. How had this situation come about?
Some ecologists told us that it was the old Christian idea of nature: the
rejection of creation as a living ecosystem and the concept of nature as
depraved, an object for exploitation and nothing more. Almost immediately young whites who were attracted by ecology were accused of
copping out on the Civil Rights movement. A diversion, black activists
cried, a means of taking the pressure off the corrupt governmental
structures that refuse to give us our rights.

What happened in the 1960s and 1970s is that, in all probability, the logic of Western culture and the meaning of the Christian
worldview that supported the institutions of Western culture were
outrun by the events of the time. The brotherhood of man may be a
noble ideal, but can it be achieved in any society that is not homogenous? Probably not, we discovered. At a certain point in the struggle
for realization, it became apparent that goals of the Civil Rights
movement could not be achieved because people did not subscribe to
them and because the goals were, after all, abstract projections of an
ideal world, not descriptions of a real world.

The collapse of the Civil Rights movement, the concern with
Vietnam and the war, the escape to drugs, the rise of power movements, and the return to Mother Earth can all be understood as

desperate efforts of groups of people to flee abstract articulations of belief and superficial values and find authenticity wherever it could be found. It was at this point that Indians became popular and the widespread and intense interest in Indians, as seen in the fantasy literature and anthologies, seemed to indicate that Americans wanted more from Indians than they did from other minority groups. For many people the stoic, heroic, and noble Indian who had lived an idyllic existence prior to contact with whites seemed to hold the key to survival and promised to provide new meanings for American life.

Although Americans who held this view were fooling themselves, they knew what they wanted. Indians who saw this interest doubly fooled themselves because they came to believe that the people were interested in them and not in the intangible experiences they were thought to represent. Thus during the early 1970s and until the mid-1980s at every meeting and convention Indian spokespersons were proudly announcing that the ensuing calendar year would truly be "The Year of the Indian." Ecological advertisements featured Indians paddling or walking across polluted streams and fields with tears running down their faces. Indians were ecstatic—and badly mistaken. People began to inquire about the basic values of Indian life and articulated their version of it to the very Indians they were quizzing. About all the Indians could do was agree and try their best to make corrections that would not insult their white friends or erode their apparent beliefs in things Indian.

The events of the summer of 1971 should have had much more impact on Indians than they did. Finding a nationwide propensity of whites who wished to dig up Indian graves should have frightened most Indians. Many years before, William Carlos Williams wrote: "The land! Don't you feel it? Doesn't it make you want to go out and lift dead Indians tenderly from their graves, to steal from them—as if it must be clinging even to their corpses—some authenticity."[1] And of course on an unconscious level that was precisely what whites did in 1971. That Christian peoples, or even quasi-Christian peoples, could commit such outrages is a measure of their spiritual desperation and unconscious yearning for a feeling of authenticity and emotional stability. But even if these grave diggers posing as amateur archaeologists were not Christian, how could the "true" Christians not have seen the danger in embracing a foreign creed and raised their voices in protest of these acts?

By 1978 the interest in traditional religions was so intense that many experienced older Indians characterized the former activists as the Indian version of "Jesus freaks." Indeed the late 1970s saw many Americans, Indian and non-Indian, blindly accept various kinds of religious doctrines without the slightest bit of critical appraisal. It was during those confusing days, we must remember, that the Jonestown tragedy took place. Many Indians who had formerly been Christians of one persuasion or another used the Western format as a means of expressing their devotion and some former AIM members, flying in to Rapid City so they could take part in the Pine Ridge sun dance, compared the sun dance with taking communion in the Christian denomination, a parallel that had absolutely no validity whatsoever.

In the 1980 presidential elections the Western religious fundamentalist right flexed its muscle and elected Ronald Reagan who stumbled through a confession that, yes indeed, he believed he had had a conversion experience and therefore deserved their votes. While the Indian correlate to the surging religious right was to be found in various Indian communities, it did not have the grim, unrelenting intolerance that characterized the white fundamentalist movement. Instead young Indians began to specialize in ways highly reminiscent of people in the old days who achieved, through visions or hard work, expertise in various badly needed community skills. Only at the fringes of Indian society, where zealous non-Indians sought to participate, was there any friction. Otherwise, the elders were greatly heartened to see the next generation adopting traditional values and customs so readily.

In ideological terms this contrast between Indian and non-Indian religious revival presents a fascinating picture. American whites are victims of a process long predicted. Friedrich W. Nietzsche and Sören A. Kierkegaard, European philosophers of the nineteenth century, both foresaw that a tragic breakdown in both vision and values was occurring in the psyche of Westerners. For Kierkegaard the solution to the problem became the exercise of an incredible power of will that he thought would lead Western peoples back to the fundamental realities as he saw them. Advocating that the individual must have "purity of heart," a solitary and well-disciplined march toward an identifiable goal, Kierkegaard believed that goodness would naturally follow the good if one so willed it.

Nietzsche announced the death of God long before the Anglican bishop John Robinson. Nietzsche's alternative was the creation of the superman, the will to power in this instance being the complete development of human powers and all talents possible. While Nietzsche saw this thrust as an individual decision, the language and temper of his ideas could easily be found in the ecstatic and demonic rantings of Adolf Hitler and National Socialism that simply insisted that the German people were supermen. Unfortunately these philosophies of will always seem to affect the ordinary citizens by vesting them with an extraordinarily destructive idea of racial superiority.

Both Kierkegaard and Nietzsche attempted to solve the problem of decay inherent with the passage of time within the Western vision of the world by using the Avis approach: try harder by doing the same things that are now outmoded but still seem reasonable. A more common sense approach to bolstering Western fortunes and moral failures came in the early years of this century when Walter Rauschenbusch (1861–1918) and others promulgated the theology of the social gospel. They visualized the fulfillment of the Christian kingdom on earth in the social reform movements of the muckraker era of American politics. Labor organization, restrictive child labor laws, pure food laws, unemployment compensation, and greatly enhanced educational opportunities became for them the realization of the Western peoples' potential for creating a heavenly society without divine intervention. The New Deal came closer than any other administration in realizing this vision but the onset of World War II shortcircuited its efforts.

When the social gospel was brought into full confrontation with the American political system in the Civil Rights movement (and there was plenty of social gospel ideology in the War on Poverty), traditional Protestant theology thwarted its realization. While advances were made in civil rights legislation, particularly in the areas of education, employment, voting rights and housing, most Americans allowed their racial prejudices to overcome their sense of compassion.

The first round of retrenchment came with the Richard Nixon/Spiro Agnew/Billy Graham theology of unquestioning submission to political decisions and the intense concentration of religious energy on achieving a personal relationship with God. Later this distinction was almost completely erased during Ronald Reagan's terms as president when the values inherent in the personal relationship turned out to be identical to the racist pandering of the Republican Party for white voters. George Bush sabotaged constructive social legislation (affirmative action, civil rights commission, etc.), appointed conservative but hardly scholarly Supreme Court Justices, and used subliminal racial themes in his campaigns and speeches. It was no accident that Willie Horton, a black man, became the symbol of the alleged Dukakis' positionof Michael Dukakis of being "soft" on crime.

Some non-Indian writers detected a turning point in the mid-1970s. Garry Wills, in two books, *Nixon Agonistes* and *Bare Ruined Choirs*, found sufficient reason to believe that a turn toward secularism within religion itself had taken place. James Michener, usually noted for long sprawling historical novels about locations, projected a search for a new conception of our position in social history, finding a religious dimension about to be revealed in *A Quality of Life*. Harvey Cox confronted secularism head-on with *The Secular City* and seemed to predict that creature of the Reagan years, the greedy yuppie who had to have it all now. A very naive interpretation of the underlying changes was found in Charles Reich's *The Greening of America*, which conceived of a benign corporate America, transformed by the entrance of movement people into the business world. More to the point, Alvin Toffler's *Future Shock* and Vance Packard's *A Nation of Strangers* forecast the impact on American behavior once computers, the population explosion, dwindling resources, and the change in sexual attitudes really took hold. Toffler and Packard were particularly worried about the increase in the rate of activity on people apart from other predicted developments. Could increasing speed in communications and the flow of information and constant migration include the same religious convictions about the world that people held two centuries ago?

Non-Indian America has fragmented during the past two decades. A small portion of people entered the New Age that has been a smorgasbord of religious experiences derived from any tradition willing to advocate its beliefs and whatever experiences could be packaged for sale to American consumers. Thus astrology, numerology, flying saucers with heavenly "space brothers," past-life regressions, a variety of martial arts techniques, various brands of shamanism, and modern versions of witchcraft fill the empty hours of the affluent fringe groups who reject Christianity but want to have some hold on religious experiences.

An increasing number of Americans have become members of the religious right, the fundamentalists. As mainline churches lose members rapidly through their constant efforts to pander to the unchurched and make themselves relevant, mindless fundamentalism makes amazing strides, even among the educated people in society. When the fundamentalists seized on abortion as an issue, they found the key to political power. Thus was created the irony of modern American life. The fundamentalists could care less about human life after birth. They unquestioningly accept American military ventures around the world and cry for more blood with each invasion or carpet-bombing of small countries. They steadfastly support the death penalty and see nothing wrong with its one-sided application to racial minorities. They close their eyes to blatant theft of American assets by government officials, savings and loan executives, and bankers, and oppose every social program that is proposed. Yet on the abortion issue they wax eloquent about the sanctity of human life as if their salvation depends on it.

Thus, through nearly two decades while American Indians were rediscovering the integrity of their traditional religions, the rest of American society has torn itself and its religious traditions apart, substituting patriotism and hedonism for old values and behaviors. Why was it so easy for American Indians to recapture the essence of their religious life and so difficult for non-Indians to regain a measure of religious experience and stability? Albert Camus explored death and suicide in *The Rebel* and gave an incisive analysis of the western religious problem that bears examining:

> The profound conflict in this century is perhaps not so much between the German ideologies of history and Christian political ideologies of history and Christian political con-

cepts, which in a certain way are accomplices, as between German dreams and Mediterranean traditions ... in other words between history and nature.

Christianity, no doubt, was only able to conquer its catholicity by assimilating as much as it could of Greek thought. But when the Church dissipated its Mediterranean heritage, it placed the emphasis on history to the detriment of nature, caused the Gothic to triumph over the romance, and destroying a limit in itself, has made increasing claims to temporal power and historical dynamism. When nature ceases to be an object of contemplation and admiration, it can be nothing more than material for an action that aims at transforming it. These tendencies—and not the real strength of mediation, which would have comprised the real strength of Christianity—are triumphing, in modern times, to the detriment of Christianity itself, by an inevitable turn of events.[2]

If, as Camus would define it, the choice for this century was between history and nature, somehow we made a very bad bargain when we chose history because it appears history has come to an end. And we are very close to destroying nature.

The religious issue in American society has been developing for several decades. It is not as simple as the old Protestant-Catholic competition nor does it reflect the former Christian-Jew diversity. American society now has a bewildering variety of sects and religious traditions. The refugees from the Vietnam War and the intense interest in Asian religions, including the martial arts so well publicized by the movies, have made Asian traditions respectable for the first time in American history. The strong interest in the esoteric traditions, astrology, etc., has broadened out the supermarket of possible religious experiences so that people feel quite at home chanting a hymn to Osiris if the occasion calls for it. The religious situation today eloquently reflects the American psyche—we create our own reality and we are absolutely free to do so. This condition, however, suggests that there is no reality and that we live in a completely intellectual world where the free choice of the individual determines the values and emotional content of experiences. We are at ground zero religiously with little possibility of a revelation to enable us to move on.

Reaching into this plate of religious linguini and making an orderly analysis are not as impossible as we might suppose because Camus has properly identified our real choices—history or nature, time or space. While we would like our personal preferences to be realized, if we have any sanity, we must admit that the world outside our perspective has a bit of substance to it and must certainly be constructed on certain principles through which history and nature are related. It is therefore our task to examine with a great deal of seriousness the possible relationships that these two ideas have and the probable configuration that a new understanding of history and nature and time and space would give us.

For the sake of comparison let us suggest the possible representatives of history and nature that we can find in America today and examine what degree of clarity they display that could help us to see new combinations and understandings about the values and directions we must take in solving our social and psychological problems. History must certainly be represented by the Christian churches, the fundamentalists having been disappointed in the recent Gulf War which many of them felt forecast Armageddon and consequently supported vigorously. Even the old tired mainline churches, the Episcopalians, Presbyterians, United Church of Christ, and others still preach in glowing terms about the coming of the Kingdom and the prominent part their respectable members will play in it. Add to this mixture the Republican Party that, by appointing second- and third-rate scholars and practitioners to the Supreme Court, believes it is now returning to the "original principles" of the Constitution, and we have pretty much the advocates of the idea that history is all important and nature is merely an inert mass to be exploited.

Identifying the groups that would naturally fall on the side of nature is more hypothetical. American Indians certainly stand out in this respect as the many quotations in anthologies demonstrate. Animal rights activists would seem to qualify as well and some of the more militant ecological and conservation organizations. It is difficult to distinguish the conservation groups who really see a value in nature and those who simply want it preserved for the sake of human enjoyment. Regardless of motive or perspective they are more reliable allies in most causes than are the churches or the political parties. Like the groups that believe in the reality of history, those people who see a value in nature and attempt to tailor their behavior accordingly share a general orientation and are not committed to any specific articulation of the idea if, indeed, they are able to derive abstract principles from their experiences.

Yet there is a profound difference between American Indians and all of these other groups. The Indian is indigenous and therefore does not have the psychological burden of establishing his or her right to the land in the deep emotional sense of knowing that he or she belongs there. Nearly half a century ago Chief Luther Standing Bear of the Sioux tribe commented on the strange feeling of alienation which the intruder experiences and applied his analysis to the American whites as follows:

> The white man does not understand America. He is too far removed from its formative processes. The roots of the tree of his life have not yet grasped the rock and soil. The white man is still troubled by primitive fears; he still has in his consciousness the perils of this frontier continent, some of its fastnesses not yet having yielded to his questioning footsteps and inquiring eyes. He shudders still with the memory of the loss of his forefathers upon its scorching deserts and forbidding mountaintops. The man from Europe is still a foreigner and an alien. And he still hates the man who questioned his oath across the continent.

> But in the Indian the spirit of the land is still vested; it will be until other men are able to divine and meet its rhythm. Men must be born and reborn to belong. Their bodies must be formed of the dust of their forefathers' bones.[3]

It is significant that many non-Indians have discerned this need to become indigenous and have taken an active role in protecting the environment.

The patriotism of the American conservative may be said to be an expression of the effort to become indigenous. Certainly many Americans chafe at the idea that only Indians should be called "Native Americans," and they argue, quite properly, that anyone born in the United States is a native American. But their allegiance is to democracy, a powerful idea, but it has no relationship to the earth upon which we walk and the plants and animals that give us sustenance. Developing a sense of ourselves that would properly balance history and nature and space and time is a more difficult task than we would suspect and involves a radical reevaluation of the way we look at the world around us. Do we continue to exploit the earth or do we preserve it and preserve life? Whether we are prepared to embark on a painful intellectual journey to discover the parameters of reconciling history and nature is the question of this generation.

Notes

1. Virginia Armstrong, *I Have Spoken* (Chicago: Swallow Press, 1971), xviii.
        It seemed to be a startling prediction of what I had thought was developing for years; combined with the series of grave-robbing incidents it is little short of prophetic.
2. Albert Camus, *The Rebel* (New York: Vintage Books, 1956), 299.
3. Luther Standing Bear, *Land of the Spotted Eagle* (Boston: Houghton Mifflin, 1933), 248.

CHAPTER 4

THINKING
IN TIME AND SPACE

The division of domestic ideologies may appear to be quite artificial to many people. Traditionally we have been taught to define differences neither by ancestral backgrounds nor cultural attitudes but by political persuasions. Conservative and liberal, terms that initially described political philosophies, have taken on the aspect of being able to stand for cultural attitudes of fairly distinct content. Liberals appear to have more sympathy for humanity, while conservatives worship corporate freedom and self-help doctrines underscoring individual responsibility. The basic philosophical differences between liberals and conservatives are not fundamental, however, because both find in the idea of history a thesis by which they can validate their ideas.

When the domestic ideology is divided according to American Indian and Western European immigrant, however, the fundamental difference is one of great philosophical importance. American Indians hold their lands—places—as having the highest possible meaning, and all their statements are made with this reference point in mind. Immigrants review the movement of their ancestors across the continent as a steady progression of basically good events and experiences, thereby placing history—time—in the best possible light. When one group is concerned with the philosophical problem of space and the other with the philosophical problem of time, then the statements of either group do not make much sense when transferred from one context to the other without the proper consideration of what is taking place.

Western European peoples have never learned to consider the nature of the world discerned from a spatial point of view. And a singular difficulty faces peoples of Western European heritage in making a transition from thinking in terms of time to thinking in terms of space. The very essence of Western European identity involves the assumption that time proceeds in a linear fashion; further it assumes that at a particular point in the unraveling of this sequence, the peoples of Western Europe became the guardians of the world. The same ideology that sparked the Crusades, the Age of Exploration, the Age of Imperialism, and the recent crusade against Communism all involve the affirmation that time is peculiarly related to the destiny of the people of Western Europe. And later, of course, the United States.

The postwar generation of which we are a part has refused to accept any alteration of this fundamental premise. It is particularly revealing that the first major doctrine enunciated as an anti-Communist foreign policy was that of containment. Through containment it was believed the spread of Communism could be restricted to certain geographical areas from which no further extensions of Communist ideologies could emanate. The anachronistic nature of this theory should have been apparent. Western political ideas came to depend on spatial restrictions of what were essentially nonspatial ideas. The inherent contradiction of opposing dissimilar definitions within a single theory proved fruitless to the colonial powers in Southeast Asia, Africa, and India, and led to unjustifiable woes in Central America and military adventurism elsewhere.

Without venturing further into the field of foreign affairs, it may be well to note in passing that the determination of two American presidents, fighting in Vietnam, not to be the "first to lose a war," when winning that war in any final sense would have meant total destruction of a land and a people, would seem to indicate the extent to which Western peoples—and particularly Americans—have taken the dimension of time or history as an absolute value. Our withdrawal from

Southeast Asia would seem to demonstrate that in most military collisions, history is clearly negated by geography. We have seen this phenomenon before in the two classic, unsuccessful attempts by Napoleon and Hitler to conquer Russia, in which that country's vast interior subdued military forces that appeared to be riding the crest of historical change. We may now be facing that phenomenon again in the Middle East.

The disclaimer of colonialism in recent years has presented Western peoples with a major dilemma. Deprived of their traditional source of wealth from the undeveloped and former colonial nations, they now have little choice but to seek ways of rechanneling their present wealth through the various forms of social organization already present domestically. A certain inertia has been achieved, perhaps unwittingly, that means a major shift in political thinking among Western peoples. The creation of wealth today is more dependent on new technology and manipulation of the tax laws than on the exploitation of untapped resources. That is not to say that exploitation of mineral and other resources will not continue. As undeveloped nations, such as those in Africa or the Middle East, continue their own growth, severe modifications of exploitation must occur, and more sophisticated forms of colonialism, such as sanctions and embargoes, must be created if Western countries are not to suffer economic collapse.

It is doubtful that many Americans understand the meaning of this shift from the colonialist attitude. At best it means the humanization of peoples who for centuries were considered merely producers of raw materials and consumers of those products they were required to purchase. At worst, the end of one form of colonialism means the beginning of a movement to feudalize political systems around the globe so as to stabilize the economic conditions of the more affluent nations. Either approach means that the ecological problem is not dealt with, the problem of technological dehumanization is not reduced, and the breakdown of individual and community identity is not reversed.

There can be little doubt that a major part of the Western world is now suffering from an increasingly complicated task of revitalizing institutions to prevent collapse. Revitalization has been primarily an effort to force outmoded institutions to respond to novel situations for which they were not created. If we take Toffler's *Future*

Shock seriously (and there does not seem to be sufficient reason to consider it a trivial analysis), or if we recognize the logical conclusions of the thinking of both Buckminster Fuller and Marshall McLuhan, we discover neither a planet Earth of the spaceship model nor an instantaneous universe of communications linking a global village, but the disappearance of time itself as a limiting factor of our experience. In a world in which communications are nearly instantaneous and simultaneous experiences are possible, it must be spaces and places that distinguish us from one another, not time nor history.

The world, therefore, is not a global village so much as a series of nonhomogeneous pockets of identity that must eventually come into conflict because they represent different historical arrangements of emotional energy. What these concentrations of emotional energy will produce, how they will understand themselves, and what minimovements will emerge from them are among the unanswered questions of our time. If we believe that religion has a presence in human societies in any fundamental sense, then we can no longer speak of universal religions in the customary manner. Rather we must be prepared to confront religion and religious activities in new and novel ways. The recognition that there is no homogeneous sense of time shared by all societies must certainly become apparent to us if it is not already clear. We can and must, therefore, create a new understanding of universal planetary history.

Beneath the minimovements of activity on the local level, we will most certainly see the emergence of religious movements that appear out of time, movements that have been somehow triggered either by the influences of the places in which they have originated or movements of restoration that seek to invoke some type of authentic religious experience to validate the identity of the small ethnic, racial, or religious group. Thus, Southern California can be the hotbed of Christian fundamentalist beliefs and at the same time support a substantial number of devil-worshippers and Satanists. Both movements are disconnected from a universal passage of time and are a product of the concentration of beliefs as modified by their human and natural environments.

Religion has often been seen as an evolutionary process in which mankind progresses from primitive superstitions to logically perfected codes of conduct, from a multiplicity of deities to a monotheistic religion with well-developed institutions and creeds honed to philosophical purity of expression. The validity of most religious traditions is believed to be their ability to explain the cosmos, not their potential to provide a wide range of spiritual experiences. But monotheism, as Nathan Soderblum has pointed out, is usually the product of the political unification of a diverse society more often than it is the result of a revelation of ultimate reality.

In the western tradition, revelation has generally been interpreted as the communication to human beings of a divine plan, the release of new information and insights when the deity has perceived that mankind has reached the fullness of time and can now understand additional knowledge about the ultimate nature of our world. Thus, what has been the manifestation of deity in a particular local situation is mistaken for a truth applicable to all times and places, a truth so powerful that it must be impressed upon peoples who have no connection to the event or to the cultural complex in which it originally made sense. The recounting of the event becomes its major value and both metaphysics and ethics are believed to be contained in the description of the event. Ultimately the religion becomes a matter of imposing the ethical perspective derived from reprocessing the religious experience on foreign cultures and not in following whatever moral dictates might have been gleaned from the experience.

The question that the so-called world religions have not satisfactorily resolved is whether or not religious experience can be distilled from its original cultural context and become an abstract principle that is applicable to all peoples in different places and at different times. The persistent emergence of religious movements and the zeal with which they are pursued would seem to suggest that cultural context, time, and place are the major elements of revelation and the content is illusory. If not illusory, it is subject to so many cultural qualifications that it is not suitable for transmission to other societies without doing severe damage to both the message of revelation and the society which receives it.

American Indians and other tribal peoples did not take this path in interpreting revelations and religious experiences. The structure of their religious traditions is taken directly from the world around them, from their relationships with other forms of life. Context is therefore all-important for both practice and the understanding of reality. The places where revelations were experienced were remembered and set aside as locations where, through rituals and ceremonials, the people could once again communicate with the spirits. Thousands of years of occupancy on their lands taught tribal peoples the sacred landscapes for which they were responsible and gradually the structure of ceremonial reality became clear. It was not what people believed to be true that was important but what they experienced as true. Hence revelation was seen as a continuous process of adjustment to the natural surroundings and not as a specific message valid for all times and places.

The vast majority of Indian tribal religions, therefore, have a sacred center at a particular place, be it a river, a mountain, a plateau, valley, or other natural feature. This center enables the people to look out along the four dimensions and locate their lands, to relate all historical events within the confines of this particular land, and to accept responsibility for it. Regardless of what subsequently happens to the people, the sacred lands remain as permanent fixtures in their cultural or religious understanding. Thus, many tribes now living in Oklahoma, but formerly from the eastern United States, still hold in their hearts the sacred locations of their history, and small groups travel to obscure locations in secret to continue tribal ceremonial life.

Other religions also have a sense of sacred places. The Holy Land has historically been a battlefield of three world religions each of which has particular sacred places it cherishes. But these places are appreciated primarily for their historical significance and do not provide the sense of permanency and rootedness that the Indian sacred places represent. European Christian shrines are often standing on the ruins of former temples and holy places of the original peoples of Europe, indicating that something of the sacred always infuses a site regardless of the religious expression that may temporarily possess it. The ancient Chinese developed an incredibly complex system of geomancy in order to make human habitations conform to the sacred landscape of China. But of all these expressions of human religious experiences, none has so faithfully remained close to the original location and original revelation as those of the tribal peoples of North America.

The nature of revelation at sacred places is often of such a personal nature as to preclude turning it into a subject of missionary activities. Thus most Indian tribes will not reveal the location of sacred places unless they are compelled through dire circumstances to do so. But having once identified a location as having sacred properties, they will not then reveal the kinds of ceremonies that are supposed to be held there. Sacred places thus inform us of the particularity of revelation—that it is not a universal message to be placed in secular or immature hands for distribution. Rather it is as intimate as our own personal thoughts that we would never utter in profane ears. (See chapter 16 for an in-depth discussion of sacred places.)

One of the features of Western religious practice has been the dependence on teaching and preaching techniques. Indeed, take away the preaching and teaching and there is very little substance left in many world religions. Christianity has been singularly involved in proclaiming the "good news" that involves the articulation of an impossibly complex scenario involving original sin, a cosmic redeemer, the catastrophic end of the planet, and transportation of the "saved" to a new heaven where presumably people will behave much better than they did on the old earth. Preaching and teaching have, as their goal, the possibility of changing individual personality and behavior, presumably in a manner more pleasing to the deity. A glance at the historical record will show that the hope of transformation is rarely realized and never seen on a large scale.

Changing the conception of religious reality from a temporal to a spatial framework involves surrendering the place of teaching and preaching as elements of religion. Rearrangement of individual behavioral patterns is incidental to the communal involvement in ceremonies and the continual renewal of community relationships with the holy places of revelation. Ethics flow from the ongoing life of the community and are virtually indistinguishable from the tribal or communal customs. There is little dependence on the concept of progress either on an individual or community basis as a means of evaluating the impact of the religious practices. Value judgments involve present community realities and not a reliance on part of future golden ages toward which the community is moving or from which the community has veered.

In conjunction with this notion of eliminating the teaching and preaching of abstract propositions, the gulf between religious reality and other aspects of community experience is not nearly as wide. A religion defined according to temporal considerations is continually placed on the defensive in maintaining its control over the interpretation of historical events. If, like the Hebrew prophets of the Old Testament, political, economic, and cultural events can be interpreted in a religious format, then religious and secular time can be made to coincide—at least for a time. But how does one continue the interpretation of history over a long period of time? The Exodus may well reveal divine intervention in addition to being a political event of great significance. Do all subsequent political events of comparable magnitude then become religious experiences? Obviously it becomes increasingly difficult to give a religious interpretation to secular events, and the basic framework of interpretation begins to beg credibility.

Western religion seems to have resolved this problem of interpretation by secularizing itself. Instead of working toward the Kingdom of God on Earth, history becomes the story of a particular race fulfilling its manifest destiny. Thus, Western history is written as if the torch of enlightenment was fated to march from the Mediterranean to the San Francisco Bay. But reaching the western edge of North America, history then must inexorably move to Japan, and it has appeared to do so, stripping the American experience of its cosmic validity. The Cold War retooled this concept so that the interpretation of the past half decade suggested that democracy was the favorite child of divine concern. But Russia is broke and America nearly so, and it takes incredible will power to pretend that history is the unfolding of a divine plan for humanity.

A variant of manifest destiny is the propensity to judge a society or civilization by its technology and to see in society's effort to subdue and control nature as the fulfillment of divine intent. This interpretation merely adopts the secular doctrine of cultural evolution and attaches it to theological language. If we factor in the environmental damage created by technology the argument falls flat. In less than two and a half centuries American whites have virtually destroyed a whole continent and large areas of the United States are now almost uninhabitable—even so we seek to "sacrifice" large rural areas to toxic waste dumps. The idea of defining religious reality along temporal lines, therefore, is to adopt the pretense that the earth simply does not matter, that human affairs alone are important.

Restructuring religious understanding to anchor experience in sacred places enables us to avoid the complications that temporal definitions create. We are left with the question of the function of religion in human society. Was it meant for us to remain tied to a particular place without an adequate technology and refusing to use the intelligence that our species obviously possesses? How do we understand religious experiences if we are confined to one or simply a few locations where religious events can take place? These questions are important but they represent a tendency to make principles absolute and describe a polarity that does not and should not exist in theological discussions. Just as the temporal world religions find a place for sacred sites, so spatial religions deal with the passage of time and the increasing complexity that it brings to human societies by attaching stories to the sacred places.

Tribal religions are actually complexes of attitudes, beliefs, and practices fine-tuned to harmonize with the lands on which the people live. It is not difficult to understand that the Hopi people, living in the arid plateau and canyonlands of northern Arizona, had need of a rain dance to ensure the success of their farming. Here place and religion have such an obvious parallel that anyone can understand the connection. It becomes exceedingly more complicated, however, when we learn that the Lummis and other tribes of the Pacific Northwest also had a rain dance. Perhaps once or twice in a person's lifetime the West Coast would have an exceedingly heavy snow storm. The snow would bury the longhouses in which the people lived, and if it remained deep for any significant period of time, the Lummis would be unable to get out and hunt and fish and would starve to death. A man with powers to make rain would then perform the rain dance, and the snow would cease falling, turning to rain that melted the snow and prevented the people from being snowbound.

Space has limitations that are primarily geographical, and any sense of time arising within the religious experience becomes secondary to present geographical existence. The hazard that appears within the spatial conceptions of religion is the effect that missionary activity has on its integrity when it tries to leave its homeland. Can it leave the land of its nativity and embark on a program of world or continental conquest without losing its religious essence in favor of purely political or economic considerations? Are ceremonies restricted to particular places, and do they become useless in a foreign land? These questions have never been critically examined within Western religious circles, because of the preemption of temporal considerations by Christian theology.

Time has an unusual limitation. It must begin and end at some real points, or it must be conceived as cyclical in nature, endlessly allowing the repetition of patterns of possibilities. Judgment inevitably intrudes into the conception of religious reality whenever a temporal definition is used. Almost always the temporal consideration revolves around the problem of good and evil, and the inconsistencies that arise as this basic relationship is defined turn religious beliefs into ineffectual systems of ethics. But it would seem likely that whereas religions that are spatially determined can create a sense of sacred time that originates in the specific location, it is exceedingly difficult for a religion, once bound to history, to incorporate sacred places into its doctrines. Space generates time, but time has little relationship to space.

The problem of religious imagery is also confounded when we shift from temporal patterns of explanation. The procedure by which religious imagery arises is still the subject of great debate among theologians. It is such a serious problem it has burst the boundaries of religious thought and become the subject of psychoanalytical investigation. How do people conceive of the symbols, doctrines, insights, and sequences in which we find religious ideas expressed? How do we come to conceive deity in certain forms and not others?

Theological explanations that depend on temporal world views would appear to be relatively helpless in examining this question. Perhaps the best that can be said is that temporal theologians place great reliance upon the poetic imagination as the source of religious symbolism. The best and most lofty considerations of a society or culture over a period of time eventually distill themselves into a poetic mythology that comes to express the community's experienced realities. That is about as close as we can come when using temporal conceptions of religious reality—eventual distillation of concepts and symbols.

If the spatial dimension of religion is considered, the answer would appear to be fairly clear. *Something is* observed or experienced by a community, and the symbols and sequences of the mythology are given together in an event that appears so much out of the ordinary experiential sequence as to impress itself upon the collective memories of the community for a sufficiently long duration of time. The basic myth may be refined to some extent, but it is not subject to very much editing because it is the common property of the community, not the exclusive property of the community's poets or religious leaders. The symbols are always representations of the concrete and the place always has precise location.

When considering the multitude of flood stories, for example, we can suggest the possibility of a planet-wide flood at some specific time, because of the appearance of the story in many diverse religious traditions. If we accept the spatial dimensions of religion can we reach reasonably profound conclusions? The flood, experienced in a number of places, gave rise to the legends that recorded memories of the flood. These accounts can be related to the geography of the region, recording the date of occupation of the location. The twist that each locale represents give us more specific information on how the religious experience was received and what it came to mean to the people indigenous to the site. Thus, instead of general principles that support one or another world religion, the flood becomes primarily a historical event with moral and ethical codes particular to the religion reporting the flood experience and explained by the complex of religious events within each tradition.

Remaining committed to temporal concepts, we can only conclude that at a certain stage in evolution it became necessary for societies—extremely diverse and with little in common—to have evolved a myth about a flood. Or, as it is the case with Christianity and Judaism, the possibility of a world flood is taken as proof that the religion is the only correct religion. It does not seem possible for adherents of these religions to conceive of the flood as a universal geological event to which each cultural tradition has attached religious significance. Theological explanations frequently become abstract, and the universal need for baptism was even once advanced as a sufficient reason for the origin of the story. Yet all religious traditions have not depended on baptism, and there seems to be no particular doctrinal need to have created a flood story in the first place.

We are virtually helpless to understand the symbols, stories, doctrines, and ideals that religions have traditionally espoused if we are content to define religion according to temporal terms of explanation. Once we leave time behind and consider the nature of geographical events of extraordinary nature, we can begin to project the possibilities for understanding the nature of religious language and the efficacy of religious doctrines as an explanation of man's religious experiences because symbols are rooted in real events in specific locations. It is, if we will consider it, a very different thing to create a religion out of the best of ideas, symbols, and explanations, and to pass down memories of religious experience absent speculation and reinterpretation.

There appears to be a peculiar relationship between thinking in temporal and spatial terms. We are inevitably involved, whether we like it or not, with time; but when attempting to explain the nature of our experiences, we are often not necessarily involved with spatial considerations once we have taken time seriously. The whole nature of the subject of ethics appears to validate this peculiarity. Ethical systems are notorious for having the ability to relate concepts and doctrines to every abstract consideration except the practical situations with which we become involved. Ethics seems to involve an abstract individual making clear, objective decisions that involve principles but not people. Ideology unleashed without being subjected to the critique to the real world proves demoniac at best. Spatial thinking requires that ethical systems be related directly to the physical world and real human situations, not abstract principles, are believed to be valid at all times and under all circumstances. One could project, therefore, that space must in a certain sense precede time as a consideration for thought. If time becomes our primary consideration, we never seem to arrive at the reality of our existence in places but instead are always directed to experiential and abstract interpretations rather than to the experiences themselves.

A great segment of the American public has been rudely pushed beyond the traditional temporal Western doctrines by the influence of the modern communications media. This is the true nature of the problem of postwar American society. The meaninglessness and alienation discernible in our generation results partially from our allowing time to consume space. The shift in thinking from temporal considerations to spatial considerations may be seen in a number of minimovements by which we are struggling to define American society. Ecology, the new left politics, self-determination of goals by local communities, and citizenship participation all seem to be efforts to recapture a sense of place and a rejection of the traditional American dependence on progress—a temporal concept—as the measure of American identity.

A great many other considerations could be made in attempting to define how our consciousness is gradually shifting away from Western cultural and religious patterns. Development schemes of the federal government began as early as the Great Depression, when the Tennessee Valley Authority marked the first departure in programming from traditional patterns—railroads, settlement, and industrial development by private parties—to federally sponsored projects to enhance regional development. Since that time, the Missouri Valley Authority, the Appalachian Development Authority, the Four Corners Development Authority, and the river compacts of states have evolved, so that geographic considerations are playing a much more important role in how we conceive social, economic, and political problems.

The field of religion has been peculiarly isolated from this development in American thought. Rather, theological considerations have fluctuated from Fundamentalism to social gospel and back. If we consider the social gospel and activist church involvement in social problems such as Civil Rights as an indication of concern with the problems of this world and land, we can find even in the theological movements of the past generation a movement away from temporal considerations.

It is doubtful if American society can move very far or very significantly without a major revolution in theological concepts. In a very real sense religious doctrines define the brooding sense of identity without which societies appear helpless to function. The present theological vacuum is being filled to a great degree by efforts to establish exotic religions in America. The great appeal of oriental religions that appear to provide a meaningful answer to contemporary questions, demonism and fascination with satanic cults, and the rejection of traditional mainline denominations for the simplicity of Fundamentalism all seem to indicate that a comprehensive effort to derive a new religious conception of the world is badly needed.

Before we can have a new theological understanding of our situation, however, the tools of analysis of religious ideas must be changed. This will require a tremendous reversal of ideas that have been held by Western peoples, particularly Christians, for many centuries. Perhaps religions can answer only a few questions concerning our existence; Christian doctrines have attempted in the past to answer everything. Perhaps we will find that the present situation makes it impossible for religion to function at all; perhaps we are stuck with psychodrama and other scientific techniques.

Many religions have been held in deepest contempt because they do not in some manner measure up to the definitions of religion as promulgated by Western/Christian ideas of the nature of religion. They were held invalid, not because they did not provide an understanding of the universe with which that particular society was confronted, but because they did not coincide with ideas held by Western society that is heavily dependent on its technology and nearly independent of its religious ideology.

In almost every instance in which other religions were considered as invalid, it was because the categories of explanation on which they were judged to be false, were those derived primarily from temporal considerations of how the world ought to be. If the categories are turned around and the Christian religion is judged by nontemporal categories, the story becomes somewhat different. In most instances Christianity has either no answer or an extremely inadequate answer to the problems that arise. The difference is notable. While Christianity can project the reality of the afterlife—time and eternity—it appears to be incapable of providing any reality to the life in which we are here and now presently engaged—space and the planet Earth.

American Indian tribal religions are among those so downgraded, because they did not fall into the easily constructed categories of religion as defined with temporal concepts and doctrines. Yet in a variety of ways the American public, searching for a sense of authenticity that it cannot find in its own tradition, is turning to American Indians as it wishes to visualize them. It is not simply the nobility of the novelists or the tragic vision of the historians that America is seeking. In a very real sense, the quest is for the religious insight of American Indians and the feeling of authenticity that Indians project.

In seeking the religious reality behind the American Indian tribal existence, Americans are in fact attempting to come to grips with the land that produced the Indian tribal cultures and their vision of community. Even if they avoid American Indians completely, those Americans seeking a more comprehensive and meaningful life are retracing the steps taken centuries before by Indian tribes as they attempted to come to grips with this land. Recently Congress discussed compensation as a principle of criminal law. The days of the oriental potentate and justice as vengeance may be closing. If so, would not the religion that sees deity as the stern judge of mankind also be fading?

In the pages to come we will deliberately place several concepts of general religious interest under examination. We shall attempt to define in Western terms that nature of Indian tribal religions as they differ in their method of framing questions from a predominantly spatial conception of reality. And we shall discuss traditional Christian solutions to these questions, comparing the two types of answers to learn if any distinct differences do in fact exist.

We cannot, of course, pretend to give an exhaustive answer to any particular question or to present a final definition of either Indian tribal religions or traditional Christian ideas. What is important is that alternative methods of asking questions or of viewing the world may arise. By learning where differences can or do occur at least one thing may become clear. Before any final solution to American history can occur, a reconciliation must be effected between the spiritual owner of the land—American Indians—and the political owner of the land—American whites. Guilt and accusations cannot continue to revolve in a vacuum without some effort at reaching a solution.

Notes

I do not pretend to make a complete analysis of the problems involved here since my original goal was to sketch out on rather broad terms the change in perspective that is required to get people to take the idea of place seriously. Most Americans, raised in a society in which history is all-encompassing, have very little idea of how radically their values would shift if they took the idea of places, both secular and sacred, seriously. In the two decades since I wrote this chapter, an amazing number of books have been published that deal, in one way or another, with sacred places. It would be interesting to see how many books preceded this one in articulating some kind of theory about the importance of specific place in our outlook and emotional lives.

CHAPTER 5

THE PROBLEM OF CREATION

Indian tribal religions and Christianity differ considerably on numerous theological points, but a very major distinction that can be made between the two types of thinking concerns the idea of creation. Christianity has traditionally appeared to place its major emphasis on creation as a specific event while the Indian tribal religions could be said to consider creation as an ecosystem present in a definable place. In this distinction we have again the fundamental problem of whether we consider the reality of our experience as capable of being described in terms of space or time—as "what happened here" or "what happened then."

Both religions can be said to agree on the role and activity of a creator. Outside of that specific thing, there would appear to be little that the two views share. Tribal religions appear to be thereafter confronted with the question of the interrelationship of all things. Christians see creation as the beginning event of a linear time sequence in which a divine plan is worked out, the conclusion of the sequence being an act of destruction bringing the world to an end. The beginning and end of time are of no apparent concern for many tribal religions.

The act of creation is a singularly important event for the Christian. It describes the sequence in which the tangible features of human existence are brought into being, and although some sermons have made much of the element of light that appears in the creation account of Genesis and the prologue of St. John's Gospel, the similarity of the two books and their use of light do not appear to be of crucial importance in the doctrine of creation. For the Christian it would appear that the importance of the creation event is that it sets the scene for an understanding of the entrance of sin into the world.

Intimately tied with the actual creation event in the Christian theological scheme is the appearance of the first people, Adam and Eve. They are made after the image of God. It is important that this point be recognized, as it has affected popular conceptions held by Christians and seems to have some relevance to central theological doctrines. As the Genesis story relates that the first people were made after God's image, Christians, although not necessarily their Hebrew predecessors and Jewish contemporaries, have popularly conceived God as having a human form. That is to say, God looks like a man. Paintings represent Him generally as an old man, deriving perhaps from the old Hebrew conception of the "Ancient of Days."

The first distinction between Indian tribal religions and Christianity would appear to be in the manner in which deity is popularly conceived. The overwhelming majority of American Indian tribal religions refused to represent deity anthropomorphically.[1] To be sure, many tribes used the term *grandfather* when praying to God, but there was no effort to use that concept as the basis for a theological doctrine by which a series of complex relationships and related doctrines could be developed. While there was an acknowledgment that the Great Spirit has some resemblance to the role of a grandfather in the tribal society, there was no great demand to have a "personal relationship" with the Great Spirit in the same manner as popular Christianity has emphasized personal relationships with God.[2]

The difference between conceiving God as an anthropomorphic being and as an undefinable presence carries over into the distinction in the views of creation. Closely following the creation of the world in Christian theology comes the disobedience of man, Adam, in eating the forbidden fruit growing on a tree in the Garden of Eden.

In this act as recorded in Genesis, humankind "fell" from God's grace and was driven out of the garden by the angry God. The major thesis of the Christian religion is thus contained in its creation story, because it is for the redemption of man that the atonement of Jesus of Nazareth is considered to make sense.

With the fall of Adam the rest of nature also falls out of grace with God, Adam being a surrogate for the whole of creation. This particular point has been a very difficult problem for Christian theologians. While it adequately explains the entrance of evil into the world, just how it could occur in a universe conceived as perfect has been difficult for theologians to answer. St. Augustine preferred to think that God Himself had taken the form of the snake that, in the story, talked Eve into eating the forbidden fruit.[3] St. Augustine's solution has not generally been accepted, even though it appears to explain the logical sequence.

Perhaps of more importance are two aspects of the Christian doctrine of creation bearing directly on us today. One aspect is that the natural world is thereafter considered as corrupted, and it becomes theoretically beyond redemption. Many Christian theologians have attempted to avoid this conclusion, but it appears to have been a central doctrine of the Christian religion during most of the Christian era. No less a thinker than Paul Tillich attempted to reconstruct the doctrine into more satisfying terms that would be acceptable to the modern world. In a rather complex analysis in his *Systematic Theology*, Tillich wrestled with the problem.

> Christianity must reject the idealistic separation of an innocent nature from guilty man. Such a rejection has become comparatively easy in our period because of the insights gained about the growth of man and his relation to nature within and outside himself. First, it can be shown that in the development of man there is no absolute discontinuity between animal bondage and human freedom. There are leaps between different stages, but there is also a slow and continuous transformation. It is impossible to say at which point in the process of natural evolution animal nature is replaced by the nature which, in our present experience we know as human, a nature which is qualitatively different from animal nature.[4]

And, as there are analogies to human freedom in nature, so there are also analogies to human good and evil in all parts of the universe. It is worthy of note that Isaiah prophesied peace in nature for the new eon, thereby showing that he would not call nature "innocent." Nor would the writer who, in Genesis, chapter 3, tells about the curse over the land declare nature innocent. Nor would Paul do so in Romans, chapter 8, when he speaks about the bondage to futility which is the fate of nature. Certainly, all these expressions are poetic-mythical. They could not be otherwise, since only poetic empathy opens the inner life of nature. Nevertheless, they are realistic in substance and certainly more realistic than the moral utopianism which confronts immoral man with innocent nature. Just as, within man, nature participates in the good and evil he does, so nature, outside man, shows analogies to man's good and evil doing. Man reaches into nature, as nature reaches into man. They participate in each other and cannot be separated from each other. This makes it possible and necessary to use the term "fallen world" and to apply the concept of existence (in contrast to essence) to the universe as well as man. [5]

Like many other Christian thinkers, Tillich cannot break the relationship between humans and the natural world in which both share a corrupt nature. Even his dependence on evolution appears to be but a temporary nod to the reflections of science, because he stands ready to label the nature of people corrupt at whatever point in the evolutionary process a human being comparable in psychological processes to ourselves emerges.

Indian tribal religions also held a fundamental relationship between human beings and the rest of nature, but the conception was radically different. For many Indian tribal religions the whole of creation was good, and because the creation event did not include a "fall," the meaning of creation was that all parts of it functioned together to sustain it. Young Chief, a Cayuse, refused to sign the Treaty of Walla Walla because he felt the rest of the creation was not represented in the transaction.

I wonder if the ground has anything to say? I wonder if the ground is listening to what is said? I wonder if the ground would come alive and what is on it? Though I hear what the ground says. The ground says, It is the Great Spirit that placed me here. The Great Spirit tells me to take care of the Indians, to feed them aright. The Great Spirit appointed the roots to feed the Indians on. The water says the same thing. The Great Spirit directs me, Feed the Indians well. The grass says the same thing, Feed the Indians well. The ground, water and grass say, the Great Spirit has given us our names. We have these names and hold these names. The ground says, The Great Spirit placed me here to produce all that grows on me, trees and fruit. The same way the ground says, It was from me man was made. The Great Spirit, in placing men on earth, desired them to take good care of the ground and to do each other no harm.[6]

The similarity between Young Chief's conception of creation and the Genesis story is striking, but when one understands that the Genesis story is merely the starting place for theological doctrines of a rather abstract nature while Young Chief's beliefs are the practical articulations of his understanding of the relationship between the various entities of the creation, the difference becomes apparent. In the Indian tribal religions, man and the rest of creation are cooperative and respectful of the task set for them by the Great Spirit. In the Christian religion both are doomed from shortly after the creation event until the end of the world.

The second aspect of the Christian doctrine of creation that concerns us today is the idea that man receives domination over the rest of creation. Harvey Cox, a popular Protestant theologian, articulates rather precisely the attitude derived from this idea of Genesis: "Just after his creation man is given the crucial responsibility of naming the animals. He is their master and commander. It is his task to subdue the earth."[7] It is this attitude that has been adopted wholeheartedly by Western peoples in their economic exploitation of the earth. The creation becomes a mere object when this view is carried to its logical conclusion—a directly opposite result from that of the Indian religions.

Whether or not Christians wanted to carry their doctrine of human dominance as far as it has been carried, the fact remains that the modern world is just now beginning to identify the Christian religion's failure to show adequate concern for the planet as a major factor in our present ecological crisis. Among the earliest scholars to recognize the Christian responsibility for our present situation of ecological chaos was Lynn White, Jr., who gave a presentation titled "The Historical Roots of Our Ecological Crisis" in 1967 before the American Association for the Advancement of Science. White presented the same previously discussed criticism of Christian theology, emphasizing the tendency of the Christian religion to downgrade the natural world and its life forms in favor of the supernatural world of the Christian postjudgment world of eternal life.[8] But he was extremely kind for a man who had his intellectual arguments honed so fine that he could have gone for the jugular vein had he wanted. White proposed that St. Francis be made the ecological saint, elevating Francis to a pedestal he did not deserve.

A number of Christians appear to be taking up White's thesis, and one frequently hears arguments that St. Francis represents the true Christian tradition. The Franciscan tradition is not a major theme of either Christian or Western thought, however, and it would appear as if advocating St. Francis as a patron of the Christian attitude toward creation is not only historically late but uncertain. White's thesis proved unbearable to Dr. René Dubos, of New York City Rockefeller University, who gave a presentation in 1969 at the Smithsonian Institution in Washington, D.C., on "A Theology of the Earth." In it Dubos disclaimed White's charge against Christianity. Dubos contended that other societies had also created ecological disasters. He felt that Christianity was therefore not to be held account-able for the shortcomings of Westerners. He buttressed his thesis by references to St. Francis and, more particularly, to St. Benedict, founder of the Benedictine Order. Dubos found that the Benedictine work rules, which at that time included draining swamps and filling in lowlands, were more suitable for modern man than St. Francis' ideas of nature worship.[9]

Dubos' valiant defense of Christian thought lacks a number of substantial considerations. While other societies did create ecologi-cal disasters, Dubos would be hard put to find in the theologies of many other religions either a command to subdue the earth or the doctrine that the creation had "fallen" and shared responsibility for a man's direct violation of divine commands. There is also little evidence that destroying wetlands is ecologically sound, a fact the Bush administration ignores as it proposes to weaken federal law against tampering with the wetlands.

Further indications of Dubos's miscalculation of Christian sincerity—and evidence, perhaps, that Christians have not yet understood the complexity of the ecological crisis—were evidenced by the liturgy of the earth created by the National Cathedral in Washington, D.C. The confession used in this liturgy exemplifies the extent to which even concerned Christians have misunderstood the seriousness of the ecological problem.

> Lord God, we say here in Your presence and before each other that we, both individually and collectively, have not been good stewards of Your earth. We have fouled the air, spoiled the water, poisoned the land, and by these acts have gravely hurt each other. We know now that this has and will cost us, and for these and all other sins we are truly sorry. Give us, we pray, the strength and guidance to undo what we have done and grant us inspiration for a new style of living.[10]

Even in this attempt to bring religious sensitivity to the problem of ecological destruction, one can see the shallow understanding of the basis of the religious attitude that has been largely responsible for the crisis. No effort is made to begin a new theory of the meaning of creation. Indeed, the popular attitude of *stewardship* is invoked, as if it had no relationship to the cause of the ecological crisis whatsoever. Perhaps the best summary of the attitude inherent in the liturgy is, "Please, God, help us cut the cost, and we'll try to find a new life-style that won't be quite as destructive." The response is inadequate because it has not reached any fundamental problem; it is only a patch job over a serious theological problem. But at least in this liturgy we humans are bad and nature is good—a marked advance over earlier conceptions.

It would be difficult to find an Indian counterpart to this proposed liturgy. In the first place, traditional religions do not have the point-counterpoint recitation of beliefs that we find in the Near Eastern traditions. Singers and individual medicine people sing specific songs that compose the ceremony. While there is the expression of humility as humans stand before the higher spiritual powers, the Indian tradition lacks the admission of individual and corporate guilt which Near Eastern religions make the central part of their doctrines. The phrase "all my relatives" is frequently invoked by Indians performing ceremonies and this phrase is used to invite all other forms of life to participate as well as to inform them that the ceremony is being done on their behalf.

There is another, more serious problem involved in the Christian doctrine of creation. For most of the history of the Christian religion, people have been taught that the description of the event of creation as recorded in Genesis is historical fact. Although many Christian theologians have recognized that at best the Genesis account is mythological, it would be fair to conclude on the basis of what is known of the Christian religion that many Christian theologians and a substantial portion of the populace take the Genesis account as historical fact.

This issue has been a particularly difficult problem in the last century in America. The 1925 Scopes trial in Tennessee is perhaps the most publicized of the incidents marking the conflict between literal believers of Genesis and those who regard it symbolically, either as an analogy or as a mythological representation of a greater spiritual reality. Because people in a number of states, most prominently California, have petitioned their state legislatures to require the Genesis account of creation in the school curriculum indicates that the desire of many Christians is to believe in spite of the evidence, not because of it.[11]

Indian tribal religions have not had this problem. The tribes confront and interact with a particular land along with its life forms. The task or role of the tribal religions is to relate the community of people to each and every facet of creation as they have experienced it. Dr. Charles Eastman, the famous Sioux physician, relates a story in which the Indian viewpoint of the historicity of creation legends is illustrated:

A missionary once undertook to instruct a group of Indians in the truths of his holy religion. He told them of the creation of the earth in six days, and of the fall of our first parents by eating an apple.

The courteous savages listened attentively, and, after thanking him, one related in his turn a very ancient tradition concerning the origin of maize. But the missionary plainly showed his disgust and disbelief, indignantly saying:

"What I delivered to you were sacred truths, but this that you tell me is mere fable and falsehood! "

"My Brother," gravely replied the offended Indian, "it seems that you have not been well grounded in the rules of civility. You saw that we, who practice these rules, believed your stories; why, then, do you refuse to credit ours?"[12]

The difference in approach goes back to the basic consideration discussed earlier. If a religion is tied to a sense of time, then everything forming a part of it must have some validity because it occurs within the temporal scheme. Christians are thus stuck with the assertion that the account of Genesis is an actual historical recording of the proceedings whether or not some of the theologians consent to such an interpretation.

Most important, perhaps, is that the major Christian theologian, the apostle Paul, made the historicity of the Genesis account the most important aspect of his theory of redemption. Paul's theory has formed a major part of the Christian teachings, and while some of the Christian sects would not agree with everything Paul wrote, he is not an insignificant figure in Christian history. Paul writes in Romans:

Sin, you see, was in the world long before the Law, though I suppose, technically speaking, it was not 'sin' where there was no law to define it. Nevertheless death, the complement of sin, held sway over mankind from Adam to Moses, even over those whose sin was quite unlike Adam's.

Adam, the first man, corresponds in some degree to the Man who was to come. But the gift of God through Christ is a very different matter from the 'account rendered' through the sin of Adam. For while as a result of one man's sin death by natural consequence became the common lot of men, it was by the generosity of God, the free giving of the grace of the One Man Jesus Christ, that the love of God overflowed for the benefit of all men.

We see, then, that as one act of sin exposed the whole race of men to God's judgment and condemnation, so one Act of Perfect Righteousness presents all men freely acquitted in the sight of God. One man's disobedience placed all men under the threat of condemnation, but one Man's obedience has the power to present all men righteous before God.[13]

It would appear that if the Genesis account of Adam's disobedience is not a historical event (that is, an event that can be located at some specific time and place on the planet), subsequent explanations of the meaning of the death of Jesus of Nazareth are without validity. We have no need to question the historical existence of Jesus of Nazareth, although that particular conflict has also consumed considerable energy in the past. But we cannot project from the historical reality of Jesus as a man existing in Palestine during the time of Augustus and his successors to affirm the historical existence of a man called Adam in a garden someplace in Asia Minor. Without the historical existence of Adam, we are powerless to explain the death of Jesus as a religious event of cosmic or historic significance.

At best we can conclude that the Christian doctrine of creation has serious shortcomings. It is too often considered not only as a historical event but also as the event that determined all other facts of our existence. It is bad enough to consider Genesis as a historical account in view of what we know today of the nature of our world. But when we consider that the Genesis account places nature and nonhuman life systems in a polarity with us, tinged with evil and without hope of redemption except at the last judgment, the whole idea appears intolerable.

There are, to be sure, numerous accounts from the various tribal religious traditions relating how an animal, bird, or reptile participated in a creation event. We have already seen how some Indian people regarded such stories and the lack of belief in the historical nature of the event. Within the tribal accounts is contained, perhaps, an even greater problem, the problem of origins of peoples and religions, which we shall take up in chapter 8. At no point, however, does any tribal religion insist that its particular version of the creation is an absolute historical recording of the creation event or that the story necessarily leads to conclusions about humankind's good or evil nature. At best the tribal stories recount how the people experience the creative process which continues today.

The relationships that serve to form the unity of nature are of vastly more importance to most tribal religions. The Indian is confronted with a bountiful earth in which all things and experiences have a role to play. The task of the tribal religion, if such a religion can be said to have a task, is to determine the proper relationship that the people of the tribe must have with other living things and to develop the self-discipline within the tribal community so that man acts harmoniously with other creatures. The world that he experiences is dominated by the presence of power, the manifestation of life energies, the whole life-flow of a creation. Recognition that the human beings holds an important place in such a creation is tempered by the thought that they are dependent on everything in creation for their existence. There is not, therefore, that determined cause that Harvey Cox projects to subdue Earth and its living things. Instead the awareness of the meaning of life comes from observing how the various living things appear to mesh to provide a whole tapestry.

Each form of life has its own purposes, and there is no form of life that does not have a unique quality to its existence. Shooter, a Sioux Indian, explained the view held by many tribal religions in terms of individuality as follows:

> Animals and plants are taught by Wakan Tanka what they are to do. Wakan Tanka teaches the birds to make nests, yet the nests of all birds are not alike. Wakan Tanka gives them merely the outline. Some make better nests than others.

In the same way some animals are satisfied with very rough dwellings, while others make attractive places in which to live. Some animals also take better care of their young than others. The forest is the home of many birds and other animals, and the water is the home of fish and reptiles. All birds, even those of the same species, are not alike, and it is the same with animals, or human beings. The reason Wakan Tanka does not make two birds, or animals, or human beings exactly alike is because each is placed here by Wakan Tanka to be an independent individuality and to rely upon itself.[14]

To recognize or admit differences, even among the species of life, does not require then that human beings create forces to forge to gain a sense of unity or homogeneity. To exist in a creation means that living is more than tolerance for other life forms—it is recognition that in differences there is the strength of creation and that this strength is a deliberate desire of the creator.

Tribal religions find a great affinity among species of living creatures, and it is at this point that the fellowship of life is a strong part of the Indian way. The Hopi, for example, revere not only the lands on which they live but the animals with which they have a particular relationship. The dance for rain, which involves the use of reptiles in its ceremonies, holds a great fascination for whites, primarily because they have traditionally considered reptiles, particularly snakes, as their mortal enemy. In this attitude and its ensuing fascination, we may illustrate, perhaps, the alienation between the various life forms that Christian peoples read into the story in Genesis. This alienation is not present in tribal religions.

Behind the apparent kinship between animals, reptiles, birds, and human beings in the Indian way stands a great conception shared by a great majority of the tribes. Other living things are not regarded as insensitive species. Rather they are "people" in the same manner as the various tribes of human beings are people. The reason why the Hopi use live reptiles in their ceremony goes back to one of their folk heroes who lived with the snake people for a while and learned from them the secret of making rain for the crops.[15] It was a ceremony freely given by the snake people to the Hopi. In the same manner the Plains Indians considered the buffalo as a distinct people, the Northwest Coast Indians regarded the salmon as a people. Equality is thus not simply a human attribute but a recognition of the creatureness of all creation.

Very important in some of the tribal religions is the idea that humans can change into animals and birds and that other species can change into human beings. In this way species can communicate and learn from each other. Some of these tribal ideas have been classified as *witchcraft* by anthropologists, primarily because such phenomena occurring within the Western tradition would naturally be interpreted as evil and satanic. What Westerners miss is the rather logical implication of the unity of life. If all living things share a creator and a creation, is it not logical to suppose that all have the ability to relate to every part of the creation? How Westerners can believe in evolution and not see the logical consequences of this doctrine in the religious life of people is incomprehensible for many Indians. Recent studies with the dolphin and other animals may indicate that Westerners are beginning to shed superstitions and consider the possibility of having communication with other life forms.

But many tribal religions go even farther. The manifestation of power is simply not limited to mobile life forms. For some tribes the idea extends to plants, rocks, and natural features that Westerners consider inanimate. Walking Buffalo, a Stoney Indian from Canada, explained the nature of the unity of creation and the possibility of communicating with any aspect of creation when he remarked:

> Did you know that trees talk? Well they do. They talk to each other, and they'll talk to you if you listen. Trouble is, white people don't listen. They never learned to listen to the Indians, so I don't suppose they'll listen to other voices in nature. But I have learned a lot from trees; sometimes about the weather, sometimes about animals, sometimes about the Great Spirit.[16]

Again we must return to the Christian idea of the complete alienation of nature and the world from human beings as a result of

Adam's immediate postcreation act in determining the Western and Christian attitude toward nature. Some theologians have felt that man's alienation from nature is a natural result of his coming to a sense of self-consciousness, and people dealing with psychological problems seem to have a tendency to emphasize the sense in which humans are alienated from nature by promulgating theories of childhood fears based on the unfolding of natural growth processes. Even Western poets have been articulating the Western fears of "I, a stranger and afraid, in a world I never made."[17]

By and large there was no fear of nature in the Indian view of the world. Chief Luther Standing Bear remarked on the "wildness" of nature in his autobiography as follows:

> We did not think of the great open plains, the beautiful rolling hills, and winding streams with tangled growth as "wild." Only to the white men was nature a "wilderness" and only to him was the land "infested" with "wild" animals and "savage" people. To us it was tame. Earth was bountiful and we were surrounded with the blessings of the Great Mystery. Not until the hairy man from the east came and with brutal frenzy heaped injustices upon us and the families that we loved was it "wild" for us. When the very animals of the forest began fleeing from his approach, then it was that for us the "Wild West" began.[18]

In some sense, part of the alienation of human beings from nature is caused by the action of humans against nature and not as the result of some obscure and corrupted relationship that came into being as a result of the human's inability to relate to the creator. It is doubtful if Western Christians can change their understanding of creation at this point in their existence. Their religion is firmly grounded in their escape from a fallen nature, and it is highly unlikely to suppose at this late date that they can find a reconciliation with nature while maintaining the remainder of their theological understanding of salvation.

We have one final aspect to cover with respect to the creation. Whether it be considered as a specific event or as a tenet of faith that need not be explained, certain empirical data exists today that was unavailable to humankind when tribal religions and Christianity originated. Modern science has in large part pierced the veil of nature. We are becoming increasingly aware of some of the basic processes of the universe to a much greater degree than was ever possible. With the explosion of the atomic bomb, humankind moved far beyond the speculations of earlier science and philosophy. It may be yet too soon to conclude that our science can determine everything about the universe. Yet the possibility of almost instantaneous destruction through misuse of science should indicate that we are close to describing in an approximate manner how the universe works.

Our further question, therefore, should concern how religious statements are to be made which are either broad enough or specific enough to parallel what we are discovering in nature through scientific experiments. Christian theology has traditionally fluctuated between the philosophical views of Plato and Aristotle. Occasionally some theologian will go to the ideas of Kant or Descartes to find a usable system to explain religious ideas in a scientific manner. Some theologians have gone so far as Alfred North Whitehead's view of the universe to find a way to describe religious ideas by the same basic form of articulation as followed in scientific circles and created *process theology*.

Which religious atmosphere, Christian or Indian, would appear to be more compatible with contemporary scientific ideas? The question may appear absurd, but it has the highest relevance for a number of reasons. First, we must determine on what basis religious ideas are considered to be mere superstitions and on what basis religious ideas are said to be either valid or possible in the world in which we live. Indian dances for rain, for example, were said to be mere superstitions; songs to make corn grow were said to be even more absurd. Today people can make plants grow with music, and the information on the power of sound vibrations is coming into its own. The principles used by Indian tribal religions have tremendous parallels with contemporary scientific experiments. This can be either coincidental, which is very difficult to prove, or it can mean that the Indian tribal religions have been dealing at least partially with a fairly accurate conception of reality, which is difficult to argue convincingly to the scientific mind.

The second reason for determining compatibility of religion and science is to lay the groundwork for bringing our view of the world back to a unified whole, if at all possible. The competition between ministers and psychoanalysts, for example, to determine the sense of spiritual or psychological infirmity in effect promotes two distinct views of reality. Karl Heim relates in his incisive book, *Christian Faith and Natural Science*, as follows:

> In cases of physiologically conditioned depression, in which the religious responses are often involved, modern medicine applies with great success the electric shock treatment, passing an electric current through leads placed in contact with the patient's temples. These are often people who in their state of depression also despaired of their spiritual salvation, who were a prey in other words to what has been called in theological literature "certainty of damnation." And lo and behold! What the minister of religion had tried in vain to achieve with comforting exhortations and encouraging words from the Bible and the Catechism has now been accomplished by the electric current! The depression has gone and the patient not only faces his life with new courage but is filled with a joyful belief in God's forgiveness and in his own eternal salvation.[19]

It would thus appear that unless some new effort in the field of religion is made to provide a more realistic understanding of the universe, there may be no solution to people's problems except manipulation by artificial means—the *1984* solution, that we all dread.

The Indian tribal religions would probably suggest that the unity of life is manifested in the existence of the tribal community, for it is only in the tribal community that any Indian religions have relevance. James Jeans, in his book *Physics and Philosophy*, suggests that a profound view of nature lies in the concept of community:

> Space and time are inhabited by distinct individuals, but when we pass beyond space and time, from the world of phenomena towards reality, individuality is replaced by community.

> When we pass beyond space and time, they [separate indi-
> viduals] may perhaps form ingredients of a single continu-
> ous stream of life.[20]

The parallel with conceptions of the basic unity of existence held
by American Indian tribal religions is striking. If the nature of the
world is a "single continuous stream of life," there is no reason to
reject the idea that one can learn to hear the trees talk. It would
be strange if they did not have the power to communicate.

R. G. Collingwood, in *The Idea of Nature*, attempts to sketch
out Alexander's cosmology as it applies to a whole continuum
of life:

> In the physical world before the emergence of life, there are
> already various orders of being, each consisting of a pattern
> composed of elements belonging to the order next below it:
> point-instants form a pattern which is the electron having
> physical qualities, electrons form an atom having higher
> chemical qualities of a new and higher order, molecules like
> those of air form wave-patterns having sonority and so on.

> Living organisms in their turn are patterns whose elements
> are bits of matter. In themselves these bits of matter are
> inorganic; it is only the whole pattern which they compose
> that is alive, and its life is the time-aspect or rhythmic
> process of its material parts.[21]

We apparently have order and orders. We have time, but a
time that is not a universal value, only a time internal to the complex
relationships themselves. Above all, we have no disruption of the unity
of the creation, only a variation on a general theme. If there is anything
to the similarity of things, it is that a sense of alienation does not exist
at a significant level.

We even have the startling statement of Whitehead about
the nature of God: "Not only does God [primordial nature] arrange the
eternal objects; he also makes them available for use by other actual
entities. This is God's function as the principle of concretion."[22] Again

we are dealing with a complexity of relationships in which no particular object is given primacy over any other object or entity. Energy or spirit and the manifestation of purposeful order seem to characterize both modern scientific speculations and Indian beliefs.

What is important is not an attempt to show that either Indian tribal religions or Christianity prefigured contemporary science, modern concern for ecological sanity, or a startlingly new idea of what the universe might eventually be. Rather we should find what religious ideas can credibly encompass the broadest field of both our thoughts and actions. We must show that religious ideas are at least not tied to any particular view of man, nature, or the relationship of man and nature that is clearly in conflict with what we know. In this sense, American Indian tribal religions certainly appear to be more at home in the modern world than Christian ideas and Westerners' traditional religious concepts.

Notes

1. Frederick Webb Hodge, *Handbook of American Indians North of Mexico*, vol. II (Lanham, Md.: Rowman & Littlefield, 1965), 366.

Something more needs to be said about anthropomorphic images. Medicine men report the existence of spiritual beings that have or take on human forms. Thus Black Elk and other Sioux mystics report that they have sat with the Six Grandfathers and counseled with them. Much more thought needs to be given to the question of whether the Indians had "gods" in the same sense as Near Eastern peoples. Was the mysterious power—*wakan tanka* in the Dakota language—the same as the spiritual power that provided life and was superior to any specific personifications of itself? If so, the ultimate representation of this sacred universe—and other sacred Indian universes—was without a deity in the Near Eastern sense.

2. For example, see Joseph Epes Brown, *The Sacred Pipe* (Norman: University of Oklahoma Press, 1953, 3–6) for Black Elk's discussion of this relationship.

3. In *The Confessions* by St. Augustine (London: Burns & Oates, 1954), the solution to the problem of evil seems to be completing the circle and suggesting that the deity himself is the tempter. Carl Jung also folds back the problem of good and evil to make a complete circle or circuit. The Plains Indian concept is considerably more complex and seems to involve

the related question of the structure of conscious life—the difference between probable future events and the realization of existing possibilities. It is too complicated to deal with here except to note that there is a considerable difference between the two traditions.

4. Paul Tillich, *Systematic Theology*, vol. II (Chicago: University of Chicago Press, 1957), 41–42.

5. Ibid.

      In all of North American Indian traditions there is, of course, no sense of "animal bondage" but rather relationships with the specific peoples of creation; hence, creation is ultimately good and humans are a part of it.

6. T. C. McLuhan, *Touch the Earth* (New York: Outerbridge & Dienstfrey, 1971), 8.

7. Harvey Cox, *The Secular City* (New York: Macmillan, 1965), 20.

8. Lynne White, Jr., "The Historical Roots of Our Ecological Crisis," paper. Ameican Association for the Advancement of Science, 1967.

9. Rene Dubois' address is published as a small booklet by the Smithsonian Institution, Washington, D.C. It is singularly instructive, however, to note that filling in marshes and wetlands destroys habitat for a significant number of species and moves the planet toward ecological unbalance. Thus, White's thesis holds even when applied to what Christians believe is their most benign behavior.

10. Quoted in an article by Louis Cassels in the Religion Section, *The Denver Post* (March 7, 1970).

11. The Creation Science Research Center in San Diego has been extremely active in submitting textbooks to the State Boad of Education which allege to give equal treatment to both Darwin and Genesis. There has apparently been some talk by people who support the center of forcing acceptance of their textbooks through court action. (Reported in *The Denver Post* Religion Section, August 12, 1972.)

12. Charles Eastman, *The Soul of the Indian* (Boston: Houghton Mifflin, 1911), 119–20.

13. Romans 5: 13–19

14. *Touch the Earth*, 18.

15. The ceremony is briefly described in *Book of the Hopi* by Frank Waters and Oswald White Bear Fredericks (Viking Press, 1963).

16. *Touch the Earth*, 23.

17. A. E. Houseman, *A Shropshire Lad* (New York: Grosset & Dunlap, 1932).

18. Luther Standing Bear, *Land of the Spotted Eagle* (Boston: Houghton Mifflin, 1933).

19. Karl Heim, *Christian Faith and Natural Science* (New York: Harper Torchbooks, 1957), 15.

20. James Jeans, *Physics and Philosophy*, Ann Arbor Papers (Ann Arbor: University of Michigan Press, 1958), 204.

21. R. G. Collingwood, *The Idea of Nature* (London: Oxford University Press, 1945), 160.

22. A. H. Johnson, *Whitehead's Theory of Reality* (New York: Dover Publications, 1962), 60–61.

CHAPTER 6

THE CONCEPT OF HISTORY

One of the major distinctions that can be made between the tribal religions taken as a group and the Christian religion that underlies Western secular thought is the extent to which the two views were dependent on the idea of history. The western preoccupation with history and a chronological description of reality was not a dominant factor in any tribal conception of either time or history. Indian tribes had little use for recording past events; the idea of keeping a careful chronological record of events never seemed to impress the greater number of tribes of the continent. While the Indians who lived in Central America had extensive calendars, the practice of recording history was not a popular one further north. "The way I heard it" or "it was a long time ago" usually prefaces any Indian account of a past tribal experience, indicating that the story itself is important, not its precise chronological location. That is not to say that Indian tribes deliberately avoided chronology. In post-Discovery times, some tribes adopted the idea of recording specific sequences of time as a means of remembering the community's immediate past experiences. The best-known method of recording these experiences was the *winter count* of the Plains Indians. A large animal hide, usually buffalo, would be specially tanned, and each year a figure or symbol illustrating the most memorable event experienced by the community would be painted on the hide. Gradually the hide became filled with representations of the years, and it would be maintained as long as there were people who could remember what the figures and symbols meant.

One could not find a very accurate concept of history in the winter counts. In general they indicated the psychic life of the community—what was important to that group of people as a group. The chances of a continuous subject matter appearing on a winter count were nil. One year might be remembered as the year that horses came to the people, the next year might be the year when the berries were extremely large, the year after perhaps the tribe might have made peace with an enemy or visited a strange river on its migrations. The chances of a series of political or military events being recorded year after year as in the Western concept of history was so remote as to preclude the origination of history as a subject matter of importance. One recent Sioux winter count, for example, does not mention a number of important treaties, and one does not even mention the battle with Custer.

Other tribes devised methods of recording community experiences similar to the winter counts. The Pimas and Tohono O'odhams of Arizona had calendar sticks on which symbols were carved. By remembering what the symbols represented, a reader could recite a short chronology of recent years. But again the ability of the reader limited the extent to which the history could be recorded.[1] Some Indian accounts involved prodigious memories and recitations of events could take weeks of ceremonial storytelling. The Delaware in post-Discovery times created a long chronology that had many political references called the *Walum Olum*. It mentioned the tribes immediately bordering the Delawares and with whom they shared a general political fate. In this sense, the Walum Olum can be said to be more complex than the Sioux and Pima/Tohono O'odham systems. However the accuracy of Western European recounting and recording events was a distant goal for the most history-conscious of the American Indian tribes.[2]

Lacking a sense of rigid chronology, most tribal religions did not base their validity on any specific incident dividing human time experience into a before and after. No Indian tribal religion was dependent on the belief that a certain thing had happened in the past that required uncritical belief in the occurrence of the event. Creation, gifts of powers and medicines, traumatic events, and the lives of great religious leaders were either events of the distant past and regarded as such or the memories of the tribe were still vivid and occupied a prominent place in the people's perspective and understanding of their situation. Salvation and religious participation in communal ceremonies did not depend on the historical validity of the event but on the ceremonies and powers that were given to the people in the event.

Culture heroes were plentiful in the tribes. Deganiwidah founded the Iroquois League some time in the pre-Discovery days. Iroquois religion and politics did not revolve around him in the traditional western religious sense, but the great law of the Iroquois held the major position in tribal religious and political life. Sweet Medicine, the Cheyenne religious figure, was believed to have received his powers in historical times, but the ceremonies he brought were important, not Sweet Medicine himself. The story of the White Buffalo Calf Woman of the Sioux happened in the distant past. The importance in the story was the reception of the Sacred Pipe, not the woman herself as a personal object of salvation or adoration.

The tribal religions had one great benefit other religions did not have and could not have. They had no religious controversy within their communities because everyone shared a common historical experience and cultural identity was not separated into religious, economic, sociological, political, and military spheres. It was never a case, therefore, of *having* to believe in certain things to sustain a tribal religion. One simply believed the stories of the elders, and these stories had significance as defining the peoples' identity. Today we can say they have specific themes, but that is our interpretation and not the way the people originally understood them. No tribe, however, asserted its history as having primacy over the accounts of any other tribe. As we have seen, the recitation of stories by different peoples was regarded as a social event embodying civility. Differing tribal accounts were given credence because it was not a matter of trying to establish power over others to claim absolute truth. To be sure, tribes that had fallen under the wide-ranging military power of the various confederacies were reminded who ran things. Under the Iroquois and Creek alliances, weaker allies had no doubt about who was in charge. But there was no coercion to convert the smaller tribes to an Iroquois or Creek conception of past historical events and their efficacy.

In the turbulent period of conflict with the whites, speeches recorded at treaty sessions, statements made to the president of the United States to remind him of previous promises, and other statements of historical importance made use of chronological references. But one cannot say, on the basis of these speeches, that a fascination with historical reality was developed through contact with whites. Rather the speeches reflect negotiations and arguments over specific proposals made by the U.S. representatives.

Perhaps the best articulation of an Indian theory of history is found in the great speech by Chief Seattle at the signing of the Medicine Creek Treaty in Washington Territory in 1854. Recognizing that the loss of lands and establishment of reservations doomed his people, the Duwamish, Seattle sadly remarked as follows:

> It matters little where we pass the remnant of our days. They will not be many. A few more moons; a few more winters— and not one of the descendants of the mighty hosts that once moved over this broad land or lived in happy homes, protected by the Great Spirit, will remain to mourn over the graves of a people once more powerful and hopeful than yours. But why should I mourn at the untimely fate of my people? Tribe follows tribe, nation follows nation, like the waves of the sea. It is the order of nature, and regret is useless. Your time of decay may be distant, but it will surely come, for even the White Man whose God walked and talked with him as friend with friend, cannot be exempted from the common destiny. We may be brothers after all. We shall see.[3]

Seattle's theory of history may be much more a recognition of life's cyclical nature than a statement of historical process. For many tribal religions the distinction would be irrelevant. The recognition of growth and decay as limiting factors in a tribe's or nation's existence is worthy of note; it runs contrary to the Western European conceptions of the Heavenly City and the Thousand-Year Reich.

The idea of world ages, held by some tribes, is comparable in many ways to the world age concepts held by people in India. The flood stories, even the most remote, gave rise to the belief that the world is periodically destroyed by flood, fire, or other natural catastrophes, and this idea was held by a number of tribes with stories of some antiquity. Some substance was given to the belief in periodic destruction by particular stories, and in this sense the people could be said to have had a conception of history. For example, the Sioux explanation was framed in familiar terminology. They held that the world was protected by a huge buffalo that stood at the western gate of the universe and held back the waters that periodically flooded the world. Every year the buffalo lost a hair on one of its legs. Every age it lost a leg. When the buffalo had lost all its legs and was no longer able to hold back the waters, the world was flooded and renewed.

The Hopi had the most comprehensive understanding of world ages, as Frank Waters and White Bear recount in *The Book of the Hopi*. These people believed that they had survived three world destructions and that each world had been marked by peculiar circumstances. Before each destruction they were given special instructions for survival, and as each new world began they received songs and ceremonies designed for living in the new world. Their ceremonial life would end with each world destruction. Other tribes had legends of similar content, although a great many tribes now appear to have had prophecies about the whites that have been so garbled and popularized as to confuse efforts to come to any conclusions as to which stories were quasi-histories and which were real prophecies.

Suffice it to say, even the closest approach to the Western idea of history by an Indian tribe was yet a goodly distance from Western historical conceptions. What appears to have survived as a tribal conception of history almost everywhere was the description of conditions under which the people lived and the location in which they lived. Migrations from one place to another were phrased in terms descriptive of why they moved. Exactly when they moved was, again, "a long time ago." The scholars have had a difficult time piecing together the maps of pre-Discovery America because of the vague nature of tribal remembrances. The Iroquois, for example, relate that they once lived on the plains but then migrated eastward. When is not important to them, but their relative hardship on the plains and eventual prosperity in the East are important.

The result of this casual attitude toward history was, of course, that history had virtually no place in the religious life of the tribe. The appearance of the various folk heroes who brought sacred ceremonies and medicines could often not be located in time at all. Only recent and specific events, such as the Cheyennes' loss of some of their sacred arrows to the Pawnees, were remembered and formed a conjunction of history and religion. But the ceremonies, beliefs, and great religious events of the tribes were distinct from history; they did not depend on history for their verification. If they worked for the community in the present, that was sufficient evidence of their validity.

In theory it is entirely possible to construct a chronological history of a tribe. This task would be accomplished by knowing the sacred places within the tribe's geography and all of the stories that are related to these places. By identifying the *before* and *after* of the stories and then arranging them on a time scale, one could project a chronology. Some exceedingly wise people in some tribes can perform this function reasonably well and some years ago the White Mountain Apaches began to develop a historical atlas of their lands that had something of this flavor. In effect, *The Book of the Hopi* is a reconstruction of a basic Hopi chronology as defined by the migrations and locations that the people remember.

In contrast, Christianity has always placed a major emphasis on the idea of history. From the very beginning of the religion, it has been the Christian contention that the experiences of humankind could be recorded in a linear fashion, and when this was done, the whole purpose of the creation event became clear, explaining not only the history of human societies but also revealing the nature of the end of the world and the existence of heaven, or a future world, into which the faithful would be welcome. Again, we have a familiar distinction. Time is regarded as all-important by Christians, and it has a casual importance, if any, among the tribal peoples.

The contrast between tribal religions and the Christian religion, therefore, can be made painfully clear with a brief and general sketch of the Christian religion itself. In a real sense, the Christian religion can be said to be dependent on the historical accuracy of the Hebrew religion as found in the sacred books of the Jews. After the death of Jesus the remaining disciples began to preach the doctrine that his crucifixion had been more than a simple execution. It was regarded by them as the culminating event in a direct sequence of events going back to the creation of the universe.

We have already seen in chapter 5 how Paul made the connection between a historical man Adam and the historical man Jesus in such a way as to explain how the disobedience of Adam had been canceled with the death of Jesus. It was within the recorded experience of the Hebrew people and the remnant peoples of the tribe of Judah, then known as the Jews, that the Christian innovation of world history took place. Two of the Gospels written to interpret the life of Jesus and his teachings had as their introductory remarks genealogies of Jesus purporting to trace his ancestry back to Adam. That they are different is cause to wonder if a biological history of his family is the intent; if it is not accurate genetics, what is it?

At any rate, the events of the Old Testament were seen as actual events of history in which a divine purpose was gradually unfolding. The idea had been inherent in Jewish religious circles prior to the advent of Christianity, but with the missionary explosion of the Christian religion, the events could be said to have taken on cosmic significance for believers of the new religion. For some time before the lifetime of Jesus, Jewish theological circles had seen the development of a curious type of literature. A large body of literature purporting to have been written by the major folk heroes of the Hebrew past began to surface, and its concern with predictions about the end of the world and the salvation of the Jews appeared to be a common feature. Such writings were called apocalyptic writings, and it is from these sources perhaps more than any others that we derive the Christian idea of a divine purpose in history and a subsequent fascination by Westerners for history.

The religion that took form around the person of Jesus came to regard the events of the past as directly prefiguring his life and teachings. To arrive at such consequences, the books of the Old

Testament were scoured for verses that might be interpreted as predicting certain events of his life. What we have in the four Gospels, therefore, is a curious mixture of historical events, parabolic teachings, and tortured proof texts from various sources in the Jewish writings. At best the Gospels, which can be said to be the first Christian effort to define the meaning of past events in terms of humankind's universal history, are exactly that—tortured.

The immediate followers who had known Jesus had come to the conclusion, apparently nurtured by Jesus himself, that their Lord would return within their own lifetime to restore the Kingdom of Israel to the glory known during the eras of David and Solomon. So impending was this feeling that the original commune in Jerusalem, headed by Jesus' brother James the Just, felt no desire or need to gather worldly goods. As a result they were soon bankrupt, and one of Paul's first acts was to take up collections from converts to bail them out of their financial difficulties.

The whole basis for the Christian belief in life after death was the alleged resurrection of Jesus after he had been dead for three days and his subsequent ascension into heaven. As the Gospels and the Acts of the Apostles were written, there can be little doubt that the primitive Christian community wished its converts to believe that Jesus in his physical body had risen upward to heaven in a cloud. Early converts saw visions in which he returned on the clouds. When Jesus failed to return within the lifetime of those who had been his closest associates, the religion should have folded. But as the original group grew smaller and the religion spread to Asia Minor, the initial prediction was continually modified so that while the basic idea had been an immediate conclusion to history through divine intervention, its immediacy gradually became symbolic, not historic.

It is now nearly two thousand years since Jesus lived and died, and there has been no return. New converts periodically become wildly enthusiastic about the impending return of Jesus, and evangelistic Christianity continuously phrases its message of mission and conversion in terms of a return of Jesus in the not-too-distant future. As the years have passed and certain milestones have been reached, Christianity has gone into traumas with the idea of imminent judgment. The arrival of the year 1000 was particularly disappointing for the thousands of people who sold their earthly goods and prepared to meet their maker. When the crisis passed and the Western world returned to normal, apologists for the religion trotted out their favorite Bible verses, attempting to smooth over the downhearted. "A thousand years is but a day in Thy sight" and other comforting verses were used to cover over the failure of Jesus to reappear.

The Christian religion looks toward a spectacular end of the world as a time of judgment and thus an end of history. It is thus theologically an open-ended proposition because it can at anytime promote the idea that the world is ending; when such an event fails to occur, the contentions can easily be retracted by resorting to philosophical warnings about the nature of time. Time thus becomes a dualistic concept for Christians. It is both divine and human; prophecies given with respect to divine time are promptly canceled by reference to human time and its distinction from divine time.

The concept of history became a rather nebulous subject matter as Christianity continued to grow. The events of the Old Testament were regarded as actual historical events, and their miraculous nature was ascribed to divine intervention on behalf of the Hebrews. As the Old Testament came closer to the days of Jesus and the writings became closed to further prophecies, with Malachi the idea of divine intervention in human affairs also appeared to slacken. The first several centuries of the Christian religion appear to have been filled with miraculous acts of God in direct assistance to the Christian martyrs. After several centuries, however, even this tendency ebbed, and with the establishment of the organizational Church as a political power in the crumbling Roman Empire, Christianity adopted the temporary doctrine that Jesus had established a "church" to supervise the affairs of men until he decided to return.

This condition of nearly total Church control over the lives of people was strengthened during the centuries that followed, and for many centuries the political struggles of Western Europe had to have Christian approval to be considered valid. The Protestant Reformation was instrumental in breaking the control of the organized Church structure over the political and economic life of Europe. Since that time, while the political structures have continued to expand their power, the relative influence of the Church has declined.

The original doctrines of Christian expansion, however, did not decline with the waning influence of the Church organization. In the first several centuries of Christian existence, one of the most popular justifications for the failure of Jesus to return to earth was his alleged admonition to his disciples to preach the message of his life to all nations. Thus, a substantial portion of the Christians believed that until every nation had heard the message of Christianity, Jesus *could not come.* In almost every generation of Christians, there was somewhere a militant missionary force seeking to convert non-Christian peoples, and this propensity to expand the religion's influence meant in realistic terms an expansion of control by the church structure over non-Christian peoples.

With the rise of secular governmental forms after the Protestant Reformation, the bitter competition between nations for lands in the newly discovered Western Hemisphere and the very violent struggles between competing interpretations of the religion following the Reformation missionary activity was seen as an arm of national politics, and the national imperialistic movements were justified on the basis of bringing the Christian religion to the "heathen." This attitude is covered more thoroughly in chapter 15. What is important for our purposes here is to note that as secular goals became more important, they were clothed in familiar terms of Western cultural attitudes, not in terms of religious reality.

Christian theology also had a direct influence on the development of the manner in which Westerners conceived the nature of the world. In the development of Christian theology, the two Greeks Plato and Aristotle were highly influential. Both of their philosophical systems sought to bring order out of the chaos of the world, and as the two major theologians of Christian history, St. Augustine and St. Thomas Aquinas, sought to reconcile Greek philosophy with Christian ideas of history, people in the West became accustomed to thinking of natural processes in terms of uniformity. In the popular mind the Old Testament was filled with highly exciting supernatural events, while the story of humankind since the life of Jesus was filled with smaller miracles and lacked the spectacular nature of Old Testament happenings.

Western history as we now have it has failed to shake off its original Christian presuppositions. It has, in fact, extended its theory of uniformity to include Old Testament events so that the history of humankind appears as a rather tedious story of the rise and fall of nation after nation, and the sequence in which world history has been written shows amazing parallels to the expansion of the Christian religion. China with its history going back far beyond the days of Abraham thus does not appear as a significant factor in world history until it begins to have relations with the West. India with even more ancient records appears on the world scene only when the British decide to colonize it, despite its brief role as a conquest goal of Alexander the Great.

We are faced today with a concept of world history that lacks even the most basic appreciation of the experiences of mankind as a whole. Unless other cultures and nations have some important relationship with the nations of Western Europe, they have little or no status in the interpretation of world history. Indeed, world history as presently conceived in the Christian nations is the story of the West's conquest of the remainder of the world and the subsequent rise to technological sophistication.

Because we cannot understand humankind from a more profound point of view, we have in recent years fallen into a number of easily avoidable difficulties. The original thrust of Christians opposing pagans translated itself many times in Christian history. Shortly after the discovery of the New World, Christianity was thought to be opposed on the one hand to the societies of the New World and on the other to the heretics of Europe. The peoples of the New World were virtually destroyed by the European invaders at the same time that Europe was being ravaged by witch-hunts, the Inquisition, and religious wars.

The tendency of placing Christianity against the social or political forms of man's secular existence continues to this day. After World War II planetary history was seen as a struggle between godless Communism and the chosen people of God—the Christian nations. At least part of the involvement of the United States in Southeast Asia was because of the influence of an important figure in the Roman Catholic Church, Francis Cardinal Joseph J. Spellman, who sought to bolster the fortunes of the Church and also subscribed to the good guys/bad guys interpretation of world events. Much of the misunderstanding of the role of the United States in postwar worlds involves this tendency to reject the Russians because of their rejection of Christianity.

A major task remains for Western man. He must quickly come to grips with the breadth of human experiences and understand these experiences from a world viewpoint, not simply a Western one. This shift will necessarily involve downgrading the ancient history of the Near East, thus serving to cut yet more subject matter away from the Christian religion. Louis Leakey's discoveries concerning early humans in Africa would seem to indicate that we are reaching a point at which the history of the Old Testament must assume a rather minor importance in the whole scheme of development. In addition to surrendering the historical Adam and his successors, we must surrender the comfortable feeling that we can find a direct line from ancient times to the modern world via the Christian religion. This involves, of course, giving up the claim by Christianity of its universal truth and validity.

Already the field of history appears to be reaching a crisis. Ancient history is taken much too casually today because it is assumed that whatever happened within human experiences could not be much different than the mythology that has grown up to explain the relics of history. We have an apparent computer of great sophistication at Stonehenge, England, and yet the traditional conceptions of life during the times when this massive structure was built continue to reflect the Western/Christian idea that nothing of major importance occurred until the advent of Western culture and its religion.

The experiences of the Hebrews do not really take precedence over the experiences and accomplishments of other peoples when viewed with an unjaundiced eye. The world abounds with ruins of incredible proportions relating hardly at all to the history of the Hebraic-Christian peoples. Yet these ruins are passed off with casual and hardly credible explanations based on the old theory of uniformity, which projects that the past had to be experienced in the way in which we experience life today.

The pyramids of Egypt are a case in point. In the popular mind of Western peoples, the pyramids were built a la Cecil B. De Mille with thousands of slaves tugging the large vine ropes up inclines to make a final resting place for the pharaoh. That the only reference to slave labor in the Old Testament remotely connected with building involves the Hebrew slaves making mud bricks is difficult for the popular mind to assimilate. It is when we go to the scholarly mind that we find even greater confusion so that our sense of human accomplishments and the meaning of history are hardly enhanced by even the best of our educated minds. Walter Fairservis, for example, rejects the concept of slave labor in pyramid building in his book *The Ancient Kingdoms of the Nile*.

> We know that there were few slaves because foreign conquests were at a minimum. The labor for the pyramids came from the peasant farmers who, at times of high Nile, were comparatively idle and could be used for public projects. In such cases they were maintained at government expense, which in view of the job to be done could not have been meager. The number of pyramids, and the years it took to build each of them, indicates that a stable arrangement between government responsibility and peasant labor had been established.[4]

The picture appears to be idyllic. In times of unemployment the benevolent pharaoh provided work for his people by having them put together what must certainly be among the most massive structures in history. But is this even a realistic picture of what happened in earlier times? That the U.S. government put forward the make-work projects of the Great Depression years does not mean that the pharaoh did likewise. The very bulk of the pyramids precludes Fairservis' solution to the problem.

The Great Pyramid of Cheops, for example, is incredible. Its base covers

> 13 acres or 7 midtown blocks of the city of New York. From this broad area, leveled to within a fraction of an inch, more than *two-and-a-half-million blocks* of limestone and granite—weighing from 2 to 70 tons apiece—rise in 201 stepped tiers to the height of a modern forty-story building.[5]

A construction project the size of this pyramid would have been a task of no mean proportions. Suppose that the workers had placed a minimum of 20 blocks of stone a day in the structure—a feat that would have been virtually impossible, yet still conceivable. Working steadily they would have assembled the 2.5 million stone blocks in about 125,000 days or 342 years. In this projection we have still not accounted for cutting the blocks, carrying them down the Nile, and bringing them to the assembly place. And we have projected a straight working project, not a summertime government make-work project as Fairservis and other scholars have assumed. If the Pilgrims had begun building a pyramid the size of the pyramid of Cheops to celebrate their safe landing in America, they would have finished the project in 1962, perhaps just in time to receive a government grant to celebrate. Is the traditional interpretation of history really an exercise in credibility?

At Aswan Dam in Egypt the people of many nations worked to save four sandstone statutes from an ancient temple from being destroyed by the waters of the dam. Engineers from nearly one hundred nations pooled their talents to save these priceless treasures. They had the benefit of helicopters, the latest in hydraulic jacks, lifts, cranes, and other modern construction equipment. Yet they had to cut the statues into smaller pieces to move them a mere 60 feet above the waters. In a quarry near Baalbek in Asia Minor, the Hadjar el Gouble stone lies squared and ready for removal. It weighs more than 4 million pounds. And primitive men are going to get their logs and ropes and move it? Hardly.

The world is, as we have noted, literally strewn with ruins of overwhelming proportions, structures that we cannot duplicate today if we wished to do so, yet the Western interpretation of world history is always skirting a straightforward effort to incorporate theories about the origin of these ruins and structures. We are fixed on a rather staid reading of human history because we are emotionally and religiously tied to the assumption, today perhaps subconsciously at least, that everything is pretty much the way people once believed centuries ago.

Even the relatively short time period of American history has been influenced by our religious heritage. There is sufficient evidence that this continent was visited by numerous expeditions prior to the arrival of Columbus. Pottery discovered in South America suggests fairly early contact between Japan and this hemisphere. Ruins in Massachusetts and Arizona may be evidence of early visits by Phoenicians and Romans. Yet up to this time scholars have adamantly refused to believe that any pre-Columbian landing took place. Even the Viking ruins in Minnesota have been buffeted by tremendous criticism and the jeers of skeptics, while the Columbian primacy has prevailed.

Cyrus Gordon, a noted scholar at Brandeis University, took a cautious stand in favor of pre-Columbian expeditions in his book *Before Columbus.* [6] He documented two possible pre-Columbian visits to the New World. Gordon's courage in dealing with a controversial subject produced great fruits during the past two decades. Today there are literally hundreds of books dealing with pre-Columbian expeditions to this continent and many of them make a great deal of sense. The best writing is being done *outside* academic circles because it covers data and theories that are not regarded as orthodox because they make uncomfortable the reigning elder statesmen of anthropology, archaeology, and history.

The reluctance of scholars to consider the possibility of pre-Columbian visits to the Western Hemisphere is but one example of the stranglehold that the one interpretation of history has had. There is, to a certain extent, a political justification in refusing to accept pre-Columbian discoveries. The land title of the United States relates back to the famous doctrine of Discovery, whereby Christian nations were allowed by the pope to claim the discovered lands of non-Christian peoples. To accept a series of pre-Columbian visitations would mean that the lands of the Western Hemisphere were hardly "discovered" by Europeans. It would call into question the interpretations and justifications given to colonization, exploitation, and genocide committed by Europeans during the last five centuries.

Christian religion and the Western idea of history are inseparable and mutually self-supporting. To retrench the traditional concept of Western history at this point would mean to invalidate the justifications for conquering the Western Hemisphere. Americans in some manner will cling to the traditional idea that they suddenly came upon a vacant land on which they created the world's most affluent society. Not only is such an idea false, it is absurd. Yet without it both Western man and his religion stand naked before the world.

It is said that one cannot judge Christianity by the actions of secular Western man. But such a contention judges Westerners much too harshly. Where did Westerners get their ideas of divine right to conquest, of manifest destiny, of themselves as the vanguard of true civilization, if not from Christianity? Having tied itself to history and maintained that its god controlled that history, Christianity must accept the consequences of its past. Secular history is now out of control and its influence has become a rather demoniac, disruptive force among nations—this is part and parcel of the Christian religion. If the lack of a sense of history can be called a shortcoming of tribal religions, as indeed it can, overemphasis on historic reality and its attendant consequences can certainly be assigned a bad grade for the Christian religion.

Notes

1. Edward Holland Spicer reproduces a Tohono O'odham calendar stick recording in this book *A Short History of the Indians of the United States* (New York: Van Nostrand Reinhold, 1969).

2. Spicer also gives a fragment of the Walum Olum.

3. *Uncommon Controversy*, a report prepared for the American Friends Service Committee (Seattle: University of Washington Press, 1970), 29.

4. Walter Fairservis, *The Ancient Kingdoms of the Nile* (New York: Thomas Y. Crowell, 1962), 89.

5. Peter Tompkins, *Secrets of the Great Pyramid* (New York: Harper & Row, 1971), 1.

6. Cyrus Gordon, *Before Columbus* (New York: Crown, 1971).

Gordon was regarded something of a traitor because he was willing to consider ideas that were outside the mainstream of doctrine laid down by the "old boy network" of American archaeology. The most telling point in his book, in my opinion, is the fact that *no* ancient peoples could have constructed astronomical tables that would predict eclipses unless they had access to observations spread over 120 degrees of arc in two directions. This suggests that there was a worldwide culture that coordinated information or that our basic ideas of astronomy were given to us as an intact body of knowledge.

CHAPTER 7

THE SPATIAL PROBLEM OF HISTORY

We have argued that not all of humankind's experiences have been encompassed within the Christian idea of history. When one confines religious history to the Old Testament, the short period covered by the New Testament, and the two thousand years of Western European history, then obviously a majority of societies and religions have been left out of the schema. It remains to be seen if the portion of history covered by Christian history really justifies the faith placed in it.

If one were to take the last two thousand years and the events of that period as representative of the validity of the Christian religion in bringing peace on Earth, then there would be little question that the religion is incapable of invoking any significant peaceful change in people or their societies. That period has been filled with continual warfare, conquest, bloodshed, and exploitation. In too many instances it was Christian pitted against Christian, leading one to conclude that the faith certainly played no favorites in choosing its victims. It has not been simply American Indians or other non-Christian peoples who have been the victims of Christians. One crusade began by sacking Constantinople, a city filled with Christians at the time.

We can avoid a prolonged examination of the Christian period; to recount the events would only appear as a deliberate indictment of the religion. It is far better to examine the nature of the Christian interpretation of history and seek to discover how and when it can be said that the Christian God does work in the affairs of people. At first glance it appears that God has not been as active in recent years as He once was. The Old Testament is filled with stories about the direct intervention of the Hebrew God in the affairs of people. These events were initially taken as actual historical facts, but in recent years an effort has been made to reinterpret them as representative of the spiritual quality of the Hebrew people and, by implication, the consequent spirituality of Christian peoples.

As Western people became more sophisticated about the nature of the universe, it became harder and harder to project exactly what the people of the Old Testament meant by seeing the action of their God in historic events. The victory of the English over the Spanish Armada (1588) was understood as an indication that God favored the Protestant English over the Catholic Spanish. While it did give rise to a plethora of religious poetry, prophecy, and theological development, it did not result in the establishment of a new religion. Even considered as a Christian renewal, Elizabethan England was not an exemplary Christian society.

Again, the victories of Russia over Napoleon and Hitler, aided each time by an unusually harsh Russian winter, might have in earlier times given rise to the idea that the Russians were especially chosen by God to be His people. Yet the theological development following those notable victories was practically nil. The American Civil War resulted in the banishment of slavery in the continental United States; yet as significant as this triumph was, it had practically no subsequent theological effect on the Christians of the land. Its major theological result could be said to have been the splitting of several major Protestant denominations into northern and southern branches, and thus if the war proved anything in a religious sphere, it proved damaging to the organizational churches.

Or we can ask what effect the numerous economic depressions in this country have had on the people's religious sensitivity. A depression as devastating as that of the 1930s visited on a nation in former times might have called forth a generation of repentant sinners and resulted in a renewal of religious faith of amazing intensity. Yet America's periodic depressions seem to call forth only bitter debates over the place and function of the federal government in the lives of citizens.

These are important questions to be asked, because of the contention of Christians that their God is specifically working in the events of mankind. In what specific way could God be said to be represented in the affairs of a person's life? This question is a penetrating one; it is not easy to point to any specific event and find incontrovertible evidence of divine intervention. The problem puzzles theologians of all stripes, and some of them have made valiant efforts to derive a sound explanation of what is meant by the idea that God is working in history.

One of the significant efforts to recapture the Christian idea of history in the postwar era was the movement known as "demythologizing" history. Originally advocated by C. H. Dodd, an English theologian, the school of history demythologizers took on a broader aspect when Rudolf Bultmann began a systematic reinterpretation of the New Testament by using the framework of Martin Heidegger's existential philosophy to eliminate the embarrassing eschatological sense of time from the New Testament. Bultmann felt that there was a basic Christian method and essence apart from any cultural values that might have crept into the text during New Testament days. His demythologizing thus involved an attempt to knock the Jewish apocalyptic flavor out of the Christian message. Under Bultmann's influence the idea grew that the events of the Bible were more symbolic than actual; the message of the coming of the Kingdom was primarily a psychological event, not an event of the real world.

In addition to Dodd and Bultmann, a movement known as the "death of God" philosophy attempted to revise and revitalize Christian theology. It was the child of Thomas J. J. Altizer. The God-is-dead theology flowered during the social turmoil of the 1960s, enjoyed a brief day in the sun and vanished quickly, much to the relief of other Christian theologians, who were not prepared to back Altizer and state that God had literally died on the cross and humankind had been godless ever since. Whatever else can be said about Altizer, one could only affirm that he took Western European history as a very valid reference point. And evaluating Western history there is a good argument to be made that Altizer was right.

Other attempts have been made to realize, at least to some extent, the nature of God's activity in human history. Some Lutherans have been content to maintain that history is "His story," which is linguistically clever but does not tell us much. Other Christians, particularly those involved in the Civil Rights, conservation and ecology, the peace movement, hunger, and even antiabortion have been willing to see the action of God reflected by the presence of the professional church in social movements. Nonclerical participants have also been very numerous in these movements; thus, the mere presence of clergy at rallies has not provided a startling renewal of theological doctrines.

Harvey Cox was among the most active clergymen in the movements of the 1960s, and if he did not have impeccable theological credentials, at least he made an effort to analyze modern society and suggest ways in which Christian peoples could speak. But even Cox with his Civil Rights experiences and work in the inner city was unable to derive a strong doctrine of God at work in history. In *The Secular City*, Cox finds that "the action of God occurs through what theologians have sometimes called 'historical events' but what might better be termed 'social change.'"[1]

Cox admonished us to engage in social movements, in effect creating a *fervor* type of history—a qualitative, group type of historical reality. His empirical evidence that this is the correct Christian theory of history is singularly misty, however, because verification of the action of God depends on the ability of the Christian to *reflect*.

> Reflection is that act by which the church scrutinizes the issues the society confronts in light of those decisive events of the past—Exodus and Easter—in which the intent of God has been apprehended by man in faith. Thus the church looks to the hints God has dropped in the past in order to make out what He is doing today.[2]

If we take the traditional conception of the events of history and attempt to locate the presence of theological dimensions, we basically arrive at Cox's conclusion, for traditional historical interpretation involves the premise that conditions were never much at variance with what we experience today. We have already seen the ridiculous conclusions attainable by applying a uniform method of arriving at descriptions of historical events. We find a benevolent pharaoh building pyramids on a part-time, make-work basis. Yet the position that Cox takes—that the Christian God is somehow tiptoeing through history dropping sly hints that are to be discerned by a church critique based on the Exodus and Easter—presents even more problems. Do people believe that the Exodus actually happened as recorded in the Bible? Is the Bible a historically accurate book with respect to the events of major importance to both the Christians and Jews?

One would suppose that the Exodus would have been a startling event in the experiences of the Hebrews. Slaves from their birth and with a heritage of slavery of nearly four centuries, they had no reason whatsoever to expect a release from their condition. Yet from the Exodus event can properly be said to have produced not only the modern Jewish religion but also Christianity and Islam—the two heretical offshoots of Jewish religious tradition. What may be surprising to many people, particularly since theologians such as Cox depend so heavily on it for their verification, is that many significant theologians do not regard the Biblical accounts of the Exodus as historical. Theodor H. Gaster, for example, characterizes the events of the Exodus as recorded in the Old Testament as a flight of fancy of undiminished proportions.

> It is obvious to any unbiased reader that this story, with its markedly religious coloration and its emphasis on super-natural "signs and wonders," is more of a romantic saga or popular legend than an accurate record. Written down centuries later than the period which it describes, it is clearly more indebted to folklore than to sober fact. [3]

Gaster, while not the final authority on the Old Testament, is not an inconsiderable figure in the scholarly world. Yet he is unwilling to grant that the Biblical record could represent a literal historical event.

Rather he understands the story as basically a romantic legend. Can Cox base his theology on a romantic legend? Can it be said then that God is not present in history at all or only within the poetic imagination that creates such romantic legends?

Gaster is a Jew, not a Christian. Johannes Pedersen is a noted Christian scholar who has specialized in Old Testament life and times. Almost every Protestant seminarian knows that *Israel: Its Life and Culture*, originally published in Swedish by Pedersen, is nearly *the* classic Christian study of early Israel. The book covers almost every aspect of Hebrew culture, illuminating many theological doctrines previously misunderstood or misinterpreted. In the book's appendix, Pedersen indicates that the Exodus is not history in the usual sense of the term but a highly colored legend meant to glorify the Jews.

> In forming an opinion of the story about the crossing of the Red Sea, it must be kept in mind as we have remarked above, that this story, as well as the whole emigration legend, though inserted as part of an historical account, is quite obviously of a cultic character, for the whole narrative aims at glorifying the god of the people at the paschal feast though an exposition of the historical event that created the people. The object cannot have been to give a correct exposition of ordinary events but, on the contrary, to describe history on a higher plane, mythical exploits which make of the people a great people, nature subordinating itself to this purpose.[4]

In other words, Pedersen finds the Exodus a historical event of no particular significance or relevance except as the Jews look backward into their past and attempt to glorify themselves. Again we have modern forms of interpretation as a basis for determining the historical reality of events of the ancient past. The assumption that humankind's experiences have remained fairly uniform and constant dominates Pedersen's considerations and negates the possibility that the Exodus might have been a real and important event.

Louis Dupré, a brilliant young Christian theologian at Georgetown University, devotes a chapter in his book *The Other*

Dimension to an excellent review of the various Christian ideas on creation. Spinning away from traditional pitfalls of logic that maintain a benevolent God and the presence of evil in the world as a dualism, Dupré illustrates by a mention of the Exodus the idea that divine intervention can never eliminate the deficiencies of people's freedom: "The separation of the waters of the Red Sea may be seen as an affliction of physical evil for the Egyptians or a miraculous escape from it for the Hebrews, but it did not affect the moral or immoral intentions of either party."[5]

One would conclude from Dupré's sentence that here is one Christian theologian who is not afraid to contend that the Exodus was a real-life, significant event of the ancient world featuring tidal waves, sweat, dust, blood, and all the grit of our existence. Where Cox and Pedersen—even Gaster—fear to affirm God working in historic events, Dupré charges right in as a true believer. Such is not the case! After making this careful distinction between the morality of freedom and the goodness of God, Dupré has a little footnote stating, "Obviously in all this I do not take a position on the historical character of this event or of any particular miracle."[6]

Can this be? Can Christian theologians tell us that their God works in and dominates history while maintaining in their footnotes that they are not prepared to affirm that anything really happened? What about the Resurrection? What kind of body did Jesus actually have? A "glorified body"? Or the body in which he walked on earth? Are Christian thinkers prepared to say? Popular Christianity, of course, is prepared to affirm almost everything it may happen to have called to its attention, including Jonah and Job, the subjects of two stories that seem to fall well within the categories of romantic legend these theologians advocated. Yet the biblical stories of Jonah, Job, and others are not central to the Bible's major premise, that God specifically chose one people from out among the peoples of the world, or that the logical conclusion to the Exodus event was the Crucifixion of Jesus and his Ascension into heaven after being dead three days. If we narrow the historical requirements of the Christian religion to affirming only two of the infinite number of events which have taken place in time and space, even then, apparently, we are left with legend and folklore.

If the major events of the Bible are to be taken not as actual events involving people, events of such significance that they could be used later as patterns by which the subsequent church could discern God dropping "hints" in the affairs of men, then what do we make of the Christian religion? Can we take it seriously? Even more, can we affirm that it is superior to any other religion, and if so, on what basis? Surely, at least, not on the basis that it tells us the true story of humankind.

Behind the Christian theory of history lies a peculiar logic of interpretation. One can see it clearly in the proposition put forward by Paul Tillich in his *Systematic Theology* as follows:

> It can be stated that in Christianity the decisive event occurs in the center of history and that it is precisely the event that gives history a center; that Christianity is also aware of the "not yet," which is the main emphasis in Judaism; and that Christianity knows the revelatory possibilities in every moment of history.[7]

In other words the Christians ask us to accept that there is a history, that there is a central event making the rest of the history intelligible, and that because there is a central event, there must necessarily be a history. The logic is clearly a precursor of the catch-22 rule. Whenever we focus on one of the very important events of that line of history, we are told by Protestants, Roman Catholics, and Jews alike that what happened was really just the growth of legend, folklore, and glorification, not a spectacular event. Yet these thinkers insist that a whole chronology of nonexistent events constitutes an important historical time line that is superior to any other explanation of human experiences.

This dilemma over the nature of history occurs and will occur whenever a religion is divorced from space and made an exclusive agent of time. Events become symbolic teaching devices, and the actual sequence of physical action that could indicate a divine intervention becomes unimportant; what is important are the moral lessons and ethical choices the legend illustrates. The Christians of another era believed that their Bible was the real record of events. While they could not geographically pinpoint the Garden of Eden, they damn sure could find Mount Sinai and Jerusalem. So they took everything as historical fact.

The contrast between Christianity and its interpretation of history—the temporal dimension—and the American Indian tribal religions—basically spatially located—is clearly illustrated when we understand the nature of sacred mountains, sacred hills, sacred rivers, and other geographical features sacred to Indian tribes. The Navajo, for example, have sacred mountains where they believe they rose from the underworld. There is no doubt in any Navajo's mind that these particular mountains are the exact mountains where it all took place. There is no beating around the bush on that. No one can say *when* the creation story of the Navajo happened, but everyone is fairly certain *where* the emergence took place.

Indian tribes combine history and geography so that they have a "sacred geography," that is to say, every location within their original homeland has a multitude of stories that recount the migrations, revelations, and particular historical incidents that cumulatively produced the tribe in its current condition. Traditional Cherokees today can still tell stories about the sacred places in Georgia and North Carolina that illuminate the tribal history. The Sioux, Cheyenne, Kiowa, and Arapaho all have traditions that describe Bear Butte in South Dakota and the Devil's Tower in Wyoming. The most notable characteristic of the tribal traditions is the precision and specificity of the traditions when linked to the landscape, a precision lacking in most other religious traditions.

The test of the extent to which a religion has a claim to historical validity, therefore, should as least partially involve its identification of the specific location and lands where the religious event that created the community took place. And that religion should stand by the historical nature of the event; it should never back off and disclaim everything while becoming furious with other peoples for not believing its claim. If the present interpretation of religious history that is accepted by many Christian theologians is maintained, we are left with a religion devoid of any significance in either time or space. History becomes a series of glorified legends that teach ethical lessons and it becomes a demoniac thing to believe that the world operates one way for religious purposes and an entirely different way for secular purposes. Leaving aside popular Christianity, which has rarely questioned anything and remains comfortable in a three-dimensional universe while astronauts walk on the moon, what effect would there be if we took the Exodus story—it really triggers the origin of three world religions—and maintained that, in fact, it records a specific happening that occurred at a definite time and in a specific space? Do we have a problem?

The problem is that one man dared to challenge the historians, theologians, and scientists on their own grounds and made the uniformitarian interpretation of history very uncomfortable. Immanuel Velikovsky,[8] a psychoanalyst and intellect of superstar magnitude, while doing research on a projected work encompassing three of Sigmund Freud's heroes, Moses, Oedipus, and Akhnaton, found evidence that Egypt had suffered a devastating catastrophe at one point in its history. The parallels between the Egyptian calamity and the accounts of the Exodus were so startling that Velikovsky began to trace other evidence of natural disaster on a global scale in the legends of peoples around the globe. By 1950 he was ready to unveil his documented conclusions on the Exodus.

In 1950 Velikovsky published *Worlds in Collision*, in which he contended that global cataclysms fundamentally changed the face of the planet in historical times, the Exodus being the event most clearly documented, thanks in part to the religious interpretation given it by the Hebrews who had seized the chance to flee Egypt in the confusion and disorder. The major thesis of the book was that Venus was a recent addition to the groups of planets circling the sun, having been ejected from Jupiter sometime earlier and was careening through our solar system for a period of centuries. During the time of the Exodus and later in the eighth century B.C., Venus came into near collision with Earth and Mars, disrupting the orbits of each and at one point saving Earth from a fatal collision with Mars.

Pointing out that prior to the second millennium B.C., there were no records of Venus as a planet by either the Hindus or Babylonians, Velikovsky asked why the most visible object in our night sky, outside of the moon, had not attracted the attention of the meticulous ancient astronomers. He replied that the only reasonable conclusion was that Venus could not be observed because it was not in the sky at that point. Ancient tales describe Venus as coming from the head of Jupiter, and other ancient records describe the struggles between the dragon and the cultural hero. Combining these features of humankind's collective memory, Velikovsky concluded that the tail of a comet doubled back in an electric field attraction with its head and would appear to people as a struggle between a hero and a reptile of enormous length and strength.

The testimony of the peoples from around the globe was compared to see if the legends bore any resemblance to the description obtained from the Near East. The legends bore out the thesis, and where they appeared to vary, the variance bolstered the thesis since the geographical location of the people changed the nature of the spectacle they would have been able to observe. Velikovsky thus unveiled a cosmic struggle between a comet and the two planets most familiar to mankind—Earth and Mars. In doing so, he called into question the psychological theories of religion as a fantasy of dream projections, raising the question of whether or not a substantial number of religions did not arise from activities taking place in the night sky and by implication offered rebuttal of the idea that natural processes have been uniform throughout earth history.

The sequence developed by Velikovsky up to the Exodus explains a substantial number of lesser and more puzzling verses that theologians have always interpreted as evidence of the Hebrew prophets' extreme poetic pretensions. It is, as briefly and accurately as possible, the following: at some time, as yet not accurately identified but before 1500 B.C., Jupiter ejected a comet of planetary size, the red spot of the planet observed today being the scar remaining on Jupiter from this incident. The comet began to travel on a highly irregular path through our solar system, menacing Earth on a number of occasions. Its bright light was the initial indication of its presence.

Eventually, Venus began to intrude on Earth's presence as it passed its perihelion and began the long distance of its elliptical orbit. In or around 1500 B.C., Earth passed through the tail of the comet. The first indication that the planet was in trouble was a rusty iron dust that covered the globe, giving the land and waters a bloody hue. The miracle of Moses turning the waters red was, therefore, not the poetic flight of a later scribe but the comet's initial effect.

As Earth went deeper into the comet's tail, hydrocarbon gases covering parts of the planet exploded in great bursts of fire.

Billions of gallons of hydrocarbons in the form of petroleum rained on parts of the planet, forming the oil fields we have tapped in recent years. Great pools of naphtha fell into depressions, caught fire, and burned for years giving the whole planet a twilight of nearly a generation. Then, as Earth went even further into the comet's tail, it was caught in an electromagnetic vise and its axis tilted, resulting in the sudden destruction of the Near East's major cities.

The catastrophe was worldwide, traumatic, and highly destructive. Rivers reversed themselves. Islands disappeared into the sea, other islands emerged. Mountains crashed skyward where peaceful strata had lain for centuries. A global hurricane ensued, leveling forests in a moment. Monstrous lakes were formed when waters jumped mountains and could not return to the seas. Arabia, once a prosperous land, and the Sahara, then populated by several large cities, were turned into desolate wastes. Part of the world lay in utter darkness, part in extended but smoky light.

The Hebrew slaves fled from the smoking ruins of Egypt as the Middle Kingdom fell in a major catastrophe. Racing for the sea of reeds, they saw the comet as a pillar of smoke during the day and a pillar of fire at night. Reaching Pi-haKhiroth at the edge of the Red Sea, they were pursued by the Pharaoh Taoui-Thom and his army. The action of the comet temporarily pulled the waters from their bed, allowing the Hebrews to cross and destroying the pharaoh's army as the waters collapsed.

The hydrocarbons of the comet's tail formed, by precipitation every morning, a nourishing substance that the Hebrews ate, thus providing them with sustenance during their flight into the Sinai desert. This was the manna from heaven of which the Bible speaks. The sun, which had previously risen in the west and set in the east, appeared to have reversed itself, now setting in the west and rising in the east. Those societies that had survived relatively intact began the laborious task of locating the new directions, making up calendars, and determining the length of the year.

Earth had only begun to recover, however, when Venus made another close approach. It was some fifty years later and coincided with Joshua's conquest of Canaan. This time the first notice of calamity occurred just prior to a battle, when a rain of meteorites pelted the Near East. Again the sun appeared temporarily to stop in the sky, and Joshua, who was just beginning a battle, used this prolonged day to achieve victory in the valley of Beth-horon.

This sequence of events, as projected in Velikovsky's *Worlds in Collision,* was more precisely developed in his companion volume *Ages in Chaos,* published some years later. Where all previous historians proudly interpreted the books of the Old Testament as divine and sublime poetry of first-rank quality, the Velikovsky thesis explained the trauma and disasters suffered by the people of the Near East and gave startling new meaning to the Bible's descriptions. The verses celebrating the power of the Lord, taken as spectacular but impossible sequences of natural events by Christian scholars, began to leap from the pages as descriptions of natural phenomena.

Ravaged by the approach of Venus twice within a fifty-year period, the nations of the world decided that they had better find a way to appease and pacify the goddess of the comet before she destroyed everything. Religions began to emphasize rites and rituals to prevent the near approach of Venus. Blood sacrifices were offered as peoples desperately sought ways to avoid continued destruction by the comet. Venus continued to cross Earth's orbit, beginning to come dangerously close to Mars so that the comet, while apparently appeased by the new religious ceremonies, was still feared by people as the initiator of destruction. A new conflict was building in the heavens as the orbits began to move closer toward a collision course.

In the days of King Uzziah, Venus missed Earth but managed to pull Mars from its orbit, sending it on a collision course with Earth. Mars was much smaller than Earth and did not have the velocity of Venus, so its approach to Earth did not result in the same degree of destruction that earlier passes of the comet had caused. Earth, which had earlier stabilized its calendar at 360 days, was forced farther out into space away from the sun, resulting in our present year of 365.25 days.

In 687 B.C. Sennacherib led his Assyrian army into Israel with the intent of conquering Jerusalem. On the evening of March 23, the first night of the Hebrew Passover, the Assyrians camped outside the city, ready to capture it the following morning. In what may have been history's most spectacular lightning bolt, the army, 185,000 strong, was destroyed when an electromagnetic charge suddenly arched between

Mars and Earth. The Hebrews had been saved twice on the same date by heavenly intervention. Is it any wonder that they used the most powerful, descriptive terms to praise their God?

Earth did not grind to a halt again, but its rotation was slowed or halted for a number of hours—the prolonged night during which the Assyrian army was destroyed. The axis was somewhat shifted again, coming back closer to its original position before the start of the catastrophes. Mars and Venus then set up an electrical field between themselves, resulting in the repositioning of Mars away from its collision course with Earth. In the sky an immense drama was enacted, as Mars and Venus set and reset fields of incredible electrical energy with respect to each other. The struggle was recounted by the Greeks as the gods intervening in the battle to take Troy.

Mars finally achieved a release from Venus and settled in its present orbit. We have pictures today from our space probes showing the terrible extent of destruction suffered by Mars from the catastrophe. The planet, with heavy scars from the rain of meteorites, looks like the moon. Venus settled in its present orbit in a highly incandescent state, gathering up remnants of its tail as thick hydrocarbon clouds that space probes have disclosed cover the planet.

Now, of course, all of this activity in the heavens was not new to Christians believing in the power of God and His role in history. They had read and believed it for centuries and had taught it as fact to generations of converts. When Velikovsky published his books documenting the catastrophes, however, Christians were not to be found defending the thesis or applauding his scholarly effort, which caused severe traumas in several sciences, including astronomy, geology, physics, and history. Rather they remained silent, while the academic community carried on what may have been history's most closed-minded, libelous attack against a thinker daring to ask separate academic fields to achieve a unity of knowledge.

Worlds in Collision was attacked by "respectable" scientists even before it was published. A concentrated effort was begun to force the Macmillan Company, Velikovsky's publisher, to stop the presses. Scholars began a boycott of Macmillan's textbook division, its most vulnerable place. Macmillan could not withstand the concerted attack and transferred the book's rights to Doubleday. A conspiracy of silence dropped over discussion of Velikovsky's works. He subsequently published *Earth in Upheaval,* which was an embarrassing revelation of geological shortcomings. The book simply took extant geological works and showed that the subject matter had been incorrectly interpreted and slanted by numerous geologists to make it conform to the then prevailing theories of geologic change based upon the interminably slow processes already defined by biologists to explain evolution.

This scientific basis of Velikovsky's work involved a recognition of the possibility that cosmic catastrophes could take place and had in historical times. These catastrophes were observed by peoples all over the globe and became part of their creation legends or myths explaining the origin of their sacrificial rites and rituals. Thus in the folklore of the ancients had been hidden important observations that were crucially important for an understanding of the nature of the universe. Scientists disagreed, however, and they began to produce facts and figures to refute Velikovsky. Fear set in among scholars, and no one stood up to demand that Velikovsky be allowed to present his views. He was subjected to bitter criticism by people who had not read his books but who had learned, from their earliest childhood, that the tales of non-Christian peoples about serpents swallowing the sun and prolonged nights of utter darkness were just pagan, hardly historical, superstitions and probably the work of the devil.

As Velikovsky unveiled his concept of the solar system, respectable scholars guffawed at his apparently wild predictions and suppositions. Practically every point he suggested was derided as being totally contrary to what science had already "proved" to be true. Scholars in the major disciplines affected by the thesis ridiculed Velikovsky, announcing satirically that if his thesis were true, it would require certain phenomena to be present, which everyone knew was not the case. All of these wild predictions, made in 1950 by Velikovsky, were universally rejected.

Then the evidence began to come in. Science had new opportunities to conduct sophisticated experiments through the initial space probe programs. New methods of dating materials began to be developed, the International Geophysical Year of 1958 was held to determine systematically certain facts about the planet, and eventually the Mars and Venus probes by space rockets were made. Universally and without exception Velikovsky's predictions and suggestions about the planets were confirmed. No other comprehensive explanation of the solar system had returned as many different accurate results as had the theory espoused in *Worlds in Collision*.

Naturally the scholars who had derided Velikovsky did not credit him with the results of his creative thought. They continued the curtain of silence while stealing his ideas as fast as they could read his books. Some of the more prominent scientists had made dramatic announcements that if Velikovsky were right, then Earth, the sun, Venus, the moon, Mars, and other heavenly bodies would have to have certain characteristics. When Velikovsky was proved correct, they promptly hedged rhetorically and dodged their embarrassment in double-talk, too chagrined or perhaps too stupid to apologize. Some of these memorable statements by noted scientists should be recorded for posterity's sake.

Velikovsky suggested that the sun was an electrically charged body. Donald Menzel, a Harvard astronomer and one of Velikovsky's most bitter critics, ridiculed the idea. He maintained that the sun cannot hold a charge above 1,800 volts if positive and a single volt if negative and said that Velikovsky's theory required a charge of 10^{19} volts, which he assured everyone was patently impossible. This was in 1952. In 1960 V. A. Bailey of Australia discovered that the sun carries a negative charge of 10^{19} volts.

Cecilia Payne-Gaposchkin, another Harvard astronomer and the scientist who reviewed Velikovsky's first book, misquoted him and then ridiculed her own misquotations. In 1950 Payne-Gaposchkin maintained that the planets could not possibly possess electrostatic charges sufficient to produce the effects Velikovsky claimed for them. Three years later in an article in *Scientific American*, she advocated a universe that was essentially a gravitating electromagnet. She never mentioned that the idea had already been advanced by Velikovsky and rejected by herself as evidence of his instability as a scholar.[9]

Velikovsky maintained that Venus, deriving from an erratic past as a comet, would be in an incandescent state. This was in direct opposition to what was "known" by science in 1950. Menzel lost no time in ridiculing Velikovsky because he was one of the leading

proponents of the theory that Venus had an extremely low temperature. In 1955 he revised his estimate of the ground temperature of
Venus, concluding that it was probably 50°C. The Venus probe of 1962
indicated that the surface temperature of Venus was some 800° F. Later
probes showed that ground temperature was closer to 1,000° F.

Because Velikovsky believed that the comet Venus erupted
from Jupiter, he predicted at a 1953 talk at Princeton that Jupiter was
probably a dark star giving off radio signals. Less than two years later,
two scientists discovered radio signals coming from Jupiter, and by
1965 Jupiter was declared a dark star. Velikovsky also predicted that
Earth would have a magnetosphere reaching as far as the moon. In 1958
the Van Allen belts were discovered, named after James Van Allen who
had only measured them and not after Velikovsky who had predicted
them.

The May 1972 issue of *Pensée,* a journal published by the
Student Academic Freedom Forum in Portland, Oregon, gave the
complete story of Velikovsky's amazing predictions and his history of
scientific persecution and derision. It devoted a considerable number
of pages to a simple listing of his suggestions about the nature of the
universe and the history of ancient peoples. Even a casual glance at the
list of Velikovsky's predictions in the face of then-accepted scientific
theory, which turned out was really dogma, is staggering to behold.
There appeared to be no doubt that Velikovsky had been vindicated.

Science and the academic community revealed themselves
as superstitious, dogmatic, narrow-minded, and spiteful little people
as a result of their treatment of Velikovsky. For nearly two and one-half
decades, they refused to allow him to discuss the theories that have
produced such a plenitude of newly verified facts about the universe
as to make the basic theory the most revolutionary explanation of the
creation we have ever seen. Some men borrowed Velikovsky's ideas
almost totally without giving him any credit or even mention. Others
reversed themselves completely without apologizing for their past
errors or acknowledging Velikovsky's earlier and correct contentions.

The most common attack leveled against Velikovsky was
that he simply made a series of lucky guesses and hit on quite a few of
them. The point that this attack missed was that every prediction he
made had to fit into his general interpretation of the nature of the solar

system. He was not simply spinning a tale and casually throwing off unrelated predictions. Everything suggested by Velikovsky originated from the implications of his thesis. His predictions involved pulling together the anomalies and inconsistencies of numerous fields of interest to form a unified view of the universe. Taken together they give us a picture of a different kind of world and a different kind of history in which things of utmost significance happen—similar to the original Christian contention that God does work in the affairs of men.

Worlds in Collision has great relevance for religious thinkers. Velikovsky's original point of departure was the belief that the Exodus was an event of worldwide significance and experienced by peoples on a global basis. His search of many peoples' folklore and their religious and cultural myths and stories indicated that celestial events viewed from different places gave rise to different descriptions of phenomena which scientifically described a definite sequence. The religious interpretation of the events varied, of course, with the respective peoples' location, language, culture, and state of existence.

With the exception of Fulton Oursler, who wrote an article for the *Reader's Digest* correlating Velikovsky's thesis with the Old Testament (a duplication of effort considering that *Ages in Chaos*, Velikovsky's second book, is a supreme demonstration of Velikovsky's skill as a biblical scholar and historian) no Christian theologian or Old Testament scholar of any note supported the consideration of the thesis that the Old Testament might be historically accurate in many respects. Christianity thus lost an opportunity to recoup its lost ground and assert the historical nature of its revelation.

Certain subtleties thus emerge that require further analysis. If Christian theologians and historians did not see the opportunities in this new evidence that events of the Bible, hitherto felt to be symbolic imagery and hyperbole, were actually historical events, what prevented them from understanding? Had they adopted the secular interpretation that all ancient stories were basically a fictional mythology devised to prove a moral point but certainly not indicative of the nature of the physical universe? Were they afraid that proving the historicity of the flood, the Exodus, and other seemingly impossible phenomena would validate corresponding legends of non-Christian traditions thereby rendering any appeal to history and geology on behalf of a particular religion moot? Or did they simply never believe the Old Testament in the first place? It is exceedingly difficult to determine why even the fundamentalists did not move to support Velikovsky's thesis.

With regard to the Exodus itself, the Makahs who live on Cape Flattery in the northwest corner of the United States have a story that one day the sea withdrew from the land and was nowhere to be found. The wise men of the tribe told everyone to build rafts and boats as quickly as possible. Some days later the sea returned in the form of a gigantic tidal wave, tossing boats and rafts all over, drowning most of the people, and forever separating portions of the tribe from each other. Geologically and geographically this phenomenon can be linked to the disappearance of the waters when Moses and the people crossed the Red Sea, suggesting that at many other places on the planet the same water tidal behavior occurred. Verification of the Exodus as a physical, historical event might then verify the Makah story, but so what? More important, if the planet is likely to be subjected to immense displacements of its land and waters, it would be better to know than to be caught thinking that a catastrophe of this magnitude was impossible.

Granted that it is a severe rupture for the theological mind to go from a conception of God slyly dropping hints for the church to discern to a belief in a cataclysmic event in which a number of religions are founded because of a belief in Divine intervention and physical salvation. But even today we have to take seriously the possibility of the planet experiencing changes of such a magnitude that they can only be credited to the action of higher powers. Every bit of evidence we have must be brought to bear on the question of how religions originate because it is not useful to pretend that while various deities once spoke to people and performed some incredible feats, they no longer do so. Religions do not rise simply because poets become too eloquent and people want to glorify their past.

World War II brought Americans into contact with parts of the world then unknown to them and unvisited by modern travelers. After the Americans had left certain islands in the South Pacific, scholars discovered that a new religion had grown up among the natives that interpreted the airplanes and machinery left by our soldiers as manifestations of their Gods. The cargo cults, as they have been called, would indicate that if an event is out of the ordinary and makes a sufficiently strong impression on people, a new religion can be called forth that seems to explain the experience regardless of how simplistic it might have appeared to more knowledgeable observers.

The Old Testament is probably extremely accurate in many respects, particularly when describing those events that changed the way people understood their world. It is difficult for many people to accept the fact that the Old Testament is primarily an effort to record first Hebrew and then Jewish history and not a volume of Divine admonitions about the nature of ultimate reality. But it is entirely possible that events recorded in the Old Testament and believed to be highly religious are also described in the legends and folklore of other people and not given the same religious significance. Our responsibility today is to discern from the many different human traditions the probable historical sequences that have shaped our modern earth and come into closer understanding of the nature of the planet on which we live.

Notes

1. Harvey Cox, *The Secular City* (New York: Macmillan, 1966), 91.
2. Ibid, 222.
3. Theodor Herzl Gaster, *Passover: Its History and Traditions* (New York: Henry Schuman, 1949), 29.
4. Johannes Pedersen, *Israel: Its Life and Culture*, vols. III–IV, translated by Geoffrey Cumberledge (London: Oxford University Press, 1959), 728.
5. Louis K. Dupre, *The Other Dimension* (Garden City, N.Y.: Doubleday, 1972), 395.
6. Ibid.
7. Paul Tillich, *Systematic Theology*, vol. II (Chicago: University of Chicago Press, 1957), 88.
8. Velikovsky's work has created a number of schools of interpretation so that his original thesis—catastrophism on a planetary scale within historic times—is reasonably acceptable today, although people within the mainstream of orthodox science do not use his name only his ideas. Among his disciples the tendency has been to advocate new cosmic scenarios that attempt to expand his original idea to include information on Saturn and other planets and hypothesize a time when our solar system had two suns. Alfred de Grazia has created his own version of solar system catastrophism that I like very much as a story but that has some severe problems when translated into the language of physics, I suspect.

Zecharia Sitchin has done the best job of analyzing the possibility of ancient astronauts and their effect on us today, and I sketch out some of his theory in chapter 9. I would, however, make an effort to combine Velikovsky's ideas with Sitchin's because I think the chronology that Velikovsky develops, from 1500 B.C. forward, still has a great deal of validity.

When he was alive, I used to send Velikovsky copies of the Indian legends and traditions that might have been useful in supporting some of his ideas. He was always very gracious in receiving them, although I don't think I ever provided him anything important.

This chapter is basically my interpretation of the ideas that Velikovsky presented in a series of books, the majority of which actually dealt with the reconstruction of ancient Near Eastern history. Any errors or misinterpretations are mine.

9. These conflicts and many others are discussed by Alfred de Grazia in an issue of the *American Behavioral Scientist* in 1964 which evolved into a book, the *Velikovsky Affair* (University Books, 1966). A group of students at Reed College produced a ten-issue series in *Pensée* magazine that reviewed all of Velikovsky's predictions and his accuracy rate as well as the inaccurate statements of his critics. I have merely discussed two of the most spectacular instances of Velikovsky's critics being wrong here in this chapter.

CHAPTER 8

ORIGIN OF RELIGION

Suppose Immanuel Velikovsky is correct? Suppose that instead of the Exodus accounts being a poetic elaboration of religious doctrine of a later time, they are fairly well-remembered accounts of the phenomena encountered by the Hebrews as they left Egypt. How then do we approach religious writings? Are they to be understood as actual events, and do we take all religious stories as having been real events at some time and someplace in man's experience? It would seem that we have a major task of discovering to what extent we can accept the historical veracity of any story of ancient times. That Velikovsky's projections about the nature of the physical world continue to produce startling verifications would tend to make us hesitate, reflect, and take another look at religious doctrines, symbolism, and beliefs.

The assumption made by theologians when discussing religious writings and their symbols and images is that world events have followed a fairly homogeneous pattern and that no particular event has happened that we cannot observe in similar pattern today. Using this assumption the Exodus does become simply another political revolt, which in later years had the fortune to be accepted as illustrating religious beliefs. But if we make this assumption, we are almost immediately faced with a more fundamental question about the origin of the religious beliefs illustrated in the stories that are found in religious traditions.

The Western conception of a homogeneous time experience apparently has many roots. Certainly one influence can be said to have been Greek philosophy and its insistence on the uniform operation of nature. This idea surfaces continually in Western thought, and it continually intrudes into theological doctrines about religion and the nature of God. So strong has this idea been that natural events have been forced into this interpretive pattern, even when the facts warranted otherwise.

For many centuries peoples of Western Europe believed that the heavens, being made by God at creation, were constant. The appearance of meteors and comets was thus a great embarrassment because these phenomena seemed to indicate that the heavens were not all that stable. Was this possible in a divinely constructed universe? Present-day astronomers are searching the records of other societies for evidence of a supernova that occurred on July 4, 1054. It was one of the spectacular events of celestial history, and it apparently lasted some three weeks and was clearly observable at various parts of the planet because it appeared quite close to the moon in its crescent phase.[1]

In at least one cave in California and on rock carvings and paintings in Arizona and New Mexico, there are representations of a crescent moon with a bright object quite near it. There are speculations that the early peoples of North America saw the supernova and made these records to verify for subsequent generations that such a thing had happened. There are very few references to this event in Europe where the social science of history was fairly advanced. The reason that there are very few records in Europe is that everyone believed that the heavens were constant. Thus people did not really see what they were seeing.

In view of this startling victory of faith over experience, is it any wonder that contemporary theories of the nature of the Exodus fall apart whenever they are examined? If people become so blinded to their observations that their beliefs override their actual experiences, would it not seem possible that the whole method of interpreting events needs drastic revision?

In another day, perhaps, the rock paintings in the American Southwest would be taken as a primitive form of religious poetry. Theologians, historians of religion, psychoanalysts, and other wise people would pour forth books about the primitive ideas of the natives who could not know that no extremely bright star exists beside the moon at its crescent. Fortunately, today we have sufficient fragmentation of knowledge so that astronomers can use Indian rock paintings as verifications that the supernova was observed.

Because it is possible, indeed highly probable, that American Indians observed and faithfully recorded a celestial event while their supposedly more civilized neighbors in Europe were gritting their teeth, reaffirming their faith in the Christian religion, and refusing to see the supernova, the whole question of the interpretation of religious symbols, doctrines, and beliefs should be reexamined. Suppose we find in the tribal traditions a memory that is not only more correct in many aspects than that of the Western religions, but suppose that we find in them the longer and more extensive history of humankind. That prospect has not been considered by Westerners. Yet it is precisely the consideration that must be made if Western societies are to be released from their religiously ethnocentric universe.

It is with this consideration in mind that we have postponed any discussion of American Indian tribal stories about creation. In the Western tradition we have been taught to regard all stories about beginnings as primitive efforts to understand how the world began. The obvious use of linear time as a determining factor in making sense of legends is so dominant in Western and Christian thought that it prevents legends being accepted on other terms.

We cannot necessarily project the thought that the early peoples in North America were any more concerned to describe the creation as an event than they were to explain any other facet of their experience as an event. The absence of a theological interpretation of history should be sufficient evidence of the Indians' refusal to use time as the determining factor when trying to understand their experiences. Where we do have legends describing world conditions, the existence of other worlds, or the existence of catastrophic conditions caused by certain factors, we cannot assume that the people are concerned primarily with the sequence of events. They might much more be concerned with describing the actual life conditions, and the apparent sequence of activity in the legends might be a fairly accurate description of what actually took place rather than a poetic elaboration of events for theological purposes.

In short, what we have previously been pleased to call creation stories might not be such at all. They might be simply the collective memories of a great and catastrophic event through which people came to understand themselves and the universe they inhabited. Creation stories may simply be the survivors' memories of reasonably large and destructive events.

The tribal religion of the Hopi Indians of Arizona is a case in point. The legends of the Hopi relate that the world as they have known it has been destroyed three times and that our present world is now reaching a time of impending destruction. This religious tradition, which has tribal variations, appears as a spiral of religious insight rather than a rigid temporal or a totally spatial understanding. The existence of the Hopi in all worlds is predicated on a particular land being given to them over which they assume a custodial function; in any specific world it involves deliberate spatial considerations. The collective memory inherent in the traditions combines time and space in a comprehensible manner, however, and one that we may be working toward today.[2]

The first Hopi world was called Topka, and it was characterized as a world of endless space. Topka was considered to be the original world, and the basic themes that are found in some of the tribal legends about the nature of creation are found in descriptions of this world. The direction of this world, according to the Hopi, was west. The living things of the creation were congenial and lived without strife. Eventually people became convinced that real differences existed between the various life forms, and men became increasingly wicked toward other species. This wickedness was erased when the world was destroyed by a rain of fire.

The Hopi survived the end of this world by living underground with the ants. As the world cooled and people were able to emerge, they discovered that the world had been rearranged. Water now existed where land had formerly been. Land stood where there had been waters. The direction of the world was west, and it was called "dark midnight."

In the second world the people and animals were not allowed to live together, so they lived separate lives. The fear that the problems of the old world would return to plague them caused this separation. Humans came to learn the arts of trade and commerce, but they used these talents to accumulate more material goods than were needed. This greed eventually led to the downfall of the second world. Earth's axis tilted, and the world spun around rapidly, destroying the natural features of the landscape. The world was stabilized only by passing through an extremely cold part of space that froze the waters into solid ice.

Everything was lifeless, and to survive the people lived underground once again. Then earth's axis changed again, and it resumed a more normal orbit of rotation around the sun. Revolution on nearly the same axis was eventually restored and the ice began to melt. The surface of the planet regained its original ability to sustain life. People emerged once again. This third world was known to the Hopi as Kuskura, and its direction was east. The new world was the scene of much activity. People had not forgotten the trade and commerce they had learned in the previous world, and substantial technology was developed. Men learned to fly through the air in *patuwvotas*, or shields, made from hide propelled by some unidentified power.

Using these flying shields, the various nations warred against one another. The warfare grew so intense that the third world was destroyed. Warned ahead of time that the world would be flooded, the Hopis constructed special cylinders of hollow reeds that floated on the flood waters. The descriptions of the flood bear close similarities with the flood stories of other nations. As the waters began to subside, the people sent out birds to find any lands remaining above the waters. Eventually the waters receded, and the various nations were assigned lands for themselves. The fourth world, the one in which we are presently living, began.

Could such a sequence of worlds have been made up in the imagination, no matter how religious that imagination, of a primitive mind that has been otherwise classified as relatively uninformed about the physical forces of the natural world? Could people have conceived the changing of directions of the world and made such a conception a primary part of their religious belief without something having happened that would justify such a belief? By *direction* of the world, we are basically talking about the rising and setting of the sun. In translating the meaning of the four Hopi worlds, we have the first two worlds in which the sun rises in the west and sets in the east, and the last two in which it rises in the east and sets in the west. All that is necessary to account for the difference in phenomena is a rotational change in direction.

Suppose that we break into this sequence and suggest that a nation of people comes into existence in one of the worlds. It begins to recognize itself as a people distinct from the other groups inhabiting the planet. A language comes into being that is relatively distinct from other languages. A religion comes into being that attempts to account for the creation of the world as the people either know it or can remember it from earlier legends. Their creation story involves the fact that the world was originally a cold and icy one. Gradually its rotation was changed, possibly by the assistance of hero figures, and the world began to warm. Eventually it warmed sufficiently to support life, and the various life forms came into being.

One day these people encounter a people who speak to them of two worlds. They are incredulous. Everyone knows that there is only one world and that it was created by changing the axis of the world, so that the ice, the original substance of the universe, gradually melted to produce their present world. When they hear stories of how the first world was destroyed by rains of fire, they are livid. Pagans, they scream. The stories of the first world are interpreted as merely childish wish projections of a people refusing to believe that the ultimate nature of the world is ice. Steps are taken to be sure that the people who believe in the first world are converted to the belief that the stories of the world's origin as a large block of ice are the absolute truth as revealed by God Himself.

That is the precise position into which non-Christians are placed when the Christian religion insists that its story of creation is descriptive of the original creation event and that their stories are superstitions that have arisen because of a great psychological need which can be filled by accepting the Christian version. Forcing the consideration of creation to be examined as if it were a specific event destroys the possibility of knowing the nature of the world with any certainty. It also presumes that the Christian account of the creation is poetic ideology typical of a certain kind of people and that this kind of people is by definition the most ancient vintage. Such conclusions are not necessarily correct. That a religious tradition may contain references to more than one type of world should indicate that the tradition is at least older than traditions speaking of only one world.

Near Eastern religions, for example, appear to have only one recallable beginning. Both Genesis and the Enuma Elish of the Babylonian records indicate a beginning in a world of waters. Do these records extend only to the third world of the Hopi? Were there societies capable of passing on a longer history of humankind in the Near East, or were they destroyed by one of the earlier catastrophes visited on the planet? The basis of perpetuating religious knowledge would appear to be a spectacular event experienced by a people who subsequently survive sufficiently long enough to pass on the tradition. In the Near East we may have peoples surviving in an area where a catastrophe did not wreak total destruction.

The Enuma Elish begins with the following description of the universe:

> When a sky above had not (yet even) been mentioned
> (And) the name of firm ground below had not (yet even) been thought of;
> (When) only primeval Apsu, their begetter,
> And Mummu and Ti'amat—she who gave birth to them all—
> Were mingling their waters in one;
> When no bog had formed (and) no island could be found;
> When no god whosoever had appeared,
> Had been named, had been determined as to (his) lot,
> Then were gods formed within them.[3]

The Enuma Elish has sometimes been regarded as the prototype of the Genesis story, sometimes as a parallel description of the creation as handed down in the Hebrew tradition. That it closely follows between Babylonian and Hebrew traditions is significant. Genesis appears to be concerned with much the same phenomena:

In the beginning God created the heaven and earth
And the earth was without form, and void; and the
darkness was upon the face of the deep. And
the Spirit of God moved upon the face of the waters.
And God said, Let there be light; and there was
light.
And God saw the light, that it was good: and God
divided the light from the darkness.
And God called the light Day, and the darkness he
called Night. And the evening and the morning
were the first day.[4]

If we closely examine these two traditions in a spatial sense rather than as a primeval event, we find that they rather specifically describe a particular condition in which there is extreme darkness. From our knowledge of the world in which we live, it would indicate extensive cloud cover. The concern of both stories would appear to be the separation of the waters so that the gods can determine and name the sky and the ground. When we understand that Genesis projects a much longer sequence of appearances and if we understand the sequence as taking place in a particular place although not necessarily limited to seven days or extended for millions of years, we face a new sense of reality.

On the second day in Genesis the waters are divided between heaven and earth. The third day plant life is created. It is not until the fifth day that animal and fish life emerge, but on the fourth day the stars, the sun, and moon are created. Clarence Darrow is supposed to have made William Jennings Bryan look foolish by asking him how the morning and evening of the first day could occur when the sun, moon, and stars were not created until the fourth day. If we view the emergence of each form mentioned in Genesis as the sequence in which things could be distinguished one from another following a monstrous flood with attendant cloud cover of unimaginable magnitude, the appearance of the sun, moon, and stars at that point at which the water vapor has allowed their light to be seen appears eminently reasonable.

The noteworthy factors in the Genesis account are that the sequence of action is not incompatible with the phenomena that would be expected in a catastrophe of major importance. Plant life, for example, develops prior to the creation of the heavens. We know that plant life would have an extremely difficult time originating without the conditions allowing photosynthesis being initiated before the origination of plants. But plants could survive for some time between periods of ordinary sunlight, if they were already in existence. While light itself is apparently present in the Genesis account prior to plant life, distinguishing the source of light comes after the emergence of plant life. We could find no better description of a planet emerging from a catastrophic event than to find light diffused in its atmosphere and people, unable to identify the source of light, still being able to recognize that somehow light and darkness had been separated.

We have an option that will apparently never be settled:is the Genesis account a refined and somehow more sublime religious statement of creation that is secondary and derivative from the Enuma Elish? Or are they really two accounts of two distinct peoples, bearing similarity to one another because of their geographic proximity to the event? Many scholars have simply foreclosed the second option, believing that the accounts are poetic attempts to describe the original creation event, instead of asking themselves whether these accounts are simply memories of one specific event in world history.

When we turn to American Indian tribal religions, we find a number of similarities also forming a pattern of interpretation. The Navajo legends begin with an account of the emergence of the Navajos or First People from the underworlds: "The first three worlds were neither good nor healthful. They moved all the time and made the people dizzy. Upon ascending into this world, the Navajo found only darkness, and they said we must have light."[5] The Navajos then separate light into constituent colors of white, blue, yellow, and black representing the colors of the sky during the twenty-four-hour period of rotation.

The Pawnees and Arickara also speak of ancient people emerging from the darkness into a lighted world. The Pueblos are led by Mother Corn (plant life) into the new world of light from the world of darkness. The Mandans climb a vine rope from the underground until a large woman proves to be too heavy for the rope and breaks it, leaving some of the people remaining under the earth. Other tribes have had variations of this general theme of emerging from the underground, where they had survived a great catastrophe or at least begun their existence in this present world as a people. There would appear to be no good reason for a number of tribes to share this story, unless there was some event behind it, even though the event was very dimly recalled in tribal memory. Perhaps the disaster of which the Near East spoke did not affect the peoples of North America, who had prepared an underground shelter for themselves in anticipation of the event. At the least we can suggest that some common experience must be shared by some of the tribes, as emergence legends among other peoples of the globe appear to be rather sparse.

The tribal religions would serve to remind us that the scope of human history cannot be encompassed within a linear time sequence running from a creation event to the present-day world. The strong possibility that different societies recall in their religious traditions various geographical histories of the planet can lead us to remember the neglected dimension of religion that has appeared in nearly every religious tradition. If we recall the thrust of Jewish history and its eschatology in the time of Jesus, we come to recognize that land, the promised land, has remained as a constant and tangible element of religious experiences of societies.

While the theology of the Old Testament appears to focus on the promised land as early as the time of Abraham, it is with the emergence of the Hebrews as a migrating nation into Canaan that the community and the land merge into a psychic and religious unity. From that time on the people orient themselves around the idea that God has given them this particular piece of land. Even those people in Jesus' time who sought the return of the Son of Man as the Jewish Messiah looked for a military hero to restore their land ownership. The translation by Christians of the fanaticism of the Jewish resistance to the Romans in the days of Jesus into a "misunderstanding" by the Jews of the nature of the Messiah has always been a difficult interpretation for the Christians to make. By substituting *heaven* for the tangible restoration of Palestine to the Jews by driving the Romans out, Christians eliminated the dimension of land from religion, and necessarily their theology had to change Hebrew tribal memories of a particular land into a generalized statement about the origin of the world.

Without the particularity of land on which it was intended that a particular people live, creation had to become an event of the beginnings of the world.

It is quite possible, therefore, that as we look for the origin of peoples, we must discover religious experiences; as we look for the origins of religions, we must discover nations of people, and whichever way we look, it is to the lands on which the people reside and in which the religions arise that is important. This possibility is what has dominated the concerns of American Indian's peoples from the very beginnings. The chance that lands would be lost meant that religious communities would be destroyed and individual identities forsaken. As sacred mountains became secularized, as tribal burial grounds became cornfields, as tribes no longer lived on the dust of their ancestors' bones, the people knew that they could not survive.

This feeling of the importance of land is also present in Western countries, but it has undergone a radical change. It has transformed itself into patriotism on the one hand and religious nationalism on the other. With this transformation, the whole nature of religion and land has been lost. Land is no longer a major element in Western religion but forms a tangential influence often manifesting itself whether or not the Christian religion intends that it do so.

The early Church centered itself in Italy in the city of Rome as surely as did the Hebrews center themselves in Jerusalem after they had conquered Canaan. Where the Jewish religion was and is centered in the Holy Land as *the* specific land of the religion, one cannot help but conclude that Rome is and has become the center of Christendom. With the Reformation the growth of national churches simply meant that each interpretation of the Christian religion had to find a home for itself and the doctrines and devotional emphases followed ethnic preferences. The peculiarites of all European theology can be understood more easily by reference to countries than by comparison of abstract creedal statements and doctrines.

With the movement of Christianity to the North American continent, and the subsequent freedom to develop religious expressions offered by this land, the possibility of constituting a Christian culture or unity vanished. Christianity shattered on the shores of this continent, producing hundreds of sects in the same manner that the tribes continually subdivided in an effort to relate to the rhythms of the land. It is probably in the nature of this continent that divisiveness is one of its greatest characteristics, a virtually uncontrollable freedom of the spirit.

The land dimension of religion must inevitably wear itself out in the respective religious traditions as they mature. What would be the nature of a religious tradition that has grown old and sophisticated on a land? The puzzlement of modern Europe would seem to indicate that the religious dimension of land is a factor that cannot be neglected. Germany was the scene of the Protestant Reformation in its most profound sense, for it was the home of Martin Luther who claimed a doctrinal superiority to everything that had preceded him. If there were to be any land, therefore, in which Christianity could have entrenched itself outside of Italy, it would probably be Germany.

Heinrich Heine in *Religion and Philosophy in Germany*, originally published in 1835, may have clearly foreseen the nature of the catastrophe that occurs when a religion grows thin on a land to which it has become a stranger.

> Christianity—and this is the fairest merit—subdued to a certain extent the brutal warrior ardor of the Germans, but it could not entirely quench it; and when the Cross, that restraining talisman, falls to pieces, then will break forth again the ferocity of the old combatants, the frantic Berserker rage whereof Northern Poets have said and sung so much. The talisman has become rotten, and the day will surely come when it will pitifully crumble to dust. The old stone gods will arise then from the forgotten ruins and wipe from their eyes the dust of centuries, and Thor with his giant hammer will arise again, and he will shatter the Gothic cathedrals.[6]

Many people have remarked that the rise of National Socialism and its attendant sense of religious fervor fulfilled Heine's vision of a Christianity that was no longer able to contain the ancient Teutonic gods.

Carl Jung suggested the existence of a collective uncon scious in which the archetypes and symbols of universal human experience were to be found. In his analysis of the nature of human spiritual problems, Jung suggested that the unconscious acted to structure solutions by presenting via dreams the archetypes representing familiar facets of our life in a type of dreams of which we became aware. His system was based on the interpretation of the dream symbols and the story in which they were found in dreams. In the period before the rise of National Socialism, Jung said that he could see in the psychological problems of his German patients the symbols of the old Germanic religious myths that were to later mark part of the development of Nazi fanaticism among the young.[7] Do we attribute the ability of young Germans to dream in ancient religious symbols to a desire to escape from Christian rigidity or perhaps to a residual power in the land itself to produce certain religious mythologies and figures?

Additional pondering on this matter brings little relief. In England there appears to be the phenomenon of ghosts. It is estimated that some ten thousand ghosts inhabit the British islands, and it is a poor castle, manor house, or moor that does not have a full complement of ghosts. Germany has a proliferation of poltergeists. How are we to account for the renewal of Druidism in England and the northern parts of France? Some people may deny that contemporary concern with witches and Druid religious practices does not conform with descriptions by scholars for ancient times. We must remember that scholars' descriptions of ancient times are primarily figments of their imaginations rather than accounts of reality.

How are we to catalog the existence of shrines of all faiths? The Shrine of Our Lady of Guadalupe Hildalgo, for example, rests on a spot already the site of ancient Indian religious practices centuries before the Christian missionaries appeared on the scene. Why is there an absence of miracles and revelations in North America when other parts of the Christian world seem to have a plentitude of religious sites? Are Fatima and Lourdes uniquely Christian, or do they represent a religious site hoary with antiquity, whose earlier religions are unknown to us today?

Students of religion have failed to recognize the unique nature of religious symbolism, its apparent correspondence with land masses, its vibrant ability to reassert itself in times of spiritual crisis, and the lack of a universal symbol system of religious experience. Perhaps the conflict of competing religions on lands has led to much of our social, political, and military conflict among peoples. It is difficult, therefore, simply to classify the cultural competition and distinctions in community values as differentials on a time scale of social evolution. Rather careful examination should be given to the nature of cultural and social disagreements and the origin of these differences in both the religious and geographical dimensions of people's lives.

If the old Germanic myths of Wotan can reassert themselves in a modern industrial state, which Carl Jung believed he could document in the rise of National Socialism in Germany, and if the practical political program of the Nazis was the conquest of additional lands for "living space" and the genetic reunification of Germanic peoples, we cannot avoid an examination of the relationship between lands, spiritual energies, and peoples. Land must somehow have an unsuspected spiritual energy or identity that shapes and directs human activities. Religions must not be simple expressions of ethical and moral codes as we have been taught. They must be more complicated manifestations of the living earth itself and this aspect of religion is something that American Indians of all the peoples on earth represented.

Popular anthologies of Indian speeches contain two basic themes: the earth is alive and everything related to it is also alive, and land consecrates human activities and makes them something more than we have power to produce. In 1912, Curley, a Crow Indian chief, refused to sell any more of his land to the federal government when it proposed another land cession. He rejected the government's offer.

> The soil you see is not ordinary soil—it is the dust of the blood, the flesh, and the bones of our ancestors. We fought and bled and died to keep other Indians from taking it, and we fought and bled and died helping the Whites.
> You will have to dig down through the surface before you can find nature's earth, as the upper portion is Crow.
> The land as it is, is my blood and my dead; it is consecrated; and I do not want to give up any portion of it.[8]

This sentiment is considerably greater than a simple allegiance to abstract religious principles, even to principles that purport to give instructions in cosmic salvation. It speaks of an identity so strong as to be virtually indistinguishable from the earth itself, the human being, as it were, completely in harmony with the Mother Earth and inseparable in every way. Nowhere else on this plant do we find this attitude and it bears further examination.

Notes

1. *Washington Post* (January 14, 1973) had a story discussing the investigation of the visibility of the Crab nebula supernova and its possible observation by the Indians of North America.

2. The best exposition of Hopi history of the four worlds is probably *Book of the Hopi* by Frank Waters and Oswald White Bear Fredericks (New York: Viking Press, 1963).

3. Milton K. Munitz ed., *Theories of the Universe* (Glencoe, Ill.: The Free Press, 1957), 9.

4. Genesis: 1:1

5. Hartley Burr Alexander, *The World's Rim* (Omaha: Bison Books, University of Nebraska Press, 1953), 13.

6. Heinrich Heine, *Religion and Philosophy in Germany* (Boston: Beacon Press, 1959), 159–60.

7. Carl Jung, "Wotan" in *Civilization in Transition, Collected Works*, vol. 10 (New York: Pantheon Books 1953–1979).

8. Ernest Thompson Seton, *The Gospel of the Red Man* (New York: Doubleday Doran, 1936), 58–59.

CHAPTER 9

NATURAL AND HYBRID PEOPLES

In 1972 when I began this book I excluded some questions that were integral to examination of the idea of land and religion. The most basic question, of course, is how we can conceive of deity at all if our religious experiences and knowledge derive primarily from the environment around us. What images do we invoke and what can we expect in the way of a relationship with Him, Her, or Them? I did not anticipate that the complexity of the subject might require considerable critical examination of the cultural context in which religions and ideas about deities appear. During the past two decades I have been able to discover a set of lesser questions that, when taken as a unified inquiry, have led me into a better understanding of how to deal with the major question of the validity and viability of religion. Still, in order to ask the proper questions, one must believe that reality is a bit different from what we have been taught to believe and in this respect I owe it all, in the last analysis, to Oral Roberts.

Several years back, in a memorable TV performance, Oral said that God was dissatisfied with Oral's ministry and had threatened that if he did not raise something like $10 million by a certain date, God would "call him home." Since the reward for faithful service for most

Christians (if we take funeral orations seriously) is to be "called home" it struck me as mighty strange that Oral was resisting this option with all his might. On reflection it also seemed strange that after some two thousand years of bribing His followers to be good with promises of eternal life, the Deity had resorted to extortion as a means of keeping people in line.

A few weeks later when I happened to be reading one of the Old Testament prophets it suddenly occurred to me that the Judeo-Christian Deity had been a pretty rough character all along. He was always throwing fits of anger over some real or imagined slight; he monitored every activity of His Chosen People to see that they were obeying some rather vague instructions he had given them; and, to hear some Protestants tell it, he had a large ledger book in which he recorded all our evil thoughts and deeds. This behavior can be described in a humorous way but it is not very funny. It suggests a Deity very closely modeled not only after a human personality but also after a personality that is unbalanced and immature.

The Judeo-Christian Deity, as a matter of fact, has emotional characteristics that are quite common and can be easily identified in contemporary human beings. He has the egotism of Henry Kissinger, the stability of Donald Trump, the generosity of Edwin Meese, and the military mind of George Bush. (We should remember that Yahweh killed some 185,000 Arabs in Sennacarib's army outside Jerusalem one night, Bush slaughtered almost as many in the prolonged bombing of Iraq during the winter of 1991. Both seem to have had the same motive—the Arabs had disregarded one of their warnings.) Having a "personal relationship" with this Deity is akin to being J. Edgar Hoover's best friend—it is safe but not satisfying.

If people are offended by these comparisons it is because they have not read their Bible objectively to see how their Deity has behaved historically. In Western society we are taught that the Deity is benign, friendly, and intent upon making us rich. So we can read Bible verses that command genocidal acts and pretend that they are merely divine bombast designed to scare us into behaving. When we step outside this cultural context and try to understand the Bible as a literal historical document, we discover that the portrait of the Deity sketched in the Old Testament is very negative and in fact may describe a psychopath like Saddam Hussein (if he is indeed what our media says he is). We find the image of a despotic Oriental monarch determined to have his way regardless of how it affects his subjects.

This uncomfortable image has been further illuminated for me by the startling contrast between Near Eastern religions on the one hand and the other world and tribal religions on the other. Near Eastern deities seem to thrive on controlling all human historical and political situations. They disregard natural law—unable to direct the activities of the physical world in a manner that would enlighten its inhabitants—and are intent on devising punishments. If there is any evidence of a karmic balancing process here, it is submerged under pictures of burning hells and blissful heavens. They are obsessed with human sexual activities and genetic purity. They demand blood sacrifices of birds, animals, and sometimes human beings as the only acceptable way of forgiving our transgressions. Such abstract concepts as redemption and atonement dominate their conversations with humans. The intellectual/devotional structure of the Near Eastern religions consists of these legalities and is presented in sophisticated arguments better raised in a courtroom than in the world as we know it. Their solution to many problems is simply to destroy the world and start over.

Only by drawing out the most realistic portrait of a deity can we begin to understand what the image really means. So let us subject the tribal conceptions of deity and religion to the same critique and scrutiny. There are serious questions whether Indian tribes actually had any conception of religion or of a deity at all. Wherever we find Indians and whenever we inquire about their idea of God, they tell us that beneath the surface of the physical universe is a mysterious spiritual power which cannot be described in human images that must remain always the "Great Mystery."

There are, on the other hand, many other entities with spiritual powers comparable to those generally attributed to one deity alone. So many in fact that they must simply be encountered and appeased, they cannot be counted. In addition all inanimate entities have spirit and personality so that the mountains, rivers, waterfalls, even the continents and the earth itself have intelligence, knowledge, and the ability to communicate ideas. The physical world is so filled with life and personality that humans appear as one minor species without much significance and badly in need of assistance from other forms of life. Almost anyone can have almost any relationship with anything else. So much energetic potency exists that we either must describe everything as religious or say that religion as we have known it is irrelevant to our concerns.

The forms of communication directed toward the deity or higher powers tell us a great deal about our emotional response to the image of God. Hymns, psalms, and chants of the Near Eastern religions are something to behold. They are, quite frankly, little more than crude attempts to flatter and deceive deities who possess preposterous egos. Omnipotent, omniscient, omnipresent, omnivorous—almost every human attribute we can conceive is expanded beyond its capability to communicate meaning and credited to the deities. We create logical inconsistencies when we try to apply the knowledge of our theology; thus, "if God is omnipotent can He make a yardstick with one end?" Christian hymns resemble nothing less than LBJ's or Nixon's White House assistants trying to convince the president of the propriety of their cause by puffing up his already considerable ego. At times, with the modern popularization of Christian ideas by televangelists, it is difficult to remember that Cole Porter's "You're the Cream in My Coffee" is not a hymn.

Indian songs and chants, on the other hand, frequently do not even mention a deity or the Great Mystery at all. They are directed to plants, birds, animals, and the earth asking for assistance in performing rather mundane tasks. When they do specifically address the Great Mysterious power, their pleas are phrased in vague terms, primarily pleading that pity be shown to them. But these pleas do not flatter; they are more in the nature of an objective admission of the fact of human finitude—a rather obvious observation.

The relationship to the natural world is also quite different between the two groups. The physical world is not often seen as a positive place in Near Eastern religions. It is a vale of tears filled with unexplained human tragedies. Animals are definitely placed beneath humans in the hierarchy of things and religious ceremonies seek to purge nature from participation in the rituals, rather than acknowledge the existence of the material world. In many ways the human body is seen as evil. The goal of life is to win eternal life where followers receive imperishable bodies in which they can do exactly the same things that were punishable offenses in the present life. This condition is known as salvation.

The Indian format is precisely the opposite. Not only the natural physical world is regarded as integral to human ambitions and activities, but also even the hypothetical geometrical structures of the world receive some form of religious acknowledgement. Thus, Indians pray to the "four directions," lay out elaborate sandpaintings to represent the cosmos, and see in pipe bowls and sweat lodges a model of the larger cosmic whole. In contrast to the practices of the Near Eastern peoples, Indians virtually eliminate the human element in their religious ceremonies and concentrate on representing the physical universe.

Of reasonable importance in each tradition are the procedures and devices for predicting the future. Both groups rely heavily on dreams for information about the future. Indians seek predictions in ceremonies in which spirits tell them, or are supposed to tell them, what may happen in the immediate future. The Near Eastern peoples have developed all manner of objective systems of prediction from astrology to tarot cards, handwriting analysis to numerology. Most of these systems are now regarded as secular, but the visit of the Three Wise Men to Bethlehem cannot have been anything except a response to these predictive elements deeply buried within the religious tradition.

These two approaches to religion are also distinguishable by their ideas about the importance of the location in which worship and other religious activities are to be held. Near Eastern religions have a propensity for building massive temples and tombs and this tradition has been emulated by Christian tendencies to construct gigantic cathedrals. Temples, churches, and synagogues separate the faithful from the secular world and from the natural world as if religion needs to be isolated from the rest of human activities. The Indian religions, on the other hand, insist on holding their ceremonies and rituals in a natural surrounding and could not have conceived of establishing a separate building especially for religious activities. The sweat lodge and the kiva are designed to represent the larger cosmos and basically have nothing to do with the subservience that characterizes churches and temples.

These two traditions are polar opposites in almost every respect and come to different conclusions about the meaning of life and the eventual disposition of the soul or personality. The Near Eastern religions seek and guarantee *salvation*, which is conceived as an escape from this planet to a place where loyal followers can enjoy eternal life filled with the delights that they were denied during this lifetime. Indians see themselves returning to nature, their bodies becoming the dust of Mother Earth, and their souls journeying to another place across the Milky Way or sometimes being reborn in a new generation of the tribe.

Although several generations of scholars have sought to devise a comprehensive theory of religions that would explain how these diametrically opposed religions are similar to each other, I can find no satisfactory explanation of what elements they have in common. Perhaps the most popular explanation is the device whereby cultural evolutionists see tribal religions as primitive efforts to come to grips with their experiences in nature and the later world religions as sublime expressions of religious knowledge. But if we examine the substance of religion as cultural evolutionists have described it, the comparison is unsatisfactory.

So-called primitive peoples do not cringe in superstition before nature and they are not fearful of natural processes. They are capable of creating situations in which they can use the forces of nature to their benefit. There is no discernible reason for primitive or tribal peoples to abandon their ceremonial life and spend their time trying to arrive at a clear description of a deity and its several powers. Religion for them is an experience and they have no reason to reduce it to systematic thought and the elaboration of concepts.

The doctrines of the world religions, expressed in the most precise phrases and elaborate concepts with every nuance of meaning represented by weighty tomes, describe virtually nothing and do not inspire anyone to do much of anything. Much as I admire the philosophical writings of Paul Tillich, the social concerns of Reinhold Niebuhr, and the sense of modernity of Harvey Cox, their theologies do not trigger off great religious feelings in me. Indeed, I suspect that the ability to describe the attributes of God may preclude the possibility of ever experiencing Him, Her, or Them. Academic orthodoxy in religious studies, however, regards the statements of the world religions as a higher evolved expression of religion primarily because the concepts are more rational. Tribal religions, with their emotional and ceremonial emphasis, are placed at the bottom of the cultural evolutionary scale because they practice rather than preach.

Unfortunately, the evolutionary framework is the only acceptable method of arranging information in Western society and it is very difficult to get anyone to break out of this context and look seriously at the data. In fact, this method of arranging data is highly suspect and more fiction than fact. The real question of determining the nature of religion is bound up with the evolutionary thesis. The traditional evolutionary interpretation of human societies assumes that one group of people was inherently brighter than the others, invented the wheel, invented written languages, established legal codes and political institutions, domesticated plants and animals, discovered metallurgy, and as a final gesture began to direct our species toward the control of nature, thereby banishing the superstitions that composed earlier expressions of religion.

Breaking free of the evolutionary context is not difficult if a person only learns to read critically and demand sensible answers to questions. As an example let us observe how Jacob Bronowski deals with the origin of wheat in the evolutionary setting:

> Before 8,000 B.C. wheat was not the luxuriant plant it is today. It was merely one of the many wild grasses that spread throughout the Middle East. By some genetic accident, the wild wheat crossed with a natural goat grass and formed a fertile hybrid.[1]

> *Emmer* (the product of this cross) crossed with another natural goat grass and produced a still larger hybrid with forty-two chromosomes, which is bread wheat. That was improbable in itself, and we know now that bread wheat would not have been fertile but for a specific genetic mutation of one chromosome.[2]

So, we have two genetic accidents, each producing a hybrid that was fertile, a sequence that would have been all but mathematically impossible. Then Bronowski leans back and fogs his high, hard fastball at us and we are expected to swallow it.

> Now we have a beautiful ear of wheat, but one which will never spread in the wind because the ear is too tight to break up. And if I do break it up, why, then the chaff flies off and every grain falls exactly where it grew. Let me remind you that is quite different from the wild wheats or from the first, primitive hybrid, Emmer. In those primitive forms the ear is much more open, and if the ear breaks up then you get a quite different effect—you get grains which will fly in the wind. The bread wheats have lost that ability. Suddenly, man and plant have come together. Man has a wheat that he lives by, but the wheat also thinks that man was made for him because only so can it be propagated. For the bread wheats can only multiply with help; man must harvest the ears and scatter their seeds; and the life of each, man and plant, depends on the other. *It is a true fairy tale* of genetics as if the coming of civilization has been blessed in advance by the spirit of the abbot Gregor Mendel.[3] (Italics added.)

It is indeed a fairy tale although we are taught to pretend that it is science, a hard-won insight into the nature of the physical world that is superior to any other explanation.

If we cannot give a better explanation of the origin of wheat than Bronowski's, how can we explain the rest of the amazing complex of civilization we have found in the Middle East? *Why* would early man or woman *bother* to harvest the wheat? If they ate the wheat raw, they would have a spectacular stomachache. If they already knew that it should be ground into flour and baked in order to break down the enzymes in the husk, where did they get that information?

We have been told that primitive peoples discovered the smelting process while baking bread. They happened to include some copper ore in their ovens and, when they completed their bakery chores for the day, discovered that they had smelted ores to produce copper or iron while making their primitive pastries. But an oven has to be in the neighborhood of 1,500°C in order to break down ore. There would be no reason to heat an oven that hot in order to bake bread.[4]

In fact, we can explain hardly anything about how civilization began. We simply find a very complex urban society when we uncover the ruins of earliest settlements anywhere in the world and we make up fairy tales to avoid asking ourselves hard questions about the origins of these ruins. It is at this point that I could well believe the theory of the ancient astronauts as bringers of culture and technology. This makes as much sense as any other explanation. At least it enables us to explain the incredible technological advances that we see so early in human history, and it helps us avoid making totally stupid statements.

Today the ancient astronaut thesis is anathema to respectable scholarship because it has been put forward in an irresponsible manner. Popular writers have simply cited a catalog of strange, unexplained items such as the large stones in Baalbek, the lines of Nazca, the dry-cell pottery battery of Mesopotamia, and citations in Ezekiel about flying wheels. These writers screamed, "Ancient astronauts!" without offering any prolonged argument that would illuminate us about exactly what these ancients did that was so important and how they have affected us today.

One writer, however, has tried to present a comprehensive view of an ancient astronaut invasion of the earth and its consequences. Zecharia Sitchin, in a four-book series, *Earth Chronicles*, reinterprets Near Eastern history with the bringing of technology, the rise of the kingship and urban settlements, and the imperial wars as if this history were the result of an intrusion from a superior civilization—certainly food for the imagination. The books, *The Twelfth Planet, The Stairway to Heaven, The Wars of Gods and Men,* and *The Lost Realm,* have an internal logic to them and illuminate some of the ruins of ancient times as well as explain social and political ideas that have continued within Western civilization for which we have only the slightest explanation.

The basic theme is that a superior civilization, finding its atmosphere is thinning and its planet threatened with extinction, comes to earth to dig gold that it plans to suspend in the atmosphere of its home planet to save it. Highly trained astronauts, once they have landed on earth, are then forced to do heavy work in gold mines in southern Africa. Finally, they rebel and demand that the head of the space mission allow them to create a "worker" to do the heavy work. After much genetic experimentation the space doctors with the cooperation of the space women produce a worker—a human being, Homo sapiens.

Soon the astronauts all want workers and the space women are occupied giving birth to workers. Space headquarters in lower Mesopotamia has domestic workers, and one day in the garden, an astronaut shows humans how to have sex. To his surprise, they discover they are fertile and that they are naked. The rest, as the preachers say, is history—human religious history in this instance. Temples are built to the respective astronauts who now adopt the posture of being gods in order to control the human population that is expanding at an incredible rate because humans rather like the idea of sex.

Some of Sitchin's ideas beg credibility. The preliminary cosmology describing the creation of the earth is difficult to believe and the mechanics of the Great Flood seem unlikely. So the narrative cannot be read uncritically. When it comes to explaining the origin of civilization and religious institutions, however, this thesis has a lot to offer. It provides a context in which virgin birth, blood offerings, the jealousies of the gods, the erection of temples and resulting institution of a priesthood, and the description of heaven as a courtroom—royal and jurisprudential—ring true.

More important, orthodox scholars had come amazingly close to reaching the same conclusions. Samuel Noah Kramer, the dean of Sumerian studies and archaeology, in his book *History Begins at Sumer*, seemed to endorse the idea that the astronauts engaged in some kind of genetic engineering in order to create lesser creatures who could work for them. Kramer observed that "Sumerian thinkers, in line with their world view, had no exaggerated confidence in man and his destiny. They were firmly convinced that man was fashioned of clay and created for one purpose: to serve the gods by supplying them with food, drink and shelter, so they might have full leisure for their divine activities."[5]

Many of Kramer's other observations, not intended to support a thesis of ancient astronauts—when he was writing there were no such things as astronauts—dovetail nicely with this thesis. The knowledge of the ancient Sumerians does not reflect any previous effort to come to grips with the natural world and devise classifications of it that would have been useful in expanding man's knowledge. Kramer is frankly puzzled at the manner in which Sumerian knowledge of the natural world is arranged.

> [I]n the linguistic field, we have quite a number of Sumerian grammatical lists that imply an awareness of numerous grammatical classifications, but nowhere do we find a single explicit grammatical definition or rule. In mathematics we find many tables, problems, and solutions, but no statement of general principles, axioms, and theorems. In what might be termed the "natural sciences" the Sumerian teachers compiled long lists of trees, plants, animals and stones. The reason for the particular ordering of the objects listed is still obscure, but certainly it does not stem from a fundamental understanding of, or approach to, botanical, zoological, or mineralogical principles and laws.[6]

In other words, what we have are the necessary inventories of information but no explanation of the scientific reasoning behind the data. This is precisely what a dominant group would make available to a lesser species if it wanted to ensure the proper operation of laboratories, farms, and cities but did not want the lesser beings to understand how the whole complex functioned. The British, among other imperial colonizers, practiced this philosophy in the Americas and later in India.

In what we have previously called "religious matter," there is a pattern not unlike what we would expect if a highly superior group were to create a lesser species having similarity to itself but were determined to emphasize the difference thereby setting themselves up a quasi-deities in order to maintain control. Kramer comments,

> From as far back as our written records go, the Sumerian theologian assumed as axiomatic the existence of a pantheon consisting of a group of living beings, man-like in form but superhuman and immortal, who, though invisible

to mortal eye, guide and control the cosmos in accordance
with well-laid plans and duly prescribed laws.[7]

And there existed a ranking of these gods that was organized along
vocational lines, precisely as we might expect our own astronauts to do
if they found themselves living on another planet with an inferior
species and felt it necessary to draft that species to perform certain
ordinary service and blue-collar functions.

> [I]t seemed reasonable to the Sumerians to assume that the
> gods constituting the pantheon were not all of the same
> importance or rank. The god in charge of the pickax or
> brickmold could hardly be expected to compare with the
> god in charge of the sun. Nor could the god in charge of
> dikes and ditches be expected to equal in rank the god in
> charge of the earth as a whole. And, on analogy, with the
> political organization of the human state, it was natural to
> assume that the head of the pantheon was a god recognized
> by all the others as king and ruler.[8]

In a ranking system this complex, one has to question why does a
pickax or an irrigation system have to have its own deity? And why do
the activities of these deities revolve around tasks that are common
occupational divisions within a civilized society?

When we compare this pantheon of powers and functions of
the early Near Eastern religions with the arrangement of the various
spirits and powers made by the tribal peoples, the contrast is even more
startling. Tribal peoples are concerned with the personification of
natural powers and neighborhood animals and classify their knowledge of higher powers by function, refusing to build a pantheon in which
various powers become subservient to others as a matter of course.
Additionally, although tribal peoples personify the forces of nature, they
do not place this personification within the context of a "personal" god.
Kramer suggests that this personal deity of the individual, the most basic
tenet of modern Christianity, originated in this ancient context in which
individual humans worked for the gods, as follows:

As they saw it, gods were like the moral rulers the world over, and no doubt had more important things to attend to. And so, as in the case of kings, man must have an intermediary to intercede in his behalf, one whom the gods would be willing to hear and favor. *The Sumerian thinkers therefore evolved the notion of a personal god, a kind of good angel to each particular individual and family head—his divine father who had begot him, as it were. It was to him, to his personal deity, that the individual sufferer bared his heart in prayer and supplication, and it was through him that he found his salvation. ..."*[9] (Italics added.)

Kramer's explanation makes sense if humans and astronauts are living together in an urban setting, the astronauts being dominant in everything. Indeed, the situation is not unlike the social arrangements in southern towns after the Civil War when blacks had to have some reliable whites to protect them against unexpected and irrational violence. Because the astronauts were presumed to have a greater life span than humans, it was natural for the space people to hold out promises of a longer life filled with the luxuries they enjoyed as a means of keeping humans in their place. It is ironic that modern American Protestants still cling to this idea and expect their deity to make good the contract.

Near Eastern religions seem to have originated as cults with the additional element that our species was created specifically to work for the outer-space visitors. It would be impossible today to trace back into our various human societies and groups to locate the genes of the astronauts that went into creating us. But modern geneticists have posited the existence of a single woman who lived in southern Africa, precisely where Sitchin says the original genetic experiments were conducted, as probably the genetic mother of us all. So perhaps we are closer to verifying Sitchin's thesis that we would suppose.

I suspect that tribal peoples would be only peripherally affected by these ancient astronaut intrusions. Most tribal peoples no social forms or beliefs that would suggest that they were part of the civilized complex that we find in the Near Eastern civilizations. Many of them do have legends about people from the skies visiting them and intermarrying with them. Much of the food-preparing knowledge and domestic skills are said to have been brought to them by remote-culture heroes who spent some time instructing the people and then departed (i.e., in Aztec legend Quetzabcoatl, a blue-eyed blond, taught them to plant corn and left them promising to return one day). Some tribes, perhaps to mark the genetic intrusions of the astronauts, divided their people into sky and earth subdivisions. The theory is not difficult to integrate into what we know of tribal traditions, technology, and social organization.

The major belief that has survived the passage of time among the peoples who were visited and created by the ancient astronauts is the expectation of eternal life. Incredible hardships have been endured by people within the religious traditions that look forward to eternal life as their reward. But as a practical matter these people do not believe this promise. Thus Oral Roberts, who should have responded to the Deity's extortion threat with a counterargument outlining his faithful service, cried copious tears on television and pleaded with his followers to fill the coffers lest he be "taken away." In the end, then, our species did not trust its divine creators and were left with the puzzling problem of making sense of human existence—and there was no good answer.

Tribal peoples, who had no difficulty with death, and saw it as part of a natural progression in the stages of life, seem to have no memory of promises of specific delights and rewards. However, they have a healthy attitude toward death that is a result of living completely within the normal earth cycles of life and death. Examining how the two traditions deal with death should enable us to further understand our relationship to the earth and the meaning of life.

Notes

1. Jacob Bronowski, *The Ascent of Man* (Boston: Little, Brown, 1973), 65.
2. Ibid, 65–66.
3. Ibid, 66.
4. This explanation of the discovery of metals, given to me as a callow undergraduate, has remained with me for over three decades. In trying to find a specific citation of how man discovered copper, I looked through dozens of books that purported to explain the rise of technology and to my surprise I found that no one tries to explain the sequence of discovery. Scholars today just water ski right across large gulfs without even bother-

ing to give an explanation. Robert James Forbes has a set of books dealing with ancient technology, which give a good idea of the technical problems of smelting and refining the various metals used very early in human history. There is no question that these processes cannot be discovered by chance; therefore, we need another and better explanation than simply the admission that at some time in the past through some undefined method we came to know how to work all kinds of metals.

5. Samuel Noah Kramer, *History Begins at Sumer* (Garden City, N.Y.: Doubleday Anchor, 1959), 104.
6. Ibid, 36.
7. Ibid, 78.
8. Ibid, 79.
9. Ibid, 107.

CHAPTER 10

DEATH AND RELIGION

The problem of integrating secular, chronological planetary history with the narrowly conceived sectarian view of history as defined by the experiences of the Hebrews and later the Christians has already been discussed in chapter 7. As Arnold Toynbee says, the difficulty is that of viewing a map of the Mediterranean and pretending that it is a map of the world. But this restricted history must have a meaning and, indeed, the purpose of restricting the data is to ensure that the events of the Old Testament and subsequent Christian history are seen as the definitive events of our species, whether in fact they are or not.

Individual Christian believers are probably not very concerned about the truth, validity, or applicability of this theological contention because it is an abstraction that has no practical bearing on their lives. It is also so commonplace in Western culture as to be uncritically accepted as a pillar of universal truth. Because the secular, political version of this restricted history suggests that Western Europeans, particularly North Americans, are God's people working their way toward Judgment Day when their sins will be forgiven and their successes applauded, average Christians simply believe that history belongs to them. What concerns individual believers most is the

promise of eternal life that is the denouement of the historical process—the whole reason that we take history seriously.

Two radically different propositions have been used to
explain individual life and the hereafter within the Christian tradition
and because there has not been a clear statement about the afterlife,
they are inevitably confused and taken as interchangeable. The Greeks
developed early the idea of the immortality of the soul. Sometimes this
doctrine was linked to reincarnation as in Plato's philosophy and
sometimes it was taken as a matter of cosmic economy. The original
Christian doctrine seems to have been the resurrection of the body—
the reconstitution of physical form in a glorified version as an award
for faithful service. Presumably this new glorified body would be freed
from the defects that presently plague us, and presumably the new
body would be free from the temptations of the flesh which constitute
one of the major barriers to achieving this new state of existence. Over
the course of Western history these two interpretations of the nature of
the afterlife have ebbed and flowed with the Greek idea of eternal life
generally achieving more popularity. Neither idea has been carefully
thought out and articulated in any intelligent format although Oscar
Cullman made a valiant effort to do so a generation ago.[1]

Popular Christianity today borrows a bit from each side of
the spectrum and the conception of the afterlife seems to be a matter of
denominational preference. Some people believe they will reach a
heavenly city, its streets paved with gold, and there they will be
inducted into a heavenly choir and spend eternity singing the same
kind of flattering hymns as they have occasionally sung here on earth.
A few televangelists believe that they will be appointed to govern large
groups of humankind, that they will be asked to judge their fellow
Christians and all pagans (raising the question whether one person's
heaven is another person's hell). In general, most visions of heaven
promulgated by North American Christians have a startling resemblance to suburban middle-class life in America sprinkled with occasional nods toward the Deity when necessary.[2]

This version of heaven is hardly credible and poses certain
conceptual problems of no small magnitude. If the afterlife has no
difficulties such as we experience in our lives on this earth, how can life
be possible and who would want to experience it? There are no polar

opposites such as good and evil, hot and cold, pain and pleasure, wisdom and ignorance. Instead we will all partake of the nice things without the bother of unpleasant things. A strong word in defense of this belief must be acknowledged. Near-death experiences of thousands of people indicate that the afterlife existence may indeed have something of this flavor, although it does not seem to have any connection with any recognizable religion that we follow today.

The radical cleavage between the two forms of existence is notable because it results in a somewhat strange posture toward death among Christians. Because life after death is so pleasant, life here is so difficult for most of us, and eternal life is our reward for being good here, one would think that the great majority of Christians would look forward to death as the final passage into a better world. If any religious people would not fear death, one would suppose, it would be Christians. But such is not the case. Of all the peoples in the world, perhaps Christians and the peoples they dominate and influence fear death more than any other part of human existence. Oral Roberts, as we have noted, wanted no part of it.

Some of this fear of death derives from the message of Christianity itself. Death was early considered as unnatural to the creation and as an evil presence resulting from the disobedience of Adam in the Garden of Eden. In the *Epistle to the Romans*, St. Paul saw death as the primary fact of human existence that had been negated by the obedience of Jesus in his mission to humanity. The logic of this idea is consistent but depends upon the historical reality of Adam and the necessity of cosmic retributive processes that, as we have already noted, are modeled after an Oriental courtroom and not taken from any observable process of the natural world. Additionally, we do not emotionally participate in the Fall of Adam or the Redemption of Jesus except insofar as we experience these things within the context of the Christian church. But the point is that Christ has not overcome death as the many preachers have declared because no one is exempted from its presence and effect.

Throughout all of Christian history, death has formed a focal point for the tangible confrontation between the people of God and the reality and powers of this world. Many people have faced death with no fear and a calm demeanor that is admirable, and their religious beliefs seem not to have helped or hindered them very much. Because eternal life was the reward particularly reserved for the believing Christian, it was not long before a whole theological network of ideas grew up around death. Traditional Roman Catholic doctrine built into the idea of confession the possibility of cancelling past sins through forgiveness by receiving the sacrament, and hence one could live a scandalous life and still reach heaven intact by reserving baptism until one's death bed or in receiving the Last Rites which wiped away all previous sins and prepared one to depart directly for heaven as the body stopped functioning. The Spanish, in slaughtering Indians, would have a priest standing by with Holy Water available as they disemboweled pregnant Indian women. If the fetus, exposed momentarily to the outside world, breathed or showed signs of life, the priest could baptize it before the soldiers smashed its head against the wall, thereby giving it an immediate audience with the Lord. Priests used to accompany the Iroquois war parties who ravaged the Huron villages in Canada in the 1600s and baptize Hurons who were in their death throes. Therefore, baptism has been understood by Christians as a mechanical entrance into the next life.

Heavily involved in the Christian concept of death has been the assertion of a day of judgment when the good and evil deeds of people would be evaluated, the good going to heaven and the evil and unbaptized people going to hell or to some intermediate place where they can congregate until released. Perhaps it was this judgmental aspect of the religion that helped to create the fear of death, for if individuals are not certain that they had lived a good life and were reasonably certain that an eternally burning hell awaited them, death would appear as a final insult of major proportions. Exactly how much of the Christian description of the afterlife depended on the other Near Eastern conceptions of life after death is not certain because the imagery of the apocalyptic vision in the New Testament seems indistinguishable from other non-Christian versions of that period.

If the focus of the religion was concentrated on the afterlife, the life of the present world necessarily took a secondary importance in the religions of the Near East. Instead of the world being the arena in which real events and personalities played themselves out to produce a meaningful and irreversible history, the events and actions of this world had a "testing-ground" aspect to them. What counted was the next life, not this one. While this thought was comforting to people caught in the lower reaches of the religious, social, economic, and political pyramids, these religions appear to be simply control measures for manipulating large populations and not a realistic appraisal of cosmic reality. In the last analysis, personal responsibility became a responsibility to the set of behaviors that would guarantee eternal life and not an ethic that would enable people to deal justly with their contemporaries.

One cannot emphasize too carefully this aspect of Western religious tradition for it was in the overemphasis on eternal life that people became separated from participation in the life cycles of the natural world and death became something to be feared. The Protestant Reformation did not improve on the early Christian and contemporary Catholic conceptions of death and the afterlife. Salvation became confused with other doctrines, in particular with the idea of predestination and the prior selection of the elect. Justification by faith alone offered no certain guidelines of living the faith. It was then that people reasoned that God would certainly bless the elect in this life as well as in the next one, and the accumulation of wealth, by whatever means possible, demonstrated that an individual or family was among the elect.

The idea of a preselected group of people who were known by God through eternity as "His People" and who, without any apparent talent or worth, were to have eternal life, presented the ultimate in cosmic injustice. It meant that the majority of people were condemned to live essentially meaningless lives and to be punished simply for the status that had been given to them at the beginning of time. It was not difficult to secularize this doctrine of the elect so that it placed religion in a role in which it simply endorsed the social and economic status quo and admitted anyone who was able to accumulate wealth—by any means possible.

The Christian doctrine of life after death had another extremely unfortunate aspect. The soul was believed to live on while the body, which was considered gross and evil, was left to decay, although it would apparently be glorified during the turmoil of the Second Coming. At any rate, by conceiving that it was possible to separate soul from body, Christians then created the most terrible of tortures to be perpetrated on those people who were suspected of heresy. Theologians believed it was proper to crush the physical body if it meant saving the immortal soul. Thus the Inquisition spared no torture in its efforts to get people to recant their heresies and confess their sins. The Inquisitors were assured that they were saving souls even if they were destroying people in the process. Many of the genocidal acts the Westerners committed against the Indians can be laid directly on the doorstep of religious fanatics who saw conversion and death as the only viable solution to the Indian problem. Near Eastern religions had centuries of practice before and after Europeans came into contact with American Indians.

In the field of secular knowledge, there is evidence of the great impact of Christian ideas about life after death. Social scientists simply project common beliefs of Westerners onto the relics of non-Western peoples, interpreting many structures and artifacts as if they represented an obsessive concern with the next life. Legends and traditions are also twisted to fit into the pattern of Western thinking as if the quest for immortality were universal. The Egyptian pyramids have generally been understood as the efforts of Egyptian pharaohs to achieve immortality in spite of the plain evidence. While some of the smaller structures of the later Egyptian period might have been used as tombs, the period of time required to build the large pyramids precludes them as resting places for individual pharaohs. The most complete Egyptian tomb yet discovered, that of Tutankhamen uncovered by Howard Carter in 1922, was a tomb cut into living rock in the Valley of the Kings and not in a pyramid.[3] Many of the objects found in the tombs were favorite possessions of the pharaohs indicating the belief that they needed these possessions in their journey to the next life. In the Christian religions, the afterlife is not an extension or natural continuation of this life but an event to be feared.

When we examine American Indian tribal religions, we find a notable absence of the fear of death. Burial mounds indicate a belief that life after death was a continuation of the life already experienced. Personal possessions, familiar tools and weapons, cooking utensils, and quite frequently food were placed near the body so that it would be sustained in the next life. It was not contemplated that the soul would have to account for misdeeds and lapses from a previously established ethical norm. All of that concern was expressed while the individual was alive. Some tribes viewed entrance into the next life as almost a mechanical process to which everyone was subject, a natural cosmic process to which all things were bound.

Many Indians perceived not only that the next life was a continuation of the present mode of existence but also that the souls of people often remained in various places where they had died or suffered traumatic events. People visiting the Sand Creek location where the Cheyennes were massacred under Colonel Chivington have told me that they can hear the cries of the women and children who are still living near this dreaded place. Indians receiving bones from museums for reburial tell about spirits of the departed speaking to them during the reburial ceremonies and thanking them for helping to get their bones from the museums so they can rest in the Mother Earth. Some decades ago I attended a burial in a Christian cemetery at Mission, South Dakota. After the body was in the grave and the several mourners were still standing at the grave, an old woman stepped forward and put an orange on the grave. The Episcopal priest who had conducted the service rushed over and took the orange away, saying, "When do you think the departed will come and eat this orange?" One of the Sioux men standing there said, "When the soul comes to smell the flowers!" No one said anything after that.

The Indian ability to deal with death was a result of the much larger context in which Indians understood life. Human beings were an integral part of the natural world and in death they contributed their bodies to become the dust that nourished the plants and animals that had fed people during their lifetime. Because people saw the tribal community and the family as a continuing unity regardless of circumstance, death became simply another transitional event in a much longer scheme of life. Some tribes made up medicine bundles containing bits of hair of the deceased, flesh or claws of the animals and birds most closely related to the family, and other intimate things of the deceased. This bundle was kept in the family dwelling for a year after the death and treated as if the person was still present with the family. In that way the trauma of losing the person was extended over a period of time and people could be comforted that, while the deceased was not visibly present, he or she was spiritually and emotionally present.

Most tribes were very reluctant to surrender their homelands to the whites because they knew that their ancestors were still spiritually alive on the land, and they were fearful that the whites would not honor the ancestors and the lands in the proper manner. If life was to mean anything at all, it had to demonstrate a certain continuity over the generations and this unity transcended death. At a treaty-signing session in the Illinois country in 1821, the Potawatomi chief, Metea, spoke of this continuity as the basic reason for his reluctance to cede the tribal lands.

> A long time has passed since first we came upon our lands, and our people have all sunk into their graves. They had sense. We are all young and foolish, and do not wish to do anything that they would not approve, were they living. We are fearful we shall offend their spirits if we sell our lands; and we are fearful we shall offend you if we do not sell them. This has caused us great perplexity of thought, because we have counselled among ourselves, and do not know how we can part with our lands.

> My father, our country was given us by the Great Spirit, who gave it to us to hunt upon, to make our cornfields upon, to live upon, and to make our beds upon when we die.[4]

This idea of identity and continuity of life lay behind the posture of many of the tribes as they approached the whites. It could be said to be a more fundamental reason than any other for the Indian resistance to white invasions of tribal land a century ago and even today. Young Chief Joseph, the famous Nez Percé leader, remained at peace with the white settlers until they began to invade his valley. When he was finally forced to fight to protect himself, he recalled the promise he had made to his father as the older Joseph lay dying.

> My son, my body is returning to my mother earth, and my spirit is going very soon to see the Great Spirit Chief. When I am gone, think of your country. You are the chief of these

people. They look to you to guide them. Always remember that your father never sold his country.

You must stop your ears whenever you are asked to sign a treaty selling your home. A few more years and the white men will be all around you. They have their eyes on this land. My son, never forget my dying words. This country holds your father's body. Never sell the bones of your father and your mother.[5]

Some people have regarded this speech of the older Joseph as merely symbolic of Indian religion, but we must recall that for tribal people symbolism is not the communicative image of Westerners but the expression of a reality that Westerners often refuse to acknowledge. This conception of land as holding the bodies of the tribe in a basic sense pervaded tribal religions across the country. It testified in a stronger sense to the underlying unity of the Indian conception of the universe as a life system in which everything had its part.

It is doubtful, however, if any of the tribal religions considered life after death to be radically changed from the life they were living. Chief Seattle, on signing the Treaty of Medicine Creek in 1854, gave a famous speech in which he summarized his beliefs about the nature of the lands his tribe had given up. If ever an Indian could have been said to have anticipated D. H. Lawrence, Albert Camus, and William Carlos Williams, Seattle's speech would certainly merit first consideration. In it he distinguished between tribal beliefs and the attitude of the Christians who were taking control of the land—at least in a legal sense.

To us the ashes of our ancestors are sacred and their resting place is hallowed ground. You wander far from the graves of your ancestors and seemingly without regret. ...

Your dead cease to love you and the land of their nativity as soon as they pass the portals of the tomb and wander way beyond the stars. They are soon forgotten and never return. Our dead never forget the beautiful world that gave them being. ...

Every part of this soil is sacred in the estimation of my people. Every hillside, every valley, every plain and grove, has been hallowed by some sad or happy event in days long vanished. The very dust upon which you now stand responds more lovingly to their footsteps than to yours, because it is rich with the blood of our ancestors and our bare feet are conscious of the sympathetic touch. Even the little children who lived here and rejoiced here for a brief season will love these somber solitudes and at eventide they greet shadowy returning spirits. And when the last Red Man shall have perished, and the memory of my tribe shall have become a myth among the White Men, these shores will swarm with the invisible dead of my tribe, and when your children's children think themselves alone in the field, the store, the shop, upon the highway, or in the silence of the pathless woods, they will not be alone. At night when the streets of your cities and villages are silent and you think them deserted, they will throng with the returning hosts that once filled and still love this beautiful land. The White Man will never be alone.

Let him be just and deal kindly with my people, for the dead are not powerless. Dead, did I say? There is no death, only a change of worlds.[6]

Again we see the fundamental conception of life as a continuing unity involving land and people. One might be tempted to suggest that as land is held by the community, the psychic unity of all the worlds is made real. We are not faced with formless and homeless spirits in this idea but with an ordered and purposeful creation in which death merely marks a passage from one form of experience to another. Rather than fearing death, tribal religions see it as an affirmation of life's reality.

A story of rather recent vintage from the Cheyenne people enables us to see more fully the communal nature of death in the tribal context.

A young man named Hugh Boyle had been killed by the Cheyennes. The authorities demanded that the Indians give up the murderers to justice. The Indians tried to settle the matter. According to their ideas, the death of Boyle might be compensated by the payment of ponies. They offered to give up a great number of horses, raising each bid as it was rejected, until the payment proposed was calculated to beggar them if it was accepted. To the ponies they added all their wealth in blankets and such other evidences of riches as an Indian may possess. They were finally made to understand that the white man did not accept a property atonement for the spilling of blood. The negotiations were carried on for some time and with difficulty, for the reason that few white men know the Cheyenne language. ... The intercourse with the people was carried on through mixed-bloods of the tribe, and it was finally made clear to them that they must give up the slayers of Boyle. But they could not give them up to die the death that kills the soul as well as the body. They believed, in common with most Indians, that when a man died his soul left the body with his last breath, and that in case a person was hanged, the soul was confined in the body with the rope. They would defend their young men from such an awful fate as was involved in the hanging by the white man's justice. The crime they neither denied nor defended. An ultimatum being sent them that they must bring in the murderers, they sent word back that a Cheyenne was not afraid to die, but would not submit to being hanged; that the two young men, Head Chief and Young Mule, would show the whites how a Cheyenne could die.

They appointed a date for the affair, September 13, 1890, and they intended that it should be magnificently spectacular. They were to bend their necks to the white man's justice, but they proposed doing it in a fashion that would impress the soldiers and the people at the agency. Special Indian Agent James A. Cooper had asked for troops, and one troop of the First Cavalry had been sent to the agency to make the arrest of the two men by force if necessary. The Cheyennes gave up diplomacy when the troops arrived, and word was sent that the two Indians would give themselves up and be ready to die. They appointed to die with their weapons in their hands. They would shoot at the soldiers, and the latter would have to kill them in defending themselves. The proposition was a rather startling one, but there was nothing to do but accept it. An attempt to arrest the men in their camps would assuredly have precipitated a bloody conflict. The proposition of the Cheyennes was for a spectacular form of suicide, and the matter was arranged on this basis. The Cheyennes accepted it all as a matter of course. The young men went about their affairs as usual, unmolested, and spent much time in visiting with and saying good-bye to their relatives. The night before the date set for the finish, there were solemn dances, in which the Indians all took part. They were to meet death as warriors and there was no reason why they should be mourned for.

The morning of the appointed day the two men were anointed by the medicine men. They painted and decorated themselves with great care, and wore all their finery. Their best horses were chosen for the ride to death, and the animals were devoted to the same fate that was to be meted out to their masters; for it was unlikely that they could escape the hail of bullets that would be sent at the doomed men. Thus, attired and mounted as warriors should be, the two rode down the slope from the northeast to the agency, where the troops were drawn up.

The agency is located on a flat, with a rather sharp declivity across Lame Deer River. The flat is almost surrounded by elevations, and on the ridge to the west the Indians, probably every one on the reservation, were assembled to see the young men demonstrate to the whites how a Cheyenne could die. Beside the agency office the troop of cavalry was drawn up; alongside of them stood the agency Indian police, close to their headquarters. The agency people were scattered about, out of what might be the line of fire when the shooting began. Never was a stage so set for so spectacular a tragedy.

At the time appointed for the coming of the men, they appeared at the top of the hill to the northeast, and dashed down the hill at the best pace their horses could make. As they rode they sang the death-song of their people, and before reaching the level ground they began shooting into the ranks of the soldiery and Indian police.

The fire was answered at once, the cavalrymen firing rapidly, but ineffectively. The Indian police, or one of them, made better practice, for one of the Indians went down with his horse in a heap just as he reached a little clump of bushes. The bullets of the police and soldiers could not find the other man. They fired at almost point-blank range, but his life was charmed. He rode shooting and singing past the cordon of troops and policemen, out beyond the agency, then turned and rode deliberately back. He had passed the troops a second time before the fire of the soldiers and the police was effective.[7]

The primary concern of the Cheyenne community was the preservation of life. When, however, it was evident that the men could not be saved, the concern shifted to preserving human dignity. The young men perfectly reflected the tribal belief, for they did not fear death, only a meaningless death that would discredit their community and violate their religious beliefs. The symbolism of dying as warriors was not something that extended beyond the grave as in the Germanic vision of the afterlife in which warriors were rewarded for their exploits by continual feasting and access to beautiful and pliant maidens. The Cheyenne response can only be understood as an affirmation of life, not as preparation for a radically different type of existence. Immortality is secondary to integrity of tribal existence in the present, and we find not a cringing fear of death but a religious community so strong as to virtually shrug off death as an enemy.

It is probably in the idea of the death song, which was found in many of the tribal religions, that the idea of death can adequately be understood. The death song was a special song sung as a man faced certain death. Often it taunted his enemies who were in the act of killing him. More often it acted as a benedictory statement by the individual to summarize and conclude his time of existence. Rather than being a feverish preparation for death it was the final affirmation of the meaning of individual existence, for it glorified the personal integrity of the person. It individualized his tribal membership in a manner bringing credit and meaning to his life as a tribal member.

One of the most famous death songs was that of Satank, the famous Kiowa chief who was being taken as a prisoner to Texas for trial after a raid against the Army. As he tore the manacles from his wrists and stabbed one of his guards Satank chanted,

O sun, you remain forever, but we Kaitsenko must die.
O earth, you remain forever, but we Kaitsenko must die.[8]

Here we find no cringing to confess sins and imagined failures. The specific events of one's life as judged by external standards pale beside this basic affirmation and acknowledgment to the rest of creation that finitude is but a role drawn by a person in this form of existence.

The singular aspect of Indian tribal religions was that almost universally they produced people unafraid of death. It was not simply the status of warrior in the tribal life that created a fearlessness of death. Rather the integrity of communal life did not create an artificial sense of personal identity that had to be protected and preserved at all costs. Many other examples could be used to show the Indians' attitude toward death. The Five Civilized Tribes of Oklahoma had their own courts in the last decades of the nineteenth century. Occasionally a member of the tribe was sentenced to death. Upon the passage of the death sentence, the condemned would be informed when and where the execution would take place. He was then released to spend his remaining days with his relatives. As the day approached he would perform any obligatory religious ceremonies, say goodbye to his relatives, and on the appointed day report to the place of execution to be killed. While this behavior was common among Indian tribes, how many Christians fully believing in the hereafter would act in comparable manner?

Some tribes had special ceremonies to be used in conjunction with the dead. The Lakota, or Sioux, for example, had a ceremony in which the sacred pipe was used, and the souls of the recently departed were kept with the tribal community to be purified and eventually released.[9] In a tragic interference with the tribal religion, the government banned this ceremony in the 1890s, causing a great trauma among the people. The Iroquois had special ceremonies in conjunction with their New Year's celebration in which the dead of the past year were remembered.[10]

In general we could say that the afterlife was not of overwhelming concern to people of the tribal religions. Vague references to the lands of the spirits, descriptions of the Milky Way as the path over which souls traveled, and concern for the departed spirits remaining, which was prevented in some tribes by burning of personal possessions, probably indicated distinct beliefs of certain tribes. No highly articulated or developed theories of the afterlife were ever necessary, and certainly none projected a life radically different than that experienced on Earth.

Some additional distinctions between tribal conceptions of the afterlife and Christian ideas can be drawn that will be particularly helpful. It is very difficult to distinguish between ideas that are primarily Christian and those that are the result of the speculations of Greek philosophy, and perhaps by reviewing one of the more recent controversies in Christian theology, we can find a way to understand the Christian posture toward death.

Oscar Cullmann, a brilliant Christian thinker, wrote a little book titled *Immortality of the Soul or Resurrection of the Dead?* He was bitterly attacked by his fellow Christians for having introduced somber and defeatist ideas into the Christian doctrine of the life to come. What Cullmann did was draw the necessary distinctions and conclusions from an examination of ideas that were primarily Christian and those primarily Greek. The differences had been blurred by generations of Christian ministers who preached popular sermons of reassurance to their congregations and used the framework of Greek philosophy to engage in speculative ventures about the afterlife.[11]

The distinction between immortality of the soul and the peculiarly Christian ideal of the resurrection of the dead is a vital one. Immortality is a Greek philosophical idea that originates primarily from the thought and teachings of Socrates. The Greeks regarded the body as only the outer garment of the soul. As a mutable part of man, the body prevented the soul from moving freely into the realm of eternal essence that for Socrates, and even more so for his disciple Plato, constituted the real world beyond that of sense perceptions. The soul was thus basically imprisoned in the body and became tainted with materialistic things because it was unable to remember its previous existence in the world of pure ideas.

For the Greek philosophers the task of the individual was to free his soul from its bondage to the body. This release could be effected in a number of ways, the pursuit of knowledge of the world of ideas being the most sublime, and every approach seemed to be based on the conception of man as the rational animal. Upon death, for the Greeks, the soul was released from the body. Cullmann placed a great deal of emphasis in his book on the distinction between the deaths of Jesus and Socrates, pointing out that death was a welcome visitor for Socrates but a dreaded and tormenting experience for Jesus.

Cullman found that death, in the Christian context, was a feared foe. Death was an event to be avoided at all costs, because it meant the cessation of identity. Cullman suggested that all men naturally fear death and that the Greek rational approach to the termination of life served only a select few who had become so enamoured of their philosophy that they could welcome death as a natural conclusion to the journey of the soul in a world in which it was a stranger.

The great innovation of Christianity, according to Cullmann, was that it preached a message of bodily resurrection in which the totality of human personality was to be reconstituted. Death was understood as the destruction of all life created by God, not the shedding of the body by an indestructible soul. Jesus's resurrection meant that God had prepared a special existence for his followers, which was apparently not available to those who had not heard or those who had but did not believe. Resurrection on the last day was therefore a singularly revolutionary concept in religion. Other religions had foreseen a continuous existence after the death experience and purported that the spirits or souls of individuals had some measure of permanency beyond the grave. Christianity was the only religion to confront directly the question of total personality survival, and it found in the fact of Jesus's resurrection a basis for overcoming the agony of death experienced by the majority of men.

Cullmann's thesis is as revolutionary today as it was when first published nearly four decades ago. It is, perhaps, the most strenuous analysis of the problem, and Cullmann grounded it well in Biblical thought using a minimum of philosophical argument and analogy for his conclusions. It is doubtful if the majority of contemporary Christians would support or believe Cullmann's distinction between immortality of the soul and the resurrection of the dead. Most people who believe themselves to be Christians are thoroughly Greek in their beliefs concerning life after death.

Tribal religions show an almost total absence of concern about either doctrine. Both doctrines would appear to tribal peoples as separating the body and the spirit of man in a detrimental manner. A majority of the tribal religions simply assume some form of personal survival beyond the grave. As Chief Seattle remarked, death is merely a changing of worlds.

Christian cemeteries reflect a curious mixture of belief, and one cannot say for certain whether they are based on the premise of the bodily resurrection or on the idea of the immortality of the soul. The use of stone gravestones indicates a determination not to allow the body to become a part of the soil. Waterproof caskets and other devices designed to preserve the body for as long as possible may indicate a belief in the resurrection of the actual body of the departed. However, the monuments to great individuals may mean that there is a desire to perpetuate people of stature in the human memories that could be interpreted as honors to great souls.

Lame Deer, in his autobiography, remarks that the old Indian graveyards had markers of wood because it was felt that the body and the wood would both return to the earth as intended. He contrasted this attitude with the granite headstones to illustrate the distinction between Christian and Indian attitudes toward death. In the very old days many of the tribes employed various means of burial, almost all of them aiming at the return of the body to the earth.[12]

Strangely enough there has been habitual conflict over the interment in Christian cemeteries of nonwhite peoples. During the Korean War, a Winnebago Indian, Sergeant Rice, was killed in action, and his body was returned to Sioux City, Iowa, for burial. But the good Christians in Sioux City forbade his burial in a cemetery reserved for whites. To the great embarrassment and grief of the family, the body remained unburied until finally accepted for burial in Arlington National Cemetery. The newspapers frequently feature stories of similar incidents involving African Americans, Indians, Chicanos, and Asians. One can only conclude that the Christian religion and its promise of the afterlife is not meant for nonwhites; Christians either do not believe in resurrection, or they exclude nonwhites from their heaven.

According to Cullmann, death has been conquered by Jesus on behalf of all humankind. As the belief in the afterlife has eroded in Western civilization, a further twist has been added to the concept of death. Western peoples avoid mention of death at all costs. Insurance peddlers always speak of taking out insurance "in case something happens." The implication, of course, is that pending an irrational and arbitrary action of God, every good, tax-paying, white citizen will live forever. This belief is rarely articulated as a formal doctrine, but we cannot help but recognize it as the fundamental approach of contemporary Western peoples toward death. If the Christian religion is a victory over death, why do Western peoples who have had the benefits of the Christian religion for two thousand years fear death? Toynbee once described death as totally "un-American," an infringement of each individual's right to life, liberty, and the pursuit of happiness.[13] As a subversive activity, death has recently come under examination by Western thinkers attempting to chart out the possible parameters of the problem. Rollo May, for example, suggests that the American preoccupation with sexual activity may in part be a response to the finality of death and the incessant concern for new sexual freedoms might be efforts directed toward a deliverance from death anxiety.

Regardless of how we attempt to explain it, the fundamental distinction between tribal religions and the Christian religion, including secular Western attitude toward death, must revolve around the conception of creation. For the tribal people, death in a sense fulfills their destiny, for as their bodies become dust once again they contribute to the ongoing life cycle of creation. For Christians, the estrangement from nature, their religion's central theme, makes this most natural of conclusions fraught with danger. Believing that they are saved and interpreting this salvation as accumulating material possessions, Western people cannot accept death except as a form of punishment by God. The Christian facing death often cries out to God, "What have I done?" The priest or clergyman has only the relentless logic of theology to present. Death is feared and rarely understood. People somehow want to see the death of their loved one as part of God's plan (i.e., God needed Elvis to sing in heaven).

It is in the face of death that Indian tribal religions have their magnificence. Big Elk, an Omaha chief, delivered a funeral oration in 1815 at the death of Black Buffalo, a fellow Omaha, and counseled his fellow chiefs as follows:

> Do not grieve. Misfortunes will happen to the wisest and best of men. Death will come and always out of season. It is the command of the Great Spirit, and all nations and people must obey. What is past and cannot be prevented should not be grieved for. ... Misfortunes do not flourish particularly in our path. They grow everywhere.[14]

While death is truly a saddening event for people of tribal religious traditions, it is an event with which every person and nation is faced and not an arbitrary, capricious exercise of divine wrath. Even today this attitude persists in Indian societies, and the natural grief occurring with the loss of a loved one is rarely translated into personal feelings of guilt, inadequacy, or sin, which appear to plague Westerners. The community regroups and continues to exist; while individuals are lonely, they are not alone.

Notes

1. Oscar Cullman's book *Immortality of the Soul or Resurrection of the Dead?* (New York: Macmillan, 1958) attempted to make sense of the idea of the afterlife in western culture. Largely, the book was ignored or not appreciated.

2. Dr. Billy Graham, for example, once speculated on how we will look in heaven. A feature story on him in *Newsweek* (July 20, 1970) quoted him as saying, "I believe in the resurrection of the body and I have in mind that in heaven we will look like what we were at our best on earth." If so, Paul Newman, Christopher Reeve, and Rachel Ward have it made here and in the life to come.

3. See Immanuel Velikovsky's *Oedipus and Akhnaton* (Doubleday, 1960) if you want an eye-opening account of Tutankhamen's tomb and why Carter and Lord Carnarvon found it so filled with wealth.

4. Virginia Armstrong, *I Have Spoken* (Chicago: Swallow Press, 1971).

5. Ibid, 94–95.

6. *Uncommon Controversy* (Seattle: University of Washington Press, 1970), 29.

7. James McLaughlin, *My Friend the Indian*, A Salisbury Press Book (Seattle, Wash.: Superior Publishing, 1970), 81–82.

8. Armstrong, *I Have Spoken*, 95.

9. See Joseph Epes Brown's *The Sacred Pipe* (Norman: University of Oklahoma Press, 1953) for a description of these ceremonies.

10. See Elisabeth Tooker, *The Iroquois Ceremonial of Midwinter* (Syracuse, N.Y.: Syracuse University Press, 1970) for more information on this type of ceremony.

11. The two choices for Western people, according to Cullman, are either to have an eternal soul that continues and possibly reincarnates or to have time itself end and the physical body restored. Neither of these choices seems to be relevant to people outside the Western tradition.

12. Almost every facet of which we have been speaking is covered in one way or another in Lame Deer's book (John Fire and Richard Erdoes, *Lame Deer, Seeker of Visions*, New York: Simon & Shuster, 1972). Rather than use extensive citations from it, I have simply suggested it as a basic source of information on tribal religious experiences.

13. As quoted in *Newsweek* (April 6, 1970).

14. Armstrong, *I Have Spoken*, 49.

CHAPTER 11

HUMAN PERSONALITY

W estern Peoples have become accustomed to thinking of religious activity as involving a radical change of human personality. This attitude is ingrained in European peoples and finds its greatest following in the United States, where a substantial number of people believe that becoming a Christian involves a radical change in the human being's constitution. In contrast to this attitude, the Indian tribal religions do not necessarily involve any significant change in human personality but encompass within the tribal cultural context many of the behavioral patterns spoken about by Christians.

The basis for Christian beliefs must certainly originate in the days of the early church. Arising in the days of turmoil of the Jewish eschatological hopes, the message of the early church was one of impending doom, the arrival of the day of judgment, and the consequent salvation of those people who believed the Christian message. The chief message of Jesus seems to have been a call for repentance by the Jews so that the Messiah could come, throw the Romans out, and reinstall the Jewish state. In this respect, Jesus and John the Baptist stood well within the Zealot tradition of Jewish sects, which looked for a radical intervention by God in history.

In the very early Christian community, the message of Jesus was transformed into a message about Jesus having been the Messiah who had come to earth, been rejected, and would return almost immediately with an angelic army to judge the world. This message was further transformed with the conversion of Paul, who later articulated a theory of cosmic redemption based on the Crucifixion of Jesus, and the subsequent beliefs that he had risen from the dead and appeared to his disciples and then to Paul on the road to Damascus.

The impending end of the world did not occur within the lifetime of even the longest-lived and immediate disciple of Jesus, and the doctrine changed once again to provide that missing explanation to hold the religious community together. One explanation of the failure of Jesus to return was that he could not come until all nations had heard the message of the Christians about the meaning of Jesus's death. Another explanation was that Jesus had intended to found a church and had given supernatural powers to the representatives of this church to exercise until his return. An even better explanation was that if people persisted in attempting to discover when the end of the world would occur, they would preempt God's options. In spite of what the Bible said it was therefore wrong to speculate on the time of the return; people simply had to wait it out and behave themselves in the meantime.

The changing time element in these various theories of the meaning of the life and message of Jesus is extremely important in understanding the nature of the Christian conception of the human personality. It indicates that the various theories were fundamentally accommodations to the incidents in the life of the early Christian community and not intended to reflect a reasoned, mature, or even rational understanding of human beings.

If we refer to the immediate urgency felt by Jesus and John in gaining the confidence of the Jews (they in fact knew that the Kingdom of Heaven was at hand), the initial demand for repentance appears as quite similar to recent power movements in American society. These power movements (i.e., the Black Panthers) anticipated a violent revolution in the United States that was to be followed by a prolonged period of peace and justice during which minority groups would control the nation and not make any of the mistakes made up to that point in American history.

In the same manner, Jesus and John called for a general repentance of the Jews so that the Messiah could come and restore the Jewish people to international sovereignty by driving out the Romans. Repentance was thus a short-term shifting of alliances of individual Jews from one religious sect of Judaism to another before the impending arrival of the last days. Their call was not an effort to bring into fruition another manner of viewing life but an attempt to restore to the Jews a sense of national pride and group integrity before the peoples of the world were judged. The Dead Sea Scrolls have made it fairly clear that Palestine at that time seemed to abound with religious communities; many of them looked forward to divine military intervention on behalf of the Jews. In this respect, the ghost dance of the American Indians of the last decade of the last century looked forward to the same type of divine intervention.

The activity of the early church was centered on continuing to call the Jews to repentance. The Jerusalem community headed by Jesus's brother James the Just thought the arrival of the kingdom so imminent that they were soon destitute of funds because everyone had stopped working in expectation of the world's end. Paul, in one of his earliest efforts to reconcile the Jerusalem community with his new doctrines, collected money to help the disciples survive. Conversion at that point must have involved simply an acknowledgment that Jesus had been the Messiah and that he was expected to return soon.

It was with the theological speculations of Paul that the Christian religion was expanded far beyond its original intent or scope. Paul viewed Jesus as representing a cosmic Christ standing as an obedient son of the deity and as a sacrificial gift atoning to God for the disobedience of Adam, presumably a historical figure who had originally corrupted human's relationship with God. Paul believed in the idea of original sin because he had provided the solution to it with his theories of cosmic atonement. Yet even with Paul, the expectation of the imminent end of the world was reflected in his efforts at counseling his new congregations as to their interim behavior.

From this initial series of concepts, additional Christian doctrines evolved; a totally coherent process of repentance, conversion, redemption, salvation, confession, absolution, and eternal life was constructed as the Christian description of the effect of the sect's religious beliefs on the human personality. Almost every category of human behavior appears to have been set into a system of distinguishing good deeds, sins, and penances through the offices of the organizational church. Sin, for example, could at least be classified into original sin, mortal sins, and venial sins, although in some Christian denominations there may be additional categories.

As Christianity gained political control over the lives of Western peoples, the Western theories of human personality began to develop. While Christianity has recently declined in its importance in the West, many of its original premises continue to exert influence over the way people think of themselves, especially in the field of religious experiences. Preaching and teaching, the fundamental form of religious activity set down by John and Jesus and emphasized by Paul, has dominated Western peoples ever since. As preaching in the Roman world was thought to be the key to one's salvation, so education, its secularized counterpart in the contemporary world, is thought to be the final answer to social ills.

Once the various Christian doctrines are taken from their original time dimension and used to form a theory of human personality coupled with the identification of sins in anticipation of the final judgment that is apparently still to come, they can be said to form the basic posture of Western peoples toward this world, the world to come, and the world's institutions. Human personality has been forced into these predetermined categories without regard to the reality of human experience. Other religious systems have been detrimentally explained in terms of the basic Christian categories of explanation. As we read in chapter 10, the Christian concern with death has been used to project a universal fear of death by all men when such fear has not necessarily been the case.

The great variety of Christian denominations that now confronts us in the religious sphere makes it virtually impossible to gain a consensus among Christians as to the meaning of the respective doctrines. Conversion may mean a quasi-miraculous event in which instant salvation is made available to the convert, or it may mean only the beginnings of an intention to live a Christian life as defined by a particular denomination. Baptism may be seen as the almost magical washing away of original and accumulated sins or as a gesture of initiation into the religious community. One can hardly determine what interpretation of any Christian doctrine would receive the support of a majority of Christian believers because it is doctrinal disagreement that creates the Christian denominations.

What we are more interested in, however, is what effect in practical terms the various sequences of the Christian life—from initial conversion to eventual salvation—have on individuals and societies. What distinguishes a Christian from any other person is difficult to determine. The track record of individual Christians and Christian nations is not so spectacular as to warrant anyone seriously considering becoming a Christian. From pope to pauper, Protestant to Catholic, Constantinople to the United States, the record is filled with atrocities, misunderstandings, persecutions, genocides, and oppressions so numerous as to bring fear into the hearts and minds of non-Christian peoples.

One aspect of Christian history that is so appalling is the almost continuous warfare between Christians. Heresy hunters seem to abound in Christian history as a regular part of its religious experience. Persecutions for religious purposes appear to dominate many periods of Christian existence. The first settlements on the shores of North America's East Coast were apparently made by people fleeing religious persecution, while settlements in the Southwest featured religious persecution of the native inhabitants, especially after their conversion.

The response of many Christians to the reminder that their religion has failed to bring peace on earth, or even a semblance of it, has been that the people who committed the numerous sins filling the pages of Western and world history were not acting in a Christian manner. If we eliminate those perpetrators of criminal activity from the Western world, we are left with a very small percentage of people who were really Christians. Why did these people remain silent while the various abuses were being committed in the name of their religion? There is apparently no answer to that question unless we conclude that there have never really been any outstanding Christians since the early days. If such is the case, then we must only conclude that the purported ability of the Christian religion to change people's hearts and minds has been a gigantic hoax, perpetrated for an unknown purpose by unknown people.

We are thus confronted with accepting the reality of Christian history and attempting to understand how it conceives its message and impact so as to warrant considering religion in the categories it has chosen to express itself. Probably a great many Christians of recent vintage would demand that Christianity be defined as establishing a personal relationship with God via a belief that Jesus, the Jewish carpenter of the first century, was his son. Certainly the multitudes of contemporary Christians who follow the evangelical and fundamentalist versions of Christianity would make such a demand.

What does this interpretation mean in human terms? Through preaching, a general description of Christian beliefs is presented to the listeners. If they decide to accept the validity of this explanation of humankind's existence, they apparently affirm their consent and, depending upon the denominational interpretation, are saved or well on their way. They are then expected to follow a Christian life that generally has great affinity to their society's cultural mores.

In some denominations the initial conversion appears to effect the guarantee of eternal life as partially described in the discussion on death in chapter 10 and featuring denominational variations that have developed over the years. Other denominations relate that the conversion allows the individual perfect freedom. Strangely the perfect freedom is almost immediately circumscribed with rules and regulations of great specificity. In practically every version of Christianity, the conversion experience or decision is followed by the exercise of individual will to act differently with respect to practical problems. One could almost say that the whole of the Christian conversion and salvation doctrines are dependent on the exercise of individual will to achieve certain standards of behavior or to make a record with respect to good and evil deeds.

Aside from the conversion experience and the exercise of individual will to follow behavior standards, the problem with the Christian conception of human behavior is that it apparently depends on the cultural context in which it exists to determine what standard of behavior the will shall follow. With only a preliminary examination of some of the positions understood as Christian over the years, one could conclude that Christianity attempts to dominate cultures and does so initially but eventually falls victim to cultural values. For a long time, for example, Christians, eschewing political involvement, were among the most persecuted peoples in the Roman world. The message emphasized that Christ's kingdom was "not of this world." Spotting the weakness in the European political structures, the doctrines suddenly changed to support the theory that Christ had given the pope total power over people's lives as his vicar on earth. No king could be crowned, no emperor installed without the pope's approval.

Expecting the momentary return of Jesus, Paul discouraged marriage among his converts but appeared to relent if it meant that they would be living in even greater sin by having intercourse in an unblessed state. From that position, marriage apparently evolved into one of the church's sacraments. The church held that position for a very long time, and monogamy became a European cultural value. The state of monogamy was held to be a Christian ideal, with marriage considered to be sealed sacramentally and divorce, which banned one from communion, sinful.

In recent years as both American and European societies have come to a greater understanding of the nature and needs of human beings, divorce has taken on a new status in Christendom. It is still frowned upon, but the wrinkles are not nearly as deep. Second, third, and fourth marriages often receive denominational blessings, and annulments for influential members of the Roman Catholic church are not a rare occurrence. We may yet see the day when it becomes a Christian doctrine that no man or woman can have more than one wife or husband *at the same time*.

Sexual intercourse was once considered sinful; the act was permissible only for purposes of procreation. Today a number of ministers advocate that more sexual freedom and premarital sex for many people is not the mortal sin that it formerly was. Marital sexual activity is now defined by a substantial number of Christians as an activity anticipated by God and encouraged by the clergy. Homosexuality, once the bane of Christianity, is now considered by some clergy as an expression of human needs, and the stigma is gradually fading in those denominations that at present do not advocate its sinlessness. Indeed in recent years the major Protestant denominations have em-

braced virtually all kinds of sexual activity, the only limits apparently
are sincerity and innovation.

Poverty was once considered a Christian virtue for it was
meant to indicate a lack of concern for the values of this world and a
concentration on the life to come. In the centuries after the Protestant
Reformation, poverty was considered indicative of sloth and other
sins, and it was seen as proof of the individual's degeneracy. The expression "poor *but* honest man" meant that a person was poor because he was
dishonest and God had refused to bless his labors. As the white populace
of Christian America has become more affluent, the concept of stewardship has been developed to explain the embarrassingly rapid
growth of wealth of a substantial number of peoples. The theory goes
that we are not really greedy, God has simply blessed us by giving us
wealth over which we are to exercise good stewardship (i.e., the
organizational church must have its cut for us to be good stewards).

These examples and many others that we can think of
illustrate at least two points. One is that once the decision is made to
exercise the human will to live a Christian life, the content of that life
is rapidly determined by the cultural values of the society in which the
convert finds him- or herself. As the cultural values change, the
doctrines also change; it becomes impossible to determine exactly how
a Christian does behave.

The other point is that as conversion is regarded as an
individual concern, so determination of the hallmarks of the Christian
life is also regarded as an individual concern. Individuals thus follow
that version of the religion that appears to be the most comforting to
them. Shopping for prestige churches as an individual climbs the
social, political, or economic ladder is not unheard of. In its practical
sense, Christianity is a religion almost wholly determined by the
culture in which it finds itself. It brings to that culture some of its ideas,
including a comforting sense of history. But in practical terms it quickly
bends to whatever forces are most dominant in that culture as individual Christians are forced to follow a course that they would imagine
to be most religious in a cultural context strange to the world of Roman-
dominated Palestine.

Because the Christian religion is conceived as personal,
individuals are both victims and victors of the religion. It is to their

personal evaluation of events and values that the religion responds. It never allows them to forget the impossibility of ultimate success for they are, after all, sinners, but it allows them to escape the consequences of that sin by making them the sole determining factor of what they shall do and what they shall consider religious activity. Ambrose Bierce once defined a Christian as one who follows Christ's teachings insofar as they are not incompatible with a life of sin. Bierce was not underestimating the practical side of the Christian religion.

Today we are suffering the impact of two thousand years of Christian individualism. Social problems continue to mount with no apparent solution in sight. Yet the United States appears to have a substantial number of devout Christians inhabiting it. We conducted a long war in Asia that was prolonged primarily for political reasons by two presidents, yet both of these men were apparently Christians in good standing. Prominent church leaders such as Dr. Billy Graham did not call them to account as being anti-Christian or non-Christians for the wastage of human life. In the Gulf War some church leaders did make an effort to prevent bloodshed, but their religious objections proved irrelevant to George Bush.

The rising rate of mental illness, especially the alarming rise in multiple murders and police brutality in civil disorders, would indicate that there is something amiss. The continued proliferation of psychologists, psychoanalysts, group therapy, psychodramas, and other phenomena indicative of attempts to heal the spiritual problems of modern people should tell us that at least part of our conception of the nature of religion has been mistaken. If Christianity saves the individual, and the evidence that it does appears to be decreasing, it must certainly be determined a failure when societies or even large numbers of human beings are concerned.

In terms of philosophical analysis, what Christian doctrines do is isolate the individual humans in a vacuum where they are confronted with a deity who is, by definition, angry. Every consideration that could be made, based on normal relationships with the world of daily experience, are not regarded as factors to be considered as part of religious experience. The individuals are then asked to make a theoretical choice whether certain factual happenings on this planet indicate a radical change of cosmic significance to the deity. Upon giving their assent, they must exercise their will to prevent the commission of further disobedience toward the deity when they face the world of daily experience. Then they are once again placed in that world and expected to respond to novel situations in a manner consistent with the concept of obedience to divine commands and purposes that remain obscured if not invisible to her.

Is there such an individual? Does the individual exist apart from his or her nation, language, family, culture, wealth, knowledge of the world, secular beliefs, and immediate situation? Traditionally Protestant theologians could conceive of such an individual. "Sinners in the hands of an angry God" characterized the sermons of this perspective, and today's evangelists who carefully orchestrate their crusades with hymns, angry sermons, threats of judgment, soothing words of comfort, efforts at healing, and psychological tricks to get the reluctant to the front row kneeling in fear and trembling are their successors. Without the ability to invoke emotion, create fear and anxiety, and promise instantaneous relief from such fear, the evangelists are helpless. It is by artificially creating that solitary individual through deliberate manipulation of his or her emotions that they give credence to their version of the Christian religion. Theologians are notably absent in the solutions of social problems, in the ongoing work of local communities, and in the examination of the nature of human personality and its problems.

When we turn from Christian religious beliefs to Indian tribal beliefs in this area, the contrast is remarkable. Religion is not conceived as a personal relationship between the deity and each individual. It is rather a covenant between a particular god and a particular community. The people of the community are the primary residue of the religion's legends, practices, and beliefs. Ceremonies of community-wide scope are the chief characteristic feature of religious activity. Religion dominates the tribal culture, and distinctions existing in Western civilization no longer present themselves. Political activity and religious activity are barely distinguishable. History is not divided into categories. It is simultaneously religious, political, economic, social, and intellectual.

There is no salvation in tribal religions apart from the continuance of the tribe itself. Being a tribal religion, there are no deviations of doctrine. Doctrine is not needed and heresies are virtually unknown. Theology is part of communal experiences needing no elaboration, abstraction, or articulation of principles. Every factor of human experience is seen in a religious light as part of the meaning of life. Tribal customs structuring relationships found to be proper for people are continued. Preconceived standards of conduct are unimportant and the assumption of the innate sinfulness of human is impossible, for the individual is judged instantaneously by his or her fellows as useful or useless according to his or her degree of participation in community affairs.

The concept of an individual alone in a tribal religious sense is ridiculous. The very complexity of tribal life and the interdependence of people on one another makes this concept improbable at best, a terrifying loss of identity at worst. It is this tribal religious individual who causes reaction among Christians whenever Indians and whites meet. For example, in *The Secular City* Cox remarks that "tribal man is hardly a personal 'self' in our modern sense of the word. He does not so much live in a tribe; the tribe lives in him. He is the tribe's subjective expression."[1] Cox concludes that "tribal naïveté must be laid to rest everywhere, and everyone must be made a citizen of the land of broken symbols."[2] In other words, if a religion or a person is different, it or he or she must be destroyed.

Religion as a tribal phenomenon can be found in Indian life in many respects. There is no demand for a personal relationship with a personal savior. Cultural heros are representative of community experience. They may stand as classic figures such as Deganiwidah, Sweet Medicine, Black Elk, Smohalla, and even Wovoka; but they never become the object of individual attention as to the efficacy in either the facts of their existence or their present supratemporal ability to affect events. The revelation that establishes the tribal community or brings to it the sacred pipes, the sacred arrows, the sacred hats, and other sacred objects is a communal affair in which the community participates but in which no individual claims exclusive franchise.

It is virtually impossible to "join" a tribal religion by agreeing to its doctrines. People couldn't care less whether an outsider believes anything. No separate religious standard of behavior is imposed on followers of the religious tradition outside of the requirements for the ceremonies—who shall do what, who may participate, who is excluded from which parts of the ceremony, who is needed for other parts of the ceremony. The customs of the tribe and the religious responsibilities to the group are practically identical, and the existence of two sets of values side by side is unthinkable. Contrast this state of affairs with Richard Nixon's stand against abortion based on his Christian reverence for life and his continuation of the Vietnam War in which thousands of lives were taken so that he would not be the first American president "to lose a war." Look at the present antiabortion advocates who also support the death penalty and refuse to provide for the poor, already born children.

The fears that Cox and others express as to the lack of a personal self among tribal peoples is unwarranted, and they indicate a lack of understanding of tribal religious beliefs and practices. One of the most notable features of Indian tribal cultures is the custom of naming individuals. Indian names stand for certain qualities, for exploits, for unusual abilities, for unique physical characteristics, and for the individual's unusual religious experiences. Every person has a name given in religious ceremonies in which his uniqueness is recognized. *Harvey Cox*, as a name, indicates that for an undetermined number of generations the male member of the genetic line has been called Cox and Harvey's parents happened to like the name Harvey. Such a name hardly indicates a personal self but at least partially denotes a breeding line.

But then consider a famous Sioux name "Man Afraid of His Horses" which properly translated means a warrior so brave and fierce that even his horses invoke fear in the enemy, a name won proudly on the field of battle and indicating a major accomplishment on behalf of the tribe. To be sure, Indian tribal religions have an individual dimension. The vision quest of many of the tribes is primarily an individual responsibility. The person fasting and praying must remain open and keenly aware that he might be chosen by the Great Mystery as a holy person, as a great and heroic warrior, as one cursed with a handicap, or have any number of other vocational responsibilities. Depending on the tribe and its traditions, the vision quest may be a relatively short-term experience. It may indicate nothing at all. Or it may require the most arduous type of life, requiring the greatest of personal sacrifices.

There is not the emotional dimension of the evangelistic crusades present in this aspect of Indian individual religious experience, however. No ranting and raving preacher threatens everlasting hellfire and damnation unless an immediate decision is forthcoming. The individual doggedly and determinedly fasts and sings sacred songs with the hope that he or she will be granted a religious vocation to serve the people.

In addition to highly personalized names and religious experiences, the individual is enabled to relate to all phases of his or her life experience through tribal religions. The Iroquois and Cherokee, for example, had sophisticated systems for dream interpretation that were part of their religious beliefs. A great majority of the tribes recognized the religious aspect of dreams and made some provision for understanding them. Western psychoanalysis has only recently come to understand the uncharted field of dream analysis as an indication of personal mental health. The Christian theologians have yet to attempt to understand the reality of dreams in spite of the appearance of dreams in both Old and New Testaments.

Individual worth was also recognized in other ways in the tribal religions. The keepers of the sacred medicine bundles, for example, were people who had been carefully watched for their personal characteristics and were chosen to share some of the tribal mysteries and responsibilities in a religious sense. The priesthoods of some of the tribes were filled with people who had been carefully trained after they had demonstrated their personal integrity. These people were chosen by the men and women responsible for maintaining the tribal religions. Young people and casual participants did not choose a religious office within the tribe as a career because they liked people, which has so often inspired the Christian clergy to become ministers.

In almost every way, tribal religions supported the individual in his or her community context, because they were community religions and not dependent on abstracting a hypothetical individual from his or her community context. One could say that the tribal religions created the tribal community, which in turn made a place for every tribal individual. Christianity, on the other hand, appears to have created solitary individuals who, gathered together every seven days, constitute the church, which then defines the extent to which the religion is to be understood and followed. With the individual as the primary focal point and his or her relationship with the deity as his or her primary concern, the group is never on certain ground as to its existence but must continually change its doctrines and beliefs to attract a maximum number of followers. It is always subject to horrendous fragmentation over doctrinal interpretations, whenever two strong-minded individuals clash.

The anthologies of Indian speeches reflect the basic Indian religious attitudes toward the nature of religion. As we review them, we find a rejection of the concept of religion as found in Western Christian understanding.

Red Cloud, for example, when told that he must become as the white men, remarked,

> You must begin anew and put away the wisdom of your fathers. You must lay up food and forget the hungry. When your house is built, your storeroom filled, then look around for a neighbor whom you can take advantage of and seize all he has.[3]

Sitting Bull, asked in Canada why he did not surrender and return to the United States to live on a reservation, replied,

> Because I am a red man. If the Great Spirit had desired me to be a white man he would have made me so in the first place. He put in your heart certain wishes and plans, in my heart he put other and different desires. Each man is good in his sight. It is not necessary for eagles to be crows.[4]

Chief Joseph once met with a U.S. commission that wanted him to cede the Wallowa valley in Oregon, which the Nez Percé owned. During the negotiations he was asked why the Nez Percé had banned missionaries from their lands. Joseph answered,

> They will teach us to quarrel about God, as Catholics and Protestants do on the Nez Percé Reservation (in Idaho) and

other places. We do not want to do that. We may quarrel with men sometimes about things on earth, but we never quarrel about the Great Spirit. We do not want to learn that.[5]

A Delaware chief complained about the Gnadenhutten massacre in 1782 when ninety Christian Indians had been killed by whites because two Indians, not of the group, had injured a white man some miles away from the settlement.

And yet these white men would be always telling us of their great Book which God had given them. They would persuade us that every man was bad who did not believe in it. They told us a great many things which they said were written in the Book; and wanted us to believe it. We would likely have done so, if we had seen them practice what they pretended to believe—and acted according to the good words which they told us. But no! While they held the big Book in one hand, in the other they held murderous weapons—guns and swords—wherewith to kill us poor Indians. Ah! And they did too. They killed those who believed in their Book as well as those who did not. They made no distinctions.[6]

Old Tassel, the famous eighteenth-century Cherokee leader, remarked on the continuous demand by the whites that the Cherokees accept the white civilization,

Much has been said of the want of what you term "civilization" among the Indians. Many proposals have been made to us to adopt your laws, your religion, your manner and your customs. We do not see the propriety of such a reformation. We should be better pleased with beholding the good effects of these doctrines in your own practices than with hearing you talk about them, or of reading your newspapers on such subjects.[7]

Red Jacket, the great Seneca orator, encountered a young missionary named Cram, who was sent by the Evangelical Missionary Society of Massachusetts to visit and convert the Iroquois. His reply to Cram's speech advocating that the Senecas accept Christianity best summarizes the tribal attitude toward the overtures of Christianity.

You say there is but one way to worship and serve the Great Spirit. If there is but one religion, why do you white people differ so much about it? Why not all agree, as you can all read the book?

Brother, we do not understand these things. We are told that your religion was given to your forefathers, and has been handed down from father to son. We also, have a religion which was given to our forefathers, and has been handed down to us, their children. We worship in that way. It teaches us to be thankful for all favors we receive; to love each other, and be united. We never quarrel about religion, because it is a matter which concerns each man and the Great Spirit.

Brother, we have been told that you have been preaching to the white people in this place. These people are our neighbors. We are acquainted with them. We will wait a little while and see what effect your preaching has upon them. If we find it does them good, makes them honest and less disposed to cheat Indians, we will consider again of what you have said.[8]

Ernest Thompson Seton compiled a series of quotations on American Indian religious behavior entitled *The Gospel of the Red Man. An Indian Bible.* The selection is designed to indicate the spiritual qualities of the various tribes and so naturally presents the best side of Indian life. One selection, however, seems to be so typical and universal an example of the nature of tribal life that is reproduced here to show how the tribal religious system worked with respect to the most modest of tribal members. Seton cites Tom Newcomb, who had been his guide in 1912 and 1914 in his travels in the West:

I tell you I never saw more kindness or real Christianity anywhere. The poor, the sick, the aged, the widows and the orphans were always looked after first. Whenever we moved camp, someone took care that the widow's lodges were moved first and set up first. After every hunt, a good-sized chunk of meat was dropped at each door where it was most needed. I was treated like a brother; and I tell you I have never seen any community of church people that was as really truly Christians as that band of Indians.[9]

The question that arises, of course, is how were the tribal religions able to produce behavior that surpassed the actions of the Christians if Christianity was to be considered as the one and true religion? Why does Christianity give rise to perpetual bickering and arguments over God and religion, which became anathema to the Indians who observed it? One cannot say that a fundamental defect is inherent in the genes of Europeans that makes them unable to follow their religious beliefs. One can only conclude that while Christianity can describe what is considered as perfect human behavior, it cannot produce such behavior.

Perhaps the closest approach that any Christian community has made to the type of behavior described by countless observers of Indian religion is that of the Amish communities of the Midwest. By every criteria that measures social integrity, the Amish appear to rank far above other communities and other denominations of Christianity. Hardly a Christian denomination can approach the record of the Amish for lack of delinquency, lack of idleness, lack of alcoholism, lack of divorce, lack of any statistic that would indicate social disintegration. Need it be noted that the Amish have settled on and related to definite lands, that they hold themselves in a tight communal setting, and that they adhere to customs with the tenacity of belief that amazes outsiders and brings them to as many clashes with civil authority as any group in the nation?

That the Amish can make their religion work indicates not so much the validity of their religion but that they have created a specific community that relates land, community, and religion into one integrated whole. To a lesser degree, the Mormons have also accomplished this task. The proper response of human personality to religious experience would seem to involve the factors that Indian tribal religions have traditionally emphasized, which the Amish and Mormons at least partially emphasize or practice, and that has distinguished American Indian people from the rest of America. In a sense then, religion must relate to land, and it must dominate and structure culture. It must not be separated from a particular piece of land and a particular community, and it must not be determined by culture.

Notes

1. Harvey Cox, *The Secular City* (New York: Macmillan, 1965).
2. Ibid, 30.
3. Ralph K. Andrist, *The Long Death* (New York: Macmillan, 1964), 134.
4. Virginia Armstrong, *I Have Spoken* (Chicago: Swallow Press, 1971), 112.
5. Ibid, 95.
6. Ibid, 33.
7. Ibid, 30.
8. Wilcomb Washburn, *The Indian and the White Man* (Garden City, N.Y.: Doubleday, 1964, 209–14) cites Red Jacket's reply to Cramm.
9. Ernest Thompson Seton, *The Gospel of the Red Man* (New York: Doubleday Doran, 1936) 26–27.

CHAPTER 12

THE
GROUP

The Christian religion's doctrine of creation was developed very early and is fundamental to the articulation of the basic Christian theology. It has since been absorbed into the general set of assumptions about the nature of the world so that few people concern themselves with the implications. The subsequent expansion of the Christological doctrines has been so extensive that their relationship to the doctrine of creation has been largely ignored or forgotten.

It may be unnecessary also to place much expectation on a renewal of the examination of history by adherents of the Christian religion. The linear conception of history as an exclusively European franchise has been so secularized and in recent years so militarized that it is no longer a wholly Christian phenomenon. While Christians abstractly maintain that God rules history, as we have seen there is no great tendency to identify exact events in which this control of history is exercised. Instead, the more Christians appear to confront the problems involved with historical interpretations the more they shy away from maintaining that any specific event has been the scene of divine activity. History, at least in its most concrete sense, has become largely a symbolic and parabolic matter.

Of more concern for the present situation with which we are confronted may be the community context in which religions arise. The present trend in Christian religion is to interpret religion and religious experience as a wholly individual phenomenon. The right wing of Christianity has embarked on a Jesus movement in which the major focus is "getting right with God" on a personal basis and an almost total neglect of the social conditions of the various nations and communities in which these believers live. In large measure, this tendency is opposed to another tradition of the Christian religion that has always placed a heavy emphasis on the existence of the church as a community of the saved and the quasi saved. The final spasm of individualism may be the logical conclusion of Christian ideas but cannot by any means be said to represent fairly the historical roots and experiences of Christianity.

The Old Testament laid down the definitions of the existence of a religious community in a number of related and rather significant doctrines. From the experience in Egypt and the ensuing trauma of the desert came the conception of the Hebrews as the Chosen People of God. In a historical sense, we can well understand that having survived a disastrous natural holocaust fairly intact would tend to make people believe that they had been particularly chosen by a deity to represent his interests here on Earth. The development of an ethical system requiring the people to act responsibly toward one another and toward the strangers in their midst may be an added feature of the conception of the Chosen People. However, the idea that religion was conceived as initially designed for a particular people relating to a specific god falls well within the experiences of the rest of humankind and may conceivably be considered a basic factor in the existence of religion.

Even within the ethical systems of the later prophets of the Hebrew religion, however, the chosen-people concept did not spill out from its ethnic boundaries. Isaiah and Jeremiah are more concerned with Israel's example as a people to the nations of the world than with a universal ethical humanism into which secular Judaism has lapsed. The absence of missionaries indicates that while the conception of God, particularly the God of Israel, may have narrowed in the centuries before the advent of Christianity, there is no impelling reason within the Hebrew religion to convert non-Hebrews to the religion of the nation.

The crisis that ensued in the doctrine of the Chosen People with the advent of Christianity was profound. If Jesus were really the Messiah and John the Baptist were Elijah, then Judgment Day should have come with the death of Jesus or shortly thereafter. Such was not the case. The community of Jesus's followers lingered on in Jerusalem for many years after his death, and it was apparently on the edge of starvation when Paul discovered their plight and sought contributions for them in Asia Minor. Inherent in the Jerusalem community's state was the problem of the salvation of a few of the Jews who had followed Jesus, and the subsequent damnation of the remainder of the Jews who had not heeded His preaching. It was essential to hold the Jerusalem community intact to maintain that the Jews had rejected their status as Chosen People and that the *real* meaning of Jesus' life and death had been to open the gates of salvation to non-Jews.

This struggle began as Paul developed his theology and the subsequent doctrines of creation, history, and atonement. Without these doctrines, preaching to the Gentiles would have been futile, as they could not have been saved at any cost. The Christian God thus became dislocated not only in time and space but also ethnically. In opening the religion to Gentiles, the whole conception of the Chosen People was radically changed from an identifiable group or nation to a mysterious conglomerate of people who could not be identified with any degree of accuracy.

Granted that during the first few centuries of Christian existence, the followers of the religion could be readily identified. It was not as religious people that they received identity, however, but as subversives, political malcontents, and enemies of the Roman Empire. The long-haired peace protesters of today and the Christians of the early Christian era share at least that peculiar feature. They both spoke of concepts totally foreign to the political structures of the society in which they lived, and both were persecuted for their beliefs. Fortunately for our day, the peace protesters did not have the exclusive concept of the invisible community that the early Christians maintained.

The existence of fellow travelers as well as identifiable Christians thrown into the arena made it necessary to develop the conception of the community of saints as a body of believers that could not be readily identified—the church. Perhaps the most standard definition of the *church* that has been advanced by Christian theologians is the *body of Christ*. That is to say, the historical aspects of Jesus as an identifiable human being were early consumed by the development of the idea of the church as the invisible body of the Christ. No one knew or could know who belonged to it until the final judgment, when everything would be revealed. As a community, then, and as a community to be identified as the Jews had once identified themselves nationally, the Christian church was virtually invisible during its ascendency to political equality in the Roman Empire.

As the empire began to disintegrate, the only institution to which people could cling was the Christian church. It had adopted the basic political structure of the old Roman administrative apparatus and transformed it into an ecclesiastical hierarchy; the transition from a social milieu primarily political to one that emphasized religious certitude was fairly smooth. In the absence of strong political leaders, Christian bishops and clergy often handled problems of local importance and concern.

By the end of the first Christian millennium, the church hierarchy had established itself as the supreme ruler of Europe. By cleverly combining a claim to divine sanction with the ambitions of rising European political leaders and the need of these leaders for divine sanctions to their authority, the professional clergy was able to solidify itself as a favored group within the continent's dominant feudal system. As the trend toward strong national governments increased, the church was able to protect itself by expanding its functions to account for the changing conditions. Ecclesiastical courts were thus set up to maintain a favored position for church officials in the face of the development of the kingdoms' secular courts.

The high point in church influence was probably the insistence that God had specifically given the governments of the world to the pope. Whom the pope recognized, therefore, was rightful ruler of the nation. The clash over this doctrine invokes familiar pictures of Henry of Germany kneeling in the snows, begging the pope's pardon for his arrogance in attempting to claim heir presumptive of the Roman Empire without the blessing of the Holy Father. For Europe, the Christian church had become the first overt conspiracy.

With the Protestant Reformation, the Christian church was shattered into a number of national organizations, each claiming a direct relationship with the essential teachings of the Christian religion to the others' detriment and degradation. Again the conception of the church as the Body of Christ was emphasized as the symbol of the community of believers, but again the most important aspect of the church was the visible organization assuming command of people's religious lives. To the degree that each church claimed primacy in delivering divine commands, it also placed less emphasis on religious experience itself and concentrated on the discipline needed to maintain itself politically and economically.

Today we inherit nearly five hundred years of church growth and organizational control over the religious lives of people. The multitude of Christian churches in America testifies to the misplaced energy that has gone into maintaining special doctrinal divergencies by disciplined organizational groups. The Lutherans in America, for example, trace themselves back to national origins in Europe rather than to any profound doctrinal differences, although doctrinal differences do occur. Among the Presbyterians, the American Civil War resulted in the creation of two churches that took opposing sides in the conflict. If, as each ecclesiastical structure would maintain, the church is the Body of Christ, Christianity is indeed in sad shape—if it is in any shape at all.

The last two decades have seen two developments in church organization that are, to say the least, baffling. The Lutherans have overcome more than a century of ethnic separatism and have been busy merging the various denominations together. The Presbyterians have resolved the Civil War division and come together again. Discussions have been held to form a "superchurch" by some of the major mainstream Protestant denominations. But the leaders of the various mainstream churches have devoted considerable time and study in preparing a calculated surrender to secular values and practices. Most ministries have given way from their male supremacy and now accept women as priests and pastors, and there is great debate on accepting and blessing homosexuality. The Episcopalians literally forced many long-time followers out of their church by insisting that everyone adopt a new form of service. Some church members, discontented with the radical changes in familiar services and doctrines, have fled to more conservative churches, and many have simply become nominal members of their denomination. Meanwhile radical evangelical churches have added new members rapidly and their message is one of total submission to whatever interpretation of the Bible the local pastor feels is appropriate. Consequently, conservative churches have found Bible verses that support American militarism, the death penalty, anti-abortion, and capitalism. Conservative Christianity today resembles nothing less than a religious auxiliary of the Republican Party.

The Christian religion's traditional claim to validity in regard to its obvious disunity is to return to the days of the early Christian church and maintain that the church is in fact invisible and made up of those who truly believe in Jesus as the Christ. It therefore becomes virtually impossible to discuss the conception of a religious community in terms of Christianity because no visible community can or does exist. Any efforts to identify failures with any of the organized denominations brings the response that the particular denomination under consideratio1 is not really *the* church. Yet that denomination collects money in the name of God, it issues pronouncements in His name, it protects its tax exemption because it is a religious group, and it plays an active part in the political decisions of the country be they the Vietnam issue, abortion, capital punishment, welfare, or whatever happens to arouse citizens' emotional involvement.

The tendency among Christian theologians is also to speak as if the denomination were in fact the church that exists invisibly and sinlessly off stage. After carefully defining the church as the Body of Christ containing true believers, true followers, and the saved or the baptized, theologians then promptly launch into exhaustive analyses of social conditions, the state of sin, the nature of the life to come, and other exotic topics with countless suggestions as to what each particular denomination can or should do about them. The abstraction that existed momentarily when conceptualizing the church generally fades in favor of budgets, fund-raising efforts, new programs of social relevancy, and new theologies of program and mission that the denomination's corporate organization must undertake if it is to carry out its ancient task of dictating to the world the conditions by which the world must exist.

The unhappy result of this practice is to make the career employees of each denomination believe that *they* are the Church and that where they appear, what they believe, how they act, and what they do constitutes the Christian religion. The recent trend of church leaders has been to become embroiled in sexuality almost to the exclusion of other concerns. Study groups of the various major Protestant denominations have advocated almost every kind of sexual activity as permissible "if it is done with love." It is not uncommon to see church pronouncements stating that even the clergy have a right to unrestricted sexual practices that would have been prohibited by both church and secular law a generation ago. Hugh Hefner should unquestionably be named as the Protestant saint of this century. One need scarcely comment on the egotism that this behavior indicates.

One cannot fault the premise of social involvement of corporate Christianity, yet one must take deep exception to both the procedures used to accomplish this end and the priorities such a path indicates. Without a continuing self-examination and reflection by the people of the respective denominations as to the nature of their involvement in social movement, the members of the churches have become increasingly alienated from their own organizations. The result of church staff and career employees delegating to themselves the power and authority to act for the whole membership has been to reduce some major denominations to a shadow of their former strength. Thus, even the most tangible indication of the existence of the Christian church, the denomination, may be disappearing in our day.

One might conclude that the departure of Christianity from its Jewish ethnicity to a universal religion maintaining that its existence is invisible and unknown while constructing elaborate organizations capable of manipulating political and economic power at a significant level has been one of the major reasons for its decline in recent years. Formal organizations seem to have an inevitable direction downward in their development as they become incapable of maintaining the original emotional commitments present at their creation. The history of Christianity would seem to indicate that attempts to form a religious community capable of maintaining an arena for religious experiences are doomed to become involved in everything but religious experiences.

The breakup of Christianity during the Reformation into national churches and the proliferation of denominations today would seem to indicate that a religious universality cannot be successfully maintained across racial and ethnic lines. The types of Christianity enjoying success in the southern United States today are hardly within the traditional experiences of two millenia of Christians. Rather they tend to reflect the cultural and political biases of the people of the region, indicating that instead of the message of universal salvation and/or fellowship, ethnicity will almost always triumph. Until contemporary Christian denominations recognize the human reality of ethnicity, they will continue to blunder into and out of contemporary situations and emerge worse for the experience.

It is in the conception of the community that Indian tribal religions have an edge on Christianity. Most tribal religions make no pretense as to their universality or exclusiveness. They came to the Indian community in the distant past and have always been in the community as a distinct social and cultural force. They integrate the respective communities as particular people chosen for particular religious knowledge and experiences. A substantial number of tribal names indicate the fundamental belief that the tribe is a chosen people distinct from the other peoples of mankind. *Dine*, the Navajo word for themselves, means *the people*. The Biloxi called themselves *taneks aya, first people*; Kiowas noted that they were *the principal people*. Washoes relate that *washui* means *person*, and Klamaths called themselves *maklaks, the people* or *the community*. The concern in almost every instance is to identify the community and distinguish its uniqueness from the rest of the creation and to emphasize "peoplehood" or personality.

Once having made this identification, the other aspects of life are then determined as a function of the community identity. For example, death in the Cheyenne sense is a demonstration of a belief in the community's continuity. No imperative to conduct religious warfare or missionary activity exists because it would mean altering the identity of the community by diluting its cultural, political, and social loyalties with the introduction of foreign elements. In the history of the early Hebrew people, we find the same concern for the maintenance of national identity as a religious function. And in both groups we find the same concern to show hospitality to a stranger as taking on an aspect of religious duty.

It is with respect to the attitude displayed toward strangers that a community's psychic identity can be determined. A community that is uncertain about itself must act in self-defense against any outsider to prevent any conceivable threat to its existence, whereas a community that has a stable identity accords to other communities the dignity of the distinct existence that it wishes to receive itself. The admonition of the early Hebrews to honor the stranger in their midst because they were once strangers in Egypt indicates the degree of community security enjoyed by the people. Their faith in the continuity of their nation precluded the destruction of others simply because they had different customs and beliefs. Logan, the Mingo chief, appealed to the Virginians for justice at the peace council following the back-country war of 1774: "I appeal to any white man to say if he ever entered Logan's cabin hungry and he gave him not meat; if he ever came cold and naked and he clothed him not."[1] Such hospitality characterized the tribal religious communities precisely because they were communities limited to specific groups, identifiable to the world in which they lived, and responsible for maintaining a minimum standard of hospitality and integrity.

The obvious benefit of a tribal religion is its coextensiveness with other functions of the community. Instead of a struggle between church and state, the two become complementary aspects of community life. The necessity of expanding the political functions of government into the social welfare field is avoided because religious duties cover the informal aspects of community concern. The coercive side of community life as we have traditionally seen it in Western democracies is blunted within tribal communities by its correspondence with religious understandings of life. Yet religious wars are avoided because of the recognition that other peoples have special powers and medicines given to them, thus precluding an exclusive franchise being issued to any one group of people.

In the closing decades of the last century, the Indian tribes could not be broken politically until they had been destroyed religiously, as the two functions supported each other to an amazing degree. Some Indians agents were able to keep control of reservations because of their use of Indian police. The tribal members would not kill their own people, and those Indians still resisting the Army refused to kill the tribal policemen. When religious ceremonies were banned and the reservations turned over to missionaries and political patronage appointees, the decline of both the traditional political leaders and the religious solidarity of the people was accomplished in a very short time.

The Indian Reorganization Act made some restoration of tribal religion possible by abolishing the rules and regulations that forbade the practice of tribal religions on the reservations. By creating corporate forms of government for political and economic ends, however, the federal government created the same problems of religious confusion in the Indian tribes that existed in America at large. A good deal of the political turmoil on the reservations today is between traditional people and more assimilated people over the use of land and resources. Traditional people generally want to use land in the same way as did their ancestors while the more assimilated people want to use it as an economic resource. The question that emerges is whether land is a "thing" to be used to generate income or a homeland on which people are supposed to live in a sacred manner.

Today with tribal governments severed from the tribal religious life, the integrity of the governments is dependent only on the ability of outside forces to punish wrongdoers. If the people of the reservation see no wrong in the actions of their tribal government in a political sense, they generally keep them in office in spite of constant failures of that government or council to act on behalf of the reservation ommunity.

Even with large defections of the tribal members to Christianity and Mormonism and with the political structure of the respective tribes frozen into quasi-corporate forms of activity, Indian tribes have shown amazing resilience in meeting catastrophes visited on them by government policies and outside interference. The primary identity of the group remains and in many cases has been perpetuated by the government with its incessant concern for administration and distribution of individual and tribal trust property. The major difference between Christianity and tribal religions thus remains active. Tribal members know who they are, and for better or for worse the whole tribe is involved in its relations with the rest of the world.

The opposite is true for Christianity. Mention the failures of either the religion or Western culture as influenced by Christian thinking, and the average Christian will tell you that Christians were not really responsible. Question any outstanding evangelist, theologian, or church leader today as to the orthodoxy of his theology or practice, and people will deny that he is remotely related to Christianity. The self-critical mechanism for analyzing behavior is thus missing from Christianity, whereas it is consumed within the tribal communities. No one will reject a tribal member as not belonging to the tribe. He may be viciously attacked as corrupt, as having assimilated, or as being a stupid traditional. He is never disclaimed as a tribal member. (This, of course, refers to tribal members and not to those, such as Chief Red Fox, who make claims on Indian ancestry without any Indian being aware of either the person or the person's claim.)

Another phenomenon existing in tribal religions that does not exist in Christianity is the absence of a paid professional religious staff. Tribal religions do not have the massive institutions that Christianity requires to perpetuate itself. While the Indian religious leaders may receive gifts for their work in conducting ceremonies, there are no pension plans, regular working hours, vacations, and the other benefits the professional Christian clergy enjoys. The Indian religious leader views his religious powers partly as a blessing and partly a curse because of added burdens of social responsibility. The Christian clergyman looks up the church hierarchical scale and begins plotting from the time of his ordination how quickly he can reach the apex of the pyramid. The scramble for rich parishes, seats on seminary faculties, appointments to church national staff positions, and boards of directors is quite irreligious and could only take place in direct opposition to the concept of religion, not as a part of it.

Indian religions consequently do not need the massive buildings, expensive pipe organs, fund-raising drives, publications, and other activities that the Christian denominations need to perpetuate themselves. The religious ceremonies of the tribal religions are carried out with a minimum of distracting activities. Many take place in sacred locations where the people can be in contact with the spiritual powers that have always guided the tribe. Other ceremonies can be performed as the occasion arises and wherever the need is shown.

Many Indian religious ceremonies have been held in apartments within the large urban areas far from the sacred lands of the tribe. Take away the large buildings and other secular achievements of Christianity, and it would vanish within a decade. Unless the Christian God is confined within a quasi-Gothic stone structure, He cannot operate. Needless to say, He does not do very well even with His real estate.

The two concepts of community are carried over into secular life. Today the land is dotted with towns, cities, suburbs, and the like. Yet very few of these political subdivisions are in fact communities. They are rather transitory locations for the temporary existence of wage earners. People come and go as the economics of the situation demand. They join churches and change churches as their business and economic successes dictate. Lawyers and doctors climbing the ladders of affluence will eventually become Episcopalians and Presbyterians. Businessmen will gravitate to those churches in which their level of secular concern is best manifested.

Within each town and city exist many denominational branches of Christianity; each competes with the others for financial and political control over an extensive portion of community affairs. People may live side by side for years having in common only their property boundaries and their status as property taxpayers. At no point do the various denominations serve to integrate cities, suburbs, or even neighborhoods. The most recent development, sharing church facilities by a number of weak denominations, and community churches too often reflect what would otherwise be regarded as community secular concerns and the perpetuation of secular ethical values.

Outside of ethnicity (i.e., the Irish, Italian, and Polish Catholic churches and the Scandinavian Lutheran churches), no unique thing distinguishes one group of Christians from another in the same manner as tribal groups are distinguishable. In the first place, the tribes have a discernible history, both religious and political. The various Indian languages have in the past acted to bind each tribe even closer. In this respect they have been paralleled by the Roman Catholic use of Latin and the ethnic use of the vernacular as liturgical languages. Latin became artificial, but the use of German, Swedish, and other languages in services meant solidification of the religious community to a real degree. In this respect some denominations of Christianity were closer to Indian tribes than they would have cared to elaborate.

Only with the use of Hebrew by the Jewish community, which in so many ways perpetuates the Indian tribal religious conceptions of community, do we find contemporary similarities. Again the conception of group identity is very strong among the Jews, and the phenomenon of having been born into a complete cultural and religious tradition is present, though many Jews, like many Indians, refuse to acknowledge their membership in an exclusive community.

Today many of the Indian tribes are undergoing profound changes with respect to their traditional solidarity. Employment opportunities away from the reservations have caused nearly half of the members of Indian communities to remove themselves from the reservations for work and educational programs leading to work. Massive economic development programs on the reservations have caused population shifts that have tended to break down traditional living groups and to cause severe strains in the old clan structure. And the tragedy of the Indian power movement is that it avoids looking realistically at this obvious change in living conditions. While Indian tribes have been able to maintain themselves in the face of sweeping technological changes, the day may be fast approaching when they too will fall before the complexity of modern life.

For that reason the future may be already a threat to Indian tribal and religious existence as it has never before appeared to be. New social, political, and religious forms must be found to enable the tribal religions to exist in a religious sense in spite of the inroads being made by the conditions of modern life. In a few selected communities, this transition is being made. In Christian perspective the Amish and perhaps the Mormons show how successfully communities can be established and maintained when they are restricted to ethnic communities residing in specific locations and preserving specific religious doctrines and ceremonial forms. The rest of Christendom and Indian religious and political leadership would do well to look at these groups as having made a realistic decision to perpetuate themselves as a community.

Surveying the past and looking for the future, the question of religion and its relationship to the social structures of humankind becomes more important. The universal and hardly identifiable conception of a religion for everyone as articulated by Christianity no longer appears to have validity. Where Christianity has most successfully entrenched itself into the lives of people, it has been on an ethnic or racial basis and has had to adopt the cultural and political outlook of the people of the land in which it has chosen to exist. In America it has become virtually impossible for Christianity to have positive effects on our society's movements. Lacking a specific people to which it could relate, Christianity has simply become a captive of the novelty of American life. To protect itself it has had to support the political structure of secular America, for without that structure the whole content of American Christianity would be meaningless.

The conflict over tax exemption of Christian churches and church property is a point in question. Would American Christianity be able to continue without its tax exemption? If there were no deductions allowed for contributions to church programs, what would be the effect on church income and programs? How would individual Christians respond to annual taxes on their massive churches, cathedrals, and investments? The fact that the churches are not willing to risk such a tax is indication enough that without a favored position in the secular world and its political and economic structures, most of what we now know as American Christianity would not and could not exist.[2]

The fundamental question of the nature of religion, therefore, must certainly involve a rejection of the structures Christianity has traditionally used to perpetuate itself and promulgate its message. For without the alliance with political structures that lend it credence and protection, Christianity would have vanished long since. It lives today because it has become so intimate a part of Western culture that its existence or reason for existence is rarely questioned. Is this condition necessarily a feature of religion as it has been experienced by humankind at various times and in various places? Is institutionalism necessary to religion in any sense? American society must honestly face and answer that question before it can understand the nature of the problems it faces.

A recent Supreme Court decision marks the irony of religion in America. Over the past two decades the Republicans have packed the Supreme Court with mediocre justices who were charged with the duty of reversing the gains made by minorities under the Earl Warren Court. In *Employment Division v. Smith* (1990) the Supreme Court ruled that the state laws covering drugs were sufficient to preclude use of peyote by members of the Native American Church.[3] In order to reach this conclusion the court had to destroy the traditional barrier between church and state that decreed that the state must prove that its laws are necessary to perform its function and that no exception can be made for religious activities. Following *Smith*, two cases involving the right of churches to control their own property in spite of city restoration and preservation ordinances were sent back to state courts with instructions to decide the cases in light of the *Smith* reasoning. There is sufficient group identity between existing Christian denominations and American Indian religious practitioners so that any effort to attack traditional tribal religions must be accomplished using principles that in fact place all religious expressions in jeopardy. Justice Antonin Scalia, in writing his opinion, stated that the Constitution of the United States would protect making golden idols and worshipping the Golden Calf—practices prohibited in the Hebrew-Christian religion for almost 3,500 years—but the Constitution would not protect anything else.[4]

Notes
1. Virginia Armstrong, *I Have Spoken* (Chicago: Swallow Press, 1971), 2.
2. When the case on church tax exemption came to court, the attorneys general of thirty-nine states filed *amicus curiae* briefs supporting continued exemption of the churches. The alleged separation of church and state does not seem so separate after all.
3. 58 LW 4433 (1990), No. 88-1213.
4. Ibid, 4435.

> Specifically, Scalia writes, "It would doubtless be unconstitutional, for example, to ban casting of 'statues that are to be used for worship purposes,' or to prohibit bowing down before a golden calf."

CHAPTER 13

CHRISTIANITY AND CONTEMPORARY AMERICAN CULTURE

We have noted previously that Christianity is often defined by the cultural context in which it appears and that, with few exceptions, it is unable to influence that culture to accept its doctrines. Intertwined with cultural and religious change is certainly the historical era in which the contact is made between a religion and a culture. Christianity may have done yeoman's service in calming the Germanic tribes and enticing them away from barbarism. But the ferocity with which Nazi ideology wreaked its havoc on Europe should cause us to wonder how much savagery Christianity actually abolished from the psychological makeup of European man.

American Christianity in particular appears to be a willing captive of American culture. The trend of recent years has only accentuated the traditional role of Christianity in American society as one of buttressing official folklore and patriotism. It is extremely difficult to discern whether American Christianity follows the culture, expressing its variations religiously, or whether it really does open up new avenues of social reality for consideration. At best we can worry that religion is in deep trouble when it finds it necessary to make itself attractive to a society in the hopes that the society will consider it worthy of its attention.

Perhaps the most publicized movement of recent years among Christians has been the Jesus movement. Theories abound as to the exact origin of this movement, but at least one reputable theory is that it came as a desperate effort by young people to get off drugs. Whether these young people were tired of drugs or whether drugs were in such short supply that they were forced to find a substitute may be the thesis of a future sociologist. At any rate, Jesus became a drug substitute for a significant number of people. Recounting how Jesus was a perpetual "high," numerous young people adopted the complete fanaticism that had characterized the earlier flower children, Civil Rights, and antiwar movements.

There does not seem to have been a theological basis of any depth within the Jesus movement. Evangelists hailed it as the greatest development in religion in recent years, foreseeing a new generation of the clean-shaven, white-buck-wearing Christians with whom they became familiar in the 1950s. Strangely, the chief characteristic of the Jesus movement was its absolutism, which led to violent intolerance of other ideas. While many of its followers proclaimed their faith in Jesus, few knew any of the details of the life of Jesus the Jewish carpenter.

A recent development of the Jesus movement has been the organization of parents to kidnap the youngsters involved in the movement and take them to debriefing stations where they are gradually returned to normal secular values and concerns. The possibility of psychic injury to participants of the movement has probably not occurred to the parents of these young people. But an additional, more serious question plagues us. How can these parents keep up the pretense of being Christians, celebrating Christmas, and doing all those other fun things that adult Christians do and then react with horror when their children join Christian communities to follow the Gospel full time? Christianity is apparently something that can be taken seriously—but not *too* seriously.

While the Jesus experience was described by ex-addicts as a "trip," one man really elaborated on this theme. The Reverend Wesley Seeliger, an Episcopalian chaplain at Texas A & M, viewed Christianity as a trip in his new frontier theology. The church, according to Seeliger, is a battered covered wagon, and God is a determined and driving trail boss. Jesus is the scout who rides out in front of the wagon train.

Seeliger's theology was published initially in a fifteen-cent cartoon format and sold more than twelve thousand copies at Texas A & M, a noted center of philosophical and theological study.

Against the frontier theology Seeliger sees the temptation of Christianity to form a settlers' theology, and this tension between rolling wagons headed westward and the sedate and comfortable life in the frontier town is apparently what has been causing a lot of our problems. In the settlers' theology, God is seen as the mayor of the old frontier town. The citizens never see Him, but they are certain He exists because they have law and order. The townspeople are scared to death of the mayor, but He keeps the old payroll coming in, and after all that's what made America great.

Meanwhile out on the prairie the old wagon train keeps rolling along. We are presently in the age of the spirit, and sure enough, there He is, the Holy Spirit as the old buffalo hunter, bringing in fresh meat to the people on the wagon train every morning. The clergy appears as the cast of characters as Wishbone and Hey Soos used to complement Mr. Favor and Rowdy Yates of the old television "Rawhide" series. They serve up that old buffalo meat whenever the people have a hankering for food. One need not comment on how this particular theology was received on the Indian reservations.

A theological development of recent vintage approaching the Western violence-prone trend of frontier theology is the emphasis on judo, karate, and other Oriental fighting skills. The Reverend Mr. Mike Crain of Brownsville, Kentucky, runs a Judo and Karate for Christ Camp. Karate is, according to Crain, useful in fighting off the devil. "We are teaching young people how to defend themselves against man," the good pastor has said. "Then we talk to them about how to defend themselves against Satan." Crain travels around the nation giving demonstrations and preaching sermons. To emphasize his point he often shatters a 300-pound block of ice.

Crain is not unique, however, because karate is the coming thing in Christian theology. Dean Blakeney, a fellow Christian who studied karate at North Georgia College and Tennessee Temple Theological Seminary, is also using karate to bring home the message of God's reconciliation with a sinful world. Blakeney apparently is further advanced in the Christian life, for besides karate he uses swords and curved Turkish Gurkha knives in his ministry. Recently he placed a potato on the stomach of one of the faithful and split it with a sword without harming the fellow Christian who, he noted, had already been saved. Then he cleaved a watermelon into two pieces with his Gurkha knife to the amazement of his audience. His final knife act on behalf of the Lord was severing a banana, which was placed near the neck of one of his disciples.

Blakeney performed all of these Christian feats in the cafeteria of the New Testament Baptist Church in Miami in the fall of 1972. His performance was clearly superior to the feats recorded in the New Testament, when Peter attempted the same feat and bungled, severing the ear of the servant of the High Priest of the temple in the Garden of Gethsemane. Blakeney lined up four concrete blocks an 1 1/2 inches thick and drove his head through them, shattering them. He explained, "These concrete blocks represent your life and one day the devil is going to try to break your life just like I did these blocks."

Blakeney's final sermonette left something to the imagination. He had four men place a 150-pound slab of ice on the stage. "I'd like to do to the devil what I'm about to do to this ice," he chanted as he gave the ice a massive and highly religious karate chop. The block of ice remained firm as Blakeney lost his first encounter with the devil. Had he had a sudden lapse of faith? Was his faith half as strong as that of Crain, who splits 300-pound blocks of ice with little emotion and considerably less pain? Or was it simply denomination differences that allowed Crain to vanquish the devil but tore victory from Blakeney's grasp?

Christians Crain and Blakeney were not alone in their belief that Christianity is relevant to athletic ability. Paul Anderson, an Olympic weightlifting champion, preached a sermon a couple of years back in which he credited his strength to his religious faith. During this historic revelation, Anderson lifted 200 pounds with one arm. Not one of his devout audience apparently felt religious enough to duplicate the feat, immediately raising the question of the relative effectiveness of the Christian faith as opposed to simple athletic training.

Other signs of the efficacy of the Christian faith were noted by the Reverend Noel Street, a British spiritual healer who visited the United States in 1970. He noted that to have a good spiritual life with mental and physical health, one must live a Christian life. Later he elaborated on this prescription, adding that one should also be a strict vegetarian, do yoga or any good regular exercise, and avoid smoking and alcohol. Like Christian karate, yoga is a difficult word to find in either the Greek or Latin versions of the Bible.

Some Christian churches have refused to venture into the new realms of religious realism with new theologies, remaining fairly close to familiar American traditions. The Cathedral of Tomorrow, for example, has followed the New Testament teachings on the talents, wisely investing its earnings in businesses. It owns the Unity Electronic Company of New Jersey, the Nassau Plastic and Wire Company of Long Island, and land for a shopping center near its headquarters in Cuyahoga Falls, Ohio. Its best investment so far, however, is the Real Form Girdle Company of Brooklyn, New York. Knowing this we can conclude that Christianity is in good shape in Cuyahoga Falls, Ohio.

The Cathedral of Tomorrow did not stop with mere business investment, however, but launched into the sale of bonds for Mackinac College, gift annuity plans, life income agreements and other security deposit agreements. The Ohio Department of Commerce, as well as six other states, has ordered a halt to these sales. Whether the Cathedral was religious or not, it was plainly an enterprising group—and that, after all, is what made America great.

The prize for merging religion and business must go, however, to the promoters of Holyland USA, a proposed fifty- million-dollar Biblical Disney-type theme park that was to be built on the Alabama Gulf coast. The original promoter of Holyland USA, a man named Bill Caywood, convinced a number of devout fundamentalists that the park would bring in an extra three million souls. Plans were made to erect a 157-foot statue of Jesus on a 57-foot base. The sculpture would be taller than the Statue of Liberty and would be visible for miles down the highway each way.

A four-thousand-seat amphitheater was to be built for the production of passion plays, but the features surrounding the central theme of the park were really what would have made it noteworthy. There was to be a Noah's Ark Kiddy Petting Zoo, a Biblical wax museum, Biblical storytellers, and a 100-foot replica of Jonah's whale. Roman chariots and drivers would be featured in daily rides for the devout believers. A Tower of Babel, Herod's Palace, Wailing Wall, a Red Sea actually able to divide, a Golden Calf (for the disbelievers?), Solomon's Temple, and a Roman catacomb were all planned. Finally, plans were made to develop an actual trip through Heaven and Hell for the more venturesome of the park's visitors. One can but speculate on the outpouring of devotion that this project would have inspired.

Other churches have not invested in businesses or developed religious theme parks, but they have adopted modern business methods. The Congregational Church in Vergennes, Vermont, provided a credit-card machine at the entrance of the church to allow parishioners to charge their gifts to the Lord. "Vergennes is literally flooded with credit cards," the Reverend Richard Ogden stated, "and since we are moving into a credit-card age, there's no reason the church should remain aloof." Theologically, perhaps, MasterCard would be most suitable.

The First Baptist Church in Hammond, Indiana, did not get its credit-card machine in time, but it did get a fleet of buses to bring people right to the church door. It owns a fleet of 108 buses that weekly carry some 2,500 worshipers to the church. The fleet covers seventy-six different routes, and the church employs a full-time mechanic. The annual budget runs close to $80,000 for the fleet of buses, which includes 6,000 gallons of gas a month and about $5,000 worth of tires annually. The minister, who has obviously found peace with the Lord, remarked, "I think so much of building church growth through transportation that I'm spending my life working with buses rather than pastoring a church. And I have no regrets." At least, he must figure, when you save a bus, it stays saved.

Christian churches in the Seattle, Washington, area preferred to dance instead of ride. In 1970 they sponsored a course on "soul," which was designed to teach African-American culture to white parishioners. For $16, an eight-week course was offered that involved learning how to move to sound blasted forth on stereophonic equipment. The idea was to get whites used to moving their bodies in conjunction with the rhythm. Many of the participants liked the course, although one lady said that she did it just to torture her husband. Christianity, as we know from the New Testament, will pit father against son, mother against daughter, wife against husband.

Other Christian churches have recently been involved in an exciting affirmation of the efficacy of the faith. Prior to the diocesan convention of the Episcopal Church in Colorado in 1970, the young priests of the diocese petitioned then-Bishop Thayer for permission to hold a peace mass for those who wanted peace in Vietnam. Bishop Thayer, a direct lineal descendent of the Apostles according to official Episcopal doctrine, is reported to have told them that there are other ways of achieving peace besides praying for it.

Sometimes even when prayer works in its mysterious ways, it places a tremendous strain on the recipients of its benefits. Oral Roberts, long-time minister of the Pentacostal Holiness Church and nationally known faith healer, joined the Methodist Church. His success in the healing arts was unparalleled in modern times, since it enabled him to build Oral Roberts University in Tulsa, Oklahoma, which now has a fine basketball team with national ratings. Roberts is also a director of the Tulsa Chamber of Commerce and a director of one of the city's largest banks. Where the Lord chose martyrdom for Peter and Paul, He obviously had bigger things in mind for Roberts. Life has not been a bed of roses for Roberts in spite of his recent rise to prominence in Oklahoma. He told a *Denver Post* reporter of the great relief he had in joining the Methodist Church and leaving behind the great burden of faith healing. Faith healing was a great burden, Roberts commented to the reporter, because people expected miracles!

Perhaps the most important Christian event of recent times was Explo 72, a giant rally held in June 1972 at the Cotton Bowl in Dallas, Texas, a city of brotherly love. It was conceived and carried out by Bill Bright of the Campus Crusade for Christ International, one of the many fundamentalist-oriented groups working on college campuses. More than seventy-five thousand gospel-preaching, sure-enough young Christians came to Dallas to conduct a historic rally on behalf of fundamentalist Christianity.

Bright is something of a wonder himself, for he surpassed all previous expositors of the gospel except Jesus himself by reducing the Christian faith to four spiritual principles: God has a plan for everyone, everyone sins, Jesus is God's method of correcting sin, and everyone must individually receive Jesus as savior. To emphasize these four spiritual principles, Bright collected a group of Christian athletes, most notably Roger Staubach, former quarterback of the Dallas Cowboys. Outside of Jesus, Staubach was apparently the hit of the event by comparing life to a football game with salvation as the goal line and the Christian as being in good field position because of Christianity. It remained uncertain whether the Christians needed a touchdown or a field goal to win the game.

Unlike the feeding of the five thousand, Explo 72 had a budget of $2.7 million and charged participants a $25 entrance fee, which was certainly an improvement over the New Testament way of doing things. For the entrance fee enough potato chips were served to make a one-ton potato chip, although apparently the *Lord* did not do so, preferring to serve individual portions. The event was billed as a religious Woodstock, and it was advertised on 800 billboards, 100,000 bumper stickers, and 5,000 T-shirts.

The festival featured all of the famous Christian personalities, including Don Wilkerson of *The Cross and the Switchblade* fame, the Chaplain of Bourdon Street, the Chaplain of Hollywood, and Dr. Billy Graham, who was honorary chairman of the great event. Graham expressed his confidence in the ability of the participants to distinguish false prophets from true ones. Folksingers Johnny Cash and Kris Kristofferson were present to serenade the assembled multitude of faithful and a band, the Armageddon Experience, helped to keep the assembled saints at a fever pitch.

The climax to Explo 72 came when the 75,000 assembled young Christians broke forth in a frenzy of religious devotion and began chanting football cheers: Gimme a J, "JJJJJJAY;" Gimme an E, "EEEEE;" Gimme an S, "ESSSSS;" Gimme a U, "UUUUUUU;" Gimme an S, "ESSSSS." Whatta ya got? "JESUS." The Sermon on the Mount pales in comparison.

Anyone who could not distinguish between Christianity and contemporary American culture on the basis of Explo 72 was simply not receiving God's signals in the great football game of life. Had not Graham himself been present as honorary chairman people might have had cause to wonder. But Graham had given his whole life to an exposition of the gospel, and although he had previously been unable to reduce it to the four spiritual principles, he was still highly regarded. Among Graham's achievements was his informal chaplaincy at the White House, which aroused the ire of Reinhold Neibuhr, who could very possibly not distinguish between true and false prophets being a liberal and all. Neibuhr protested that Graham and the White House prophets were reducing religion to a civil obedience course that helped to cover problems, not solve them.

Graham was very hurt at this charge, remarking that he was simply a personal friend of the president and not a political man. He later said that he would vote for Richard Nixon, basing his choice on the president's obvious morality and integrity. Perhaps Graham felt that a man who could remain oblivious to Watergate, the ITT affair, the Lockheed loan, the Hughes loan to his brother, and who would maintain a committee to reelect him months after his reelection must have the highest morals in the nation. Dr. Graham felt that his presence at the White House in no way endorsed the policies of the president. When asked to comment on the Vietnam situation Graham replied that he spoke out only on the moral issues.

Graham's role in contemporary Christian thinking is buttressed by his lack of doubt. Having never attended a seminary, he did not have the opportunity to study Christian history or doctrine and had no chance to be led astray by the facts. He once related that he had no doubts whatsoever about Christianity since 1949 when he was converted on a golf course in Florida—calling into question, perhaps, Roger Staubach's theology, which viewed Christianity and life as football games. Some years ago when Graham addressed a men's group in England, he compared life to a golf course in which one need only follow the rules to be greeted by the Lord after the game was over. (Perhaps the greatest golfer of them all?)

While Graham is probably the most admired Christian in the modern world, it is difficult to distinguish his theological position as a religious leader and judge of morality from his participation in American cultural forms. He apparently swallows almost all of the traditional mythologies of American life without any critical analysis of whether they in fact relate to the Christian religion. In 1971 he was the grand marshal of the Rose Bowl parade, and he has consistently used sports metaphors as vehicles for his preaching. Graham supports athletics because "the Bible says leisure and lying around are morally dangerous for us." But Graham contended, "Sports keeps us busy; athletes, you notice, don't take drugs." How any adult in this day and age can make that statement is perhaps the most incredible aspect of Graham's view of the world.

In the political arena it was virtually impossible to tell Graham from the rest of Nixon's aides. When the president came to the University of Tennessee in 1970—one of the few campuses he dared to visit—to address Graham's revival meeting, a choir of 5,500 voices sang "How Great Thou Art" as Nixon was seated awaiting Graham's introduction. There remains some question as to which "thou" the choir was trumpeting. The avowed purpose of inviting Nixon to speak in Tennessee was to "show the younger generation that the president is listening to them." This attitude meshes with his interpretation of religion as a buttress of civil and political structures. He was reported in *Newsweek* to have said, "I'm for change, but the Bible teaches us to obey authority."

Graham's crusade frequently is held in conjunction with other events of less theological stature. During his appearance at Madison Square Garden in 1969, a special hall was set up near the Garden where rock and roll interspersed with confessions of faith continued all night after the famous evangelist's sessions. Poor Graham was thus connected with at least some of those who did not take the command to obey seriously. But the participants apparently "dug" the session. "It's amazing to hear those band members talk about Christ," one young visitor to the hall was heard to remark. The Reverend John Guest, leader of the sessions, called it "getting back to the biblical principle of going where the people are." He probably could have added that the Christian church itself was founded on a rock.

The confusion between Christianity and American culture is not simply a phenomenon of evangelical and right-wing Christianity. The liberal counterpart has made its contribution to making Christianity relevant to the modern world. The Lutheran Youth Congress meeting in San Diego in 1972 originated the Jesus cheer later repeated at the Cotton Bowl.

In 1970 the United Church of Christ in Chicago held an unusual ordination ceremony that indicated it also had seen the light and was trying to make religion relevant to American culture. The ordinand wore a multicolored vest with seventeen symbols representing his "concerns" sewn on it. Included were symbols of joy and sorrow, a black fist, a Star of David, a peace symbol, a herald's trumpet, and wheat seeds. Two leotarded dancers conducted a "moving prayer" against a background of shifting images projected on the walls of the museum in which the service was held. Kent Schneider, the newly ordained minister, "celebrated." He is director of the Chicago Center for Contemporary Celebration and will teach others to celebrate. He noted, "Celebration is an idea whose time has come." We will drink to that.

Celebration may be the name of the game over on the left wing of the Christian spectrum as football cheers seem to characterize the right wing. The Reverend Harvey Cox, author of *Secular City* and the liberal guru of the Boston area, decided in 1970 to combine all the elements of religion into one massive presentation. Choosing a congruence of holy days, Jewish Passover and Orthodox Easter, Cox gathered his disciples at The Boston Tea Party, a converted warehouse discotheque near Fenway Park. A projector flashed images on the walls to represent pictorially the agony of Vietnam, while participants wrote graffiti on the walls of the building. A rock band called the Apocrypha played "I Can't Get No Satisfaction," and at daybreak the crowd rushed into the streets, chanting, "Sun, sun, sun." Liberal Christianity had finally come of age. Right on, as the liturgy of the day related.

Women's Liberation has even intruded itself into what has normally been a male domain. In November 1972 a group of women from the Roman Catholic, Presbyterian, Methodist, Episcopal, United Church of Christ, and other denominations held a "sister celebration" at the Washington Square Methodist Church in New York City. Choosing Reformation Day, the traditional commemoration of Martin Luther's nailing of his ninety-five theses on the church door, the women wrote their own unique service. It featured the "liberation of apples."

The service began with the reading of the Genesis account of the creation and fall but rapidly assumed a relevant status. "We were told that we were agents of evil, corrupters of perfect creation," the leader chanted. "We fell for all that," the congregation replied in unison. "We were told that we were subordinate beings, derived from man, not uniquely created," the leader continued. "We fell for all that," the faithful responded. The service featured apple juice, which was tagged the "ferment of freedom." The women added a new myth of

Lilith, who was first created coequal with Adam but abandoned him because she refused to be subservient to him. God, a male chauvinist if ever there was one, then created Eve for Adam, a more compliant female who would minister to Adam's needs. Then Eve apparently climbed the apple tree, jumped over the garden wall, and left Adam standing there. This version does add dimension to the traditional Christian story of the creation.

The flexibility of the conception of Jesus appears to be another feature of contemporary Christianity. The Reverend Cecil Maxey of Parker, Colorado, for example, believes that Jesus wore short hair, not long hair, and has preached sermons against long hair. He was asked why the portraits of Jesus show him with long hair. "That's just an artist's conception, and you know how artists are," he replied. Maxey stated that the first paintings of Jesus were done hundreds of years after his death, and he is convinced that Jesus had short hair. Maxey, in charge of the First Baptist Church, is installing swimming pools, tennis courts and a miniature golf course to provide an "opportunity to witness."

It is very unfortunate that Maxey has discredited the portraits of Jesus, for that raises a serious problem for the people in Jerusalem. The Rockefeller Museum there has a skeleton whose anklebone has a steel nail driven through it. The relic was discovered in 1969, but its existence was kept secret until 1971. The relic is called the Yehochanan bone because it was found in a coffin with that title inscribed on it. When the discovery became known, scholars from around the world wrote to ask if the skeleton was that of Jesus. The Jerusalem scholars, on the basis of anthropologist Nico Haas's report of his findings on the structure of the skull, have determined that the skeleton is not that of Jesus. The skull, according to Haas, bore no resemblance to "Christ as we know him from portraits." Perhaps the anthropologist should join Maxey's congregation.

From Jesus freaks to portraits of Jesus, contemporary Christianity rocks with efforts to clarify its faith, define its beliefs, and make itself relevant to the modern world. Yet the tensions existing in its divergent branches, and the cancerous growth of splinter sects via television and radio evangelism, make it virtually impossible to understand. The advent of electronic communications has made radio and television religious programs so popular and lucrative that a significant number of evangelists have done very well financially in building up their own private denominations. Younger evangelists are now pushing Graham and Roberts into the past, creating gaudier, more spectacular programs for bringing the faithful into the fold.

A number of years ago the evangelical world was shattered when Marjoe Gortner, a well-known evangelist, became the subject of a documentary movie based on his experiences as a traveling evangelist. He had been brought up from early childhood as a religious prodigy, gaining great fame as a prototype of Christian youth. Then the fascination grew thin, and Marjoe decided to blow the whistle on the circuit that had proven so lucrative to his fellow evangelists. The movie revealed the money-mad preacher casually and perhaps cynically shearing his sheep. The greatest fears of the fundamentalists were thus realized, and the old Elmer-Gantry image seems doomed to follow them.

The movie *Marjoe* appeared perhaps at an auspicious time. Revivalists had been getting somewhat out of hand, as witness Reverend Ike. Better known as the Reverend Frederick J. Eikerenkoetter II in respectable Christian circles, Reverend Ike likes money. For a time he was simply another poor evangelist, but he soon developed a theology second to none in the modern world. Discovering that most people were already in hell, Ike began telling his congregations to give him money, basing his message on the belief that the Bible says all things are possible. Combining a fascinating style with the propensity for greed found scattered among the unsaved, Ike is reported to spend $1,000 a week on clothes, and because this is rather expensive overhead to maintain, he asks his congregations for money to pay the bills. They cough it up. As for Jesus, who is the standard product of other evangelists, "One thing even Jesus didn't do," Ike preaches, "he didn't save the world."

As the various branches of American Christianity gather to continue to grow. Dr. Carl F.H. Henry, a noted Christian theologian, sees a rise of atheism on a world basis. "Without a recovery of those lively spiritual convictions and vitalities through which the church itself came into historical existence," Henry maintains, "Christianity is unlikely long to remain either a serious contender among world religions or an effective alternative to Communist or any other ideology. " The fall of the Iron Curtain and the Berlin Wall revealed that Communism never was a viable ideology. What message does Western Christianity have for those who believed and practiced their religions not because they were politically correct or economically advantageous but because they offered hope and a sense of community?

Therein lies the problem. Western Christians continue to view their religion as an alternative to personally disliked political, social, and economic theories. The alternative to the potsmoking environs of Woodstock is, for right-wing Christianity, a crew cut, weightlifting, quarterbacking, and Christian folksinging rally in the Cotton Bowl with Jesus cheers. A religious Woodstock, as the promoters called it.

Contemporary American Christianity can quite possibly be understood as having two major, apparently mutually exclusive, emphases. The right-wing, evangelical, and fundamentalist spectrum of Christianity dwells almost exclusively and fanatically on the figure of Jesus and on the familiar theology of the old-time religion. However, its actual scholarly knowledge of Jesus and his times, the nature of the Roman world, and the movement of the early Church is practically nil. The less it knows about the human being Jesus, the more comfortable it is because it is the idealized, law-abiding, goody-goody projections of themselves, which they call Jesus, that forms the object of their devotion.

The predominance of whites in the right wing of Christianity and their perpetual identification of Christianity as the opponent and mortal enemy of Communism, Socialism, freethinking, long hair, and other symbolic foes makes their version of Christianity little more than a sacred patriotism seeking to restore the imagined elegance of the last century to American society. Their position with respect to social problems is generally to ignore them. Graham, their leading spokesman, sees poverty and race problems as indications of the coming of the end of the world. He already finds twenty-eight signs that the end is imminent, and he speculates that he would perhaps receive a favored place in the universe after Judgment Day as his reward, as ruler of a planet perhaps. He notoriously avoids the Bible verses having to do with Christ being present in the prisons, among the hungry and poor, and living with the oppressed.

The left wing is almost the opposite of its counterpart. It is probably best represented by the more traditional denominations such as the Presbyterians, Methodists, United Church of Christ, Episcopalians, and Roman Catholics. Perhaps the Greek Orthodox church should also be included in this category. For such denominations the mention of Jesus is both an embarrassment and a disappointment. Their primary theology can be summarized as a church theology. Every theological question presenting itself is solved by asking what the church should do about it. Inherent in their attitude is the presumption that they are by definition the world's religious and respectable people. They feel the only task remaining in the field of religion is to find a way to make their church relevant to the outside world. Most of them would take the Second Coming of Jesus as a personal affront indicating that God had lost confidence in their ability to solve problems.

The left wing thrives on social movements and fads of all kinds. Let someone advocate the use of hoola hoops to illustrate a theological point, and they swarm to his corner. These churches see their task as making American society respond to people, not as making American society change its basic presuppositions. They have set aside large amounts of money for self-determination by minority groups as well as for studies to determine how to assist the wealthy of the world in filling their leisure time. Planning new liturgies and new ministries, they feel impelled to issue a pronouncement on each and every event occurring on the planet. Much of the social movement of the past two decades has been made possible by the work of these churches, and in that respect they are probably more in tune with the state of American society than their fellow Christians on the right.

Today we find that the right wing of Christianity is growing quite fast, while the left wing, battered from indiscriminate support of demagogues in the power movements, is losing both members and financial support. Garry Wills in *Bare Ruined Choirs* has outlined the extent of internal dissension within the Roman Catholic branch of Christendom, and one might only note that its basic problem is that of reconciling itself to the world of the nineteenth century. In spite of its most optimistic emotions, it has not yet begun to comprehend the twentieth century or its most advanced twentieth-century man, Teilhard de Chardin.

Intertwined in both branches of Christendom is the fast-rising pentecostal movement, which finds its meaning in the underground church of the left and in some of the healing evangelicals on the right. Walter Hollenwerger has compiled a four-thousand-page handbook on pentecostalism that discusses the phenomena to be encountered in this movement. Speaking in tongues, healing, and other activities can be found among pentecostals of all persuasions, and if anything, the movement testifies to the human need for experience in religion.

While Christians are tearing themselves apart on the left or avoiding contact with the real world on the right, we are witnessing the rather frightening revival of demonism, devil worship, the astrological and numerological sciences, and other manifestations of the occult. Both the pope and Billy Graham agree that this is the devil's work, but the persistence of such ancient forms of religious experience in the modern world can testify more to the desperate nature of the spiritual crisis rather than the active work of the devil. Even the devil can certainly think up something new in two-thousand years.

Theologies come and go. Black theology apparently attempts to interpret the black experience in American society in religious terms. Carl McIntyre, a right-wing Christian, sponsors rallies in the nation's capital extolling the Christian virtues of killing one's enemies. Women's theologies, gay theologies, frontier theologies, and especially athletic theologies abound. At what point does America echo the plaintive cry of the Boston policeman who was assigned to guard Cox's Easter celebration, "This is not religion, it is chaos."

It is chaos. The world in which Christianity arose no longer exists in its social and political sense. Even the world in which most of today's theologians grew to adulthood no longer exists. The old certainties have become stumbling blocks and the question is not whether one can make Christianity relevant in the modern world. The question is whether the modern world can have any valid religious experiences or knowledge whatsoever. The traditional assumption that Christianity represented the highest form of evolved religion can no longer be considered valid. Nor can the contention that it is the revealed truth of God, perhaps the only revealed truth.

The majority of Christian leaders today do not derive their

claim to the office of religious leader from their ability to project spiritual values. More often they have been educated and trained to assume the reins of church leadership. Or they have attracted large followings by simplifying the nature of religion into four spiritual principles or other formulas that are eagerly sought by people as a divine form of life insurance. The old charisma that attached to the truly religious man has been negated by the rapid pace of the modern world and is an extreme rarity today.

Instead of observing other religions and finding that they are "close" to Christianity, Christians would be wise to begin a search for religious experience and certainty itself regardless of the consequences. If there is no means by which the modern world can come into religious integrity, we should accept our condition and shoulder our responsibility of humane treatment of one another as victims of an incomprehensible universe. But if we find our way religiously we should have the courage to accept the revelation that comes and live in the manner it commands us.

In 1972, when I was writing the first version of this book, I made a deliberate effort to keep track of the nonsensical things that were being promulgated about contemporary American Christianity. I do regret that I did not continue to keep a clippings file on the antics of American Christianity during the past two decades. The ridiculous and the sublime have manifested themselves in such amusing ways that an update of this chapter would have been a delightfully funny writing assignment. However, most people know of the developments in the recent past when several televangelists quarreled as their audiences and contributions began to wane, and we saw revelations of unsuspected proportions regarding their sexual and financial adventures.

Oral Roberts, of course, topped the list of nonsense when he announced that God was trying to extort several million dollars from him. I was tempted at the time to announce that I also had spoken with God, that he was mightily displeased with Oral and distrusted his stewardship, and wanted everyone to send their contributions to me. Unfortunately, I had another agenda at the time, but it would have been fun.

The rise of New Age spiritualism has most definitely intruded into the behavior patterns of contemporary Christianity. Hardly a day goes by that my work is not interrupted by a renegade Protestant minister who wants me to send him to an Indian medicine man for spiritual counseling or by the news that some Christian church is now vesting its bishops and pastors in buckskins and feathers or purchasing crystals for its rituals. Groups of American Indians have now made presentations at most of the Christian church national meetings and given their version of the reverence for nature. And a considerable number of Christian clergy have tried to do some version of the sweat lodge or vision quest.

All of these things, taken together, make it seem as if we are now approaching a time when a new kind of religion will make itself manifest to us. If we view all of this struggling for meaning in a world in which institutions and beliefs are rapidly eroding, then it seems likely that people are merely sorting out the correlation between beliefs and experiences. Thus the religions that depend on the articulation of doctrinal propositions to maintain themselves are doomed to disappear beneath their own silliness. Those religious traditions that depend primarily upon invoking some kind of experience that is qualitatively distinct from everyday feelings will become the vehicles for religious expression in the future. All of this is to say that we will continue to see unqualified nonsense as the major product of the Christian churches; Jimmy and Tammy Faye Bakker are only the first of the clowns to enter the arena.

Notes

These anecdotes derive from the late 1960s and early 1970s and represent the ludicrous nature of religion when it is tied so intimately to a popular culture. The antics of Christians, particularly televangelists, became so outrageous that I stopped keeping newspaper clippings of their activities. It is my opinion that popular American Christianity is the greatest of all blasphemies in world history. To imply, as we so often do, that the Creator and sustainer of the whole cosmos has an intimate interest in who wins our sports championships or that He/She/They devote a considerable amount of time in bringing us riches, social status, and sexual pleasures is about as obscene as it can get. What is so amazing, however, is our total inability to look at ourselves critically and devise some minimum standard of decency that we attribute to our society and our deity.

CHAPTER 14

TRIBAL RELIGIONS AND CONTEMPORARY AMERICAN CULTURE

W̶e have seen some examples of the deviations created in religious behavior when a culture defines a religion. In a great many areas, tribal religion defined culture. This aspect of Indian life can be seen fairly clearly in the speeches and attitudes of the old chiefs and warriors. Their refusal to consider land as a commodity to be sold and their insistence that the lands held a great and sacred place in their hearts and the hearts of their people must be understood in its context of the last century, when they faced the momentous decisions of giving up some of their lands in an effort to preserve the remainder of it for themselves and their children.

There can be no doubt that not only times have changed but also cultures since the white man first set foot on the continent. Tribal cultures have shifted to confront the changes forced on the people by the tidal wave of white settlement. The recent Indian activist movement has attempted to recoup the lost ground and return to the culture, outlook, and values of the old days. The fundamental question facing tribal religions is whether the old days can be relived— whether, in fact, the very existence of an Indian community in the modern electronic world does not require a massive task of relating traditional religious values and beliefs to the phenomena presenting themselves.

One small example might indicate the extent to which this problem is a daily irritation to Indian people. In some of the traditional pueblos, modern conveniences are rejected, even electricity. The children of the pueblo attend the public school system, however, and have become accustomed to having cold milk. For the children to have cold milk at home, the pueblo must install electricity. But this innovation will violate the people's religious beliefs. A generation gap of no small distance emerges. What decision do the tribal elders make about the nature of the tribal religion and the demand of the little children for cold milk?

Again and again Indian people are faced with a puzzling unveiling of the distinctions between the Western Christian world and themselves. Sacred bundles of the tribe reside in the state museum; for centuries they were revered by the people, serving to focus their attentions on their religious experience as a people. During the period of religious oppression, the government forbade the practice of Indian religions, and one day the sacred bundle was given or sold to the museum or stolen from the tribe. Everyone had given up on the idea that they would ever again be allowed to practice their own religion, and the sacred bundles were considered as the remaining artifacts of paganism. In a scene being played out across the country today the younger people of the tribe, trying to revive the tribal religion, need the sacred bundles. An old man has been found who has preserved the tribal religion. He is old, and unless he can train the young, the religion will be lost. What can be done? The sacred bundles are no longer in Indian hands. Do we storm the museum? Will the whites understand why we need the sacred bundles back?

We have been taught to look at American history as a series of land transactions involving some three hundred Indian tribes and a growing U.S. government. This conception is certainly the picture that emerges when tribal officials are forced to deal with federal officials, claims commissioners, state highway departments, game wardens, county sheriffs, and private corporations. Yet it is hardly the whole picture. Perhaps nearly as accurate would be the picture of settlement phrased as a continuous conflict of two mutually exclusive religious

views of the world. The validity of these two religious views is yet to
be determined. One, Christianity, appears to be in its death throes. The
other, the tribal religion, is attempting to make a comeback in a world
is as different from the world of its origin as the present world is
different from the world of Christian origins. Can tribal religions
survive? Can they even make a comeback?

Even where the two religious systems have clashed, the
picture is not clear as to villain and hero. Father A. M. Beede, a
missionary to the Sioux at Fort Yates, North Dakota, told Seton, "I am
convinced now that the Medicine Lodge of the Sioux is a true Church
of God, and we have no right to stamp it out."[1] Yet they did try to stamp
it out while recognizing the wrong they were doing.

Some Christian missionaries successfully bridged the cultural gap and became more important to the tribes than most of their
own members. The Reverend Samuel Worcester, a missionary to the
Cherokees in the 1830s, remained a faithful friend to the tribe in
defiance of the State of Georgia. He persisted in his recognition of the
Cherokees as a people, following their cultural development, obeying
their laws, and giving continual assistance. For his loyalty he was
imprisoned by Georgia, and his appeal for release was heard in the U.S.
Supreme Court in the famous case *Worcester v. Georgia*[2] in which Chief
Justice John Marshall gave the definitive statement on the status of
Indian tribes under the Constitution.

At the opposite end of the spectrum is the Reverend John M.
Chivington, an infamous Methodist minister from Denver, Colorado.
Chivington served briefly as a colonel in the Colorado Volunteers
during the Civil War. Finding no Johnny Rebs to fight, he turned his
attentions to the Indians. He planned, led, justified, and celebrated the
massacre at Sand Creek, Colorado, in an unexpected dawn attack on a
friendly band of Cheyenne and Arapaho Indians in which hundreds of
helpless people were needlessly slaughtered. The actions of the Colorado
Volunteers remain, even today, as one of the most barbaric examples
of human behavior.

Between these two extremes are hundreds of cases of Christian people who reflected well both their religious beliefs and their
cultural values in their relationships with Indians. Some were staunch
defenders of the tribes they knew; others behaved in a rigid, authori-

tarian manner without a trace of human feeling. In fairness one cannot judge the religion of the whites as either good or bad when it came into contact with the tribal religions, only that no consistent set of values ever emerged as peculiarly and gloriously Christian.

After four centuries of pressure and religious imperialism, many tribal religions disappeared. Some disappeared because the tribes were destroyed or were reduced to such few members that the survivors, dropping their own religion, joined larger tribes and accepted the practices of the host tribe. It has only been in fairly recent times that a number of religions have emerged that cross tribal lines. Foremost of these has been the Native American Church, which uses peyote in its ceremonies. Although universally respected among Indians, the Native American Church has come afoul of the drug laws of the various states and now faces severe repression. Oppression of the people who use peyote sacramentally, connecting them with the drug war, is ludicrous. Very few people belong to the Native American Church and its services are always held in the most isolated locations and attended by a handful of people. Traffic in peyote is almost nonexistent, and it has been used successfully in helping Indians escape from alcoholism. But it is, culturally and theologically, foreign to American culture and consequently is seen as a threat to social stability.

The establishment of reservations generally involved the creation of mission stations at agency headquarters. Some of the treaties gave the missionaries lands on which they promised to build schools, houses for teachers, hospitals, and farms. The tribes failed in many cases to appreciate that allowing the missionaries to enter the tribal lands would inevitably result in religious conflict and dissension among tribal members. We have already seen how Chief Joseph refused to have missionaries around fearing that they would teach the people to quarrel about God.

As the reservations became more permanent, the churches devoted themselves wholeheartedly to converting the people. Religious controversies increased, and missionaries soon became one of the most vocal forces in demanding that tribal political activity be suppressed because it was apparent to them that the religious and political forms of tribal life could not be separated. Soon plans were underfoot to ban tribal religious ceremonies. The ignorance of the

Indian agents assisted the missionaries in their endeavors because they interpreted any Indian ceremonial as a war dance.

By the time of the Allotment Act of 1887 (Dawes Act), almost every form of Indian religion was banned on the reservations. In the schools the children were punished for speaking their own language. Anglo-Saxon customs were made the norm for Indian people; their efforts to maintain their own practices were frowned on, and stern measures were taken to discourage them from continuing tribal customs. Even Indian funeral ceremonies were declared to be illegal, and drumming and any form of dancing had to be held for the most artificial of reasons.

The record of Indian resistance is admirable. When people saw that they could no longer practice their ceremonies in peace, they sought subterfuge in performing certain of the ceremonies. Choosing an American holiday or Christian religious day when the whites would themselves be celebrating, traditional Indians often performed their ceremonies "in honor of" George Washington or Memorial Day, thus fulfilling their own religious obligations while white bystanders glowed proudly to see a war dance or rain dance done on their behalf. The Lummi Indians from western Washington, for example, continued some of their tribal dances under the guise of celebrating the signing of their treaty. The Plains Indians eagerly celebrated the Fourth of July because it meant that they could often perform Indian dances and ceremonies by pretending to celebrate the signing of the Declaration of Independence.

In 1934 under the Indian Reorganization Act, Indian people were finally allowed religious freedom. The missionaries howled in protest, but the ban on Indian religious ceremonies was lifted. Traditional Indians could no longer be placed in prison for practicing old tribal ways. Ceremonies began to be practiced openly, and there were still enough older Indians alive that a great deal of tribal religious traditions were regained. The great Black Elk, today perhaps the best remembered of the Sioux holy men, was still alive in 1934. It is said that he had frequent conferences with the holy men from other parts of the tribe living on different reservations.

For several decades the tribal religions held their own in competition with the efforts of the Christian missionaries. But a whole new generation had grown up, educated in mission and government schools and living according to the bureaucrats' dictates; these young Indians rigorously rejected old religious activities as a continuation of paganism. Yet as more Indians went off the reservation, went to war, attended college, and lived in the cities, the situation began to change. The Indian people had always been somewhat in awe of Western technology. It seemed to imply that their god was more powerful than their tribal religions and medicine. The great expansion of the American Indian horizon in the 1950s had a tremendous effect on attitudes toward tribal religions, which provided a very important link with the tribal past. Often through healing ceremonies performed by the holy people of the tribe, sicknesses were cured that urban white doctors could not cure. In one decade many American Indians began to see that whites and their Christian religion had fatal flaws.

In the last several decades tribal religions have seen a renewal that astounds many people. The Pueblos of New Mexico and the Navajos of Arizona managed to retain much of their ceremonial life throughout the period of religious suppression. The Hopi in particular preserved many of their ceremonies with relative purity. The Apaches also kept a number of their tribal ceremonies. In the Northwest some of the tribes kept their ceremonies by holding them in secret on the isolated reservations lacking sufficient federal resident staff to prohibit them. These tribes quite frankly continued their ceremonies by making them once again a total community affair to which everyone was expected to come.

Other tribes have experienced an increasing interest recently as specific ceremonies become the objects of people's affection. Naming ceremonies in some tribes have become more numerous as urban Indians seeking a means of preserving an Indian identity within the confusion of the city have asked reservation people to sponsor naming ceremonies for them. They travel sometimes thousands of miles and spend thousands of dollars to be able to participate in such events.

Religious conflict has become pronounced on some reservations as Christian Indians have had to make room for traditional Indians in tribal affairs. The continuous conflict on the St. Regis Mohawk Reservation in upstate New York is a classic example of such strife. For nearly two centuries the Roman Catholic church dominated the affairs of the Mohawks who remained on this side of the border after the Revolutionary War. Edmund Wilson recounts how he visited a cemetery where many of the Christian Mohawks sat silently in the night, listening to the songs and activities of the traditional Mohawks being held a short distance away. Such was the overt situation until recently.

In 1972 open conflict broke out at St. Regis as the impending wave of traditionalism threatened the political stability of a few figurehead Christian Mohawks who had been dominating tribal affairs for nearly a generation. The largest Indian newspaper in North America, *Akwesasne Notes*, operated by traditional Mohawks on a sharing-the-cost-by-contribution basis, was harassed continuously. Questions were raised about whether Canadian Mohawks and their adopted friends should be allowed to live on the reserve. The fundamental question was that of defining contemporary Mohawk culture and outlook. The traditionals appeared to be strongly appealing to the rest of the people. In 1989 and 1990 violence broke out in Mohawk country as traditional people attempted to forestall the installation of gambling on their reservations. Both the Canadian and U.S. governments were placed in a difficult situation because it appeared as if tribal sovereignty and the viability of the tribal government was at stake. There is no question that the traditional Mohawks held the high moral ground, but there was also the difficulty of recognizing the informal, traditional government because it would not endorse the continued intrusions into community life that the organized tribal council condoned.

As tribal religions emerge and begin to attract younger Indians, problems of immense magnitude arise. Many people are trapped between tribal values constituting their unconscious behavioral responses and the values that they have been taught in schools and churches, which primarily demand conforming to seemingly foreign ideals. Alcoholism and suicide mark this tragic fact of reservation life. People are not allowed to be Indians and cannot become whites. They have been educated, as the old-timers would say, to think with their heads instead of their hearts.

Additional problems face any revival of tribal religions that originated in times when the tribes were small and compact. Whenever a band got too large to support itself and required a large game source to feed everyone, it simply broke into smaller bands of people. The two bands would remain in contact with each other. Often they would share war parties and ceremonials of some importance. At treaty signing times they would congregate and act as a national unit. Their primary characteristic, however, was their manageability. For political decisions, religious ceremonies, hunting and fishing activities, and general community life, both the political and religious outlook of the tribe, was designed for a small group of people. It was a rare tribal group that was larger than one thousand people for any extended period of time.

Today tribal membership is determined on quite a legalistic basis, which is foreign to the accustomed tribal way of determining its constituency. The property interests of descendants of the original enrollees or allottees have become determining factors in compiling tribal membership rolls. People of *small Indian blood quantum,* or those descended from people who were tribal members a century ago, are thus included in the tribal membership roll. Tribes can no longer form and reform on sociological, religious, or cultural bases. They are restricted in membership by federal officials responsible for administering trust properties who demand that the rights of every person be respected whether or not that person presently appears in an active and recognized role in the tribal community. Indian tribal membership today is a fiction created by the federal government, not a creation of the Indian people themselves.

In the 1860s the Navajo bands who were gathered up and marched to New Mexico to be imprisoned by Kit Carson numbered somefour thousand people. The basis of their unity as a people was similarity of language and occupation in a commonly defined area. It was not a political unity. When they were returned to Arizona and given a reservation in the most desolate part of the state, they then fictionally became a distinct tribe, although they had previously composed several distinct independent bands. Today that same tribe numbers close to 200,000 people. The Navajo have not had sufficient time to develop an expanded religious or political structure to account for this tremendous population explosion.

The Oglala Sioux once formed a large-numbered tribe but one that was dominated by a series of brilliant and charismatic chiefs such as Red Cloud, Crazy Horse, American Horse, Standing Bear, and

Little Wound. They had a number of bands virtually acting indepen-dently of each other. Thus Crazy Horse and his people spent most of their time in Montana with the Cheyennes fighting Custer while Red Cloud and his people were living in South Dakota several hundred miles away from that area. It would have been absurd for Red Cloud to have signed a treaty for the Oglala Sioux without having Crazy Horse and the other chiefs also signing for the tribe.

Today the Oglala Sioux number at least fifteen thousand people, perhaps twenty thousand. A substantial number live off the reservation and participate only sporadically in community life. Yet the people must find a way to define what it means to be an Oglala Sioux in today's world. When such a process is rigidly controlled by federal officials fearful that the Sioux may gain control over their lives, then incidents such as the confrontation at Wounded Knee in 1973 are inevitable.

While the AIM received a lion's share of the publicity at Wounded Knee, it was merely the external symbolic group of which the public was made aware. AIM had been asked to come to the reservation to mount the protest by members of the Oglala Sioux Civil Rights Association, a group formed a year earlier to protest conditions on the reservation brought about by the tribal council's refusal to guarantee civil rights to individual Indians. Cooperating with the two groups was the Black Hills Treaty Rights Council. This council was composed of the elder traditional leaders on the reservation who had tried to preserve the older form of tribal political organization. They had been working all their lives to see that the federal government fulfills its commitments to the Oglalas as promised in the Treaty of 1868 and the Agreement of 1876.

The situation was further complicated by two other organi-zations supporting the protest. One, the Landowner's Association, was composed of individual Indians who owned allotments of land and wished to use their lands in community cooperatives to form grazing units for the local communities. The BIA, with the concurrence of the tribal council, had placed their lands in larger grazing units and leased these large units to white cattle ranchers. The individual Indians were thus deprived of the use of their lands and were given small rental checks by the federal government. They were kept in a perpetual state of poverty while the white ranchers enjoyed the benefits of economic prosperity during the great rise in the price of beef.

The fourth group involved in the protest was the Inter-District Council. As the conditions on the reservation grew worse during 1972, the people of the different reservation districts formed their own shadow government known as the Inter-District Council. They had representatives from every one of the eight districts on the reservation and were discussing ways to get a federal law passed to give the people of the local communities political control over their lives through a new constitution. Naturally the existing tribal council and the BIA were violently opposed to such a reform because it would have unseated the tribal council and reduced the power of the bureaucrats. During the Wounded Knee confrontation the Inter-District Council tried desperately to get the federal government to understand how the conditions on the reservation had led to the protest and how the protest could be peacefully resolved.

Perhaps the most important aspect of the Wounded Knee protest was that the holy men of the tribe and the traditional chiefs all supported the AIM activists and younger people on the issues that they were raising. Some people were fearful of the violence that threatened their lives, but the strong ceremonial life and the presence of medicine men in the Wounded Knee compound diffused a great deal of the criticism that would have been forthcoming from members of the other Indian tribes. No Indian could keep up a sustained criticism of the confrontation upon knowing that the people at Wounded Knee had their sacred pipes and that the medicine men from both the Pine Ridge and the neighboring Rosebud Sioux reservations were performing the ceremonies.

The Wounded Knee protest was dreaded by Indians but it was not unexpected. The federal government had taken the original rolls of the allotment period and insisted that the descendants of those original allottees be considered members of the tribe whether they had sufficient Indian blood to qualify for membership or whether they lived in the communities on the reservation. The internal social mechanisms that ordinarily would have operated to define community membership were forbidden by federal law—if they operated, they were given no legal status or recognition.

We have just begun to see the revival of Indian tribal religions at a time when the central value of Indian life—its land—is under incredible attack from all sides. Tribal councils are strapped for funds to solve pressing social problems. Leasing and development of tribal lands is a natural source of good income. But leasing of tribal lands involves selling the major object of tribal religion for funds to solve problems that are ultimately religious in nature. The best example of this dilemma is the struggle over the strip-mining at Black Mesa on the Navajo and Hopi reservations. Traditional Indians of both tribes are fighting desperately against any additional strip-mining of the lands. Tribal councils are continuing to lease the lands for development to encourage employment and to make possible more tribal programs for the rehabilitation of the tribal members.

A substantial portion of every tribe remains solidly within the Christian tradition by having attended mission schools. They grew up in a period of time when any mention of tribal religious beliefs was forbidden, and they have been taught that Indian values and beliefs are superstitions and pagan beliefs that must be surrendered before they can be truly civilized. They stand, therefore, in much the same relationship to the tribal religion as educated, liberals now stand to the Christian and Jewish religions. Both groups have lost their faith in the mysterious, the transcendent, the communal nature of religious experience. They depend on a learned set of ethical principles to maintain some semblance of order in their lives.

A great many Indians reflect the same religious problem as do the young whites who struggled through the last several decades of social disorder. They are somehow forced to hold in tension beliefs that are not easily reconciled. They have learned that some things are true because they have experienced them, that others are true because everyone seems to agree that they are true, and that some things are insoluble and cannot be solved by any stretch of the imagination.

One of the primary aspects of traditional tribal religions has been the secret ceremonies, particularly the vision quests, the fasting in the wilderness, and the isolation of the individual for religious purposes. This type of religious practice is nearly impossible today. The places currently available to people for vision quests are hardly isolated. Jet planes pass overhead. Some traditional holy places are the scene of strip-mining, others are adjacent to superhighways, others are parts of ranches, farms, shopping centers, and national parks and forests. The struggle of the Taos people to get their sacred Blue Lake away from the Department of Agriculture indicates the tenuous nature of some tribal religious practices in a world of complicated transportation services and radio and television.

If modern conditions were not sufficient to prevent the continuance of traditional ceremonies, the U.S. Supreme Court has made it almost impossible to perform some ceremonies on federal lands. In 1988 in *Lyng v. Northwest Indian Cemetery Protective Association*,[3] the Court dealt with the question of whether the Forest Service could construct a 6-mile segment of road for the convenience of the logging industry in the high country of Northern California where the Yurok and Karok tribes traditionally conducted religious ceremonies. Relying on the American Indian Religious Freedom Resolution, the Indian demonstrated to the Forest Service and to the lower courts that to construct the road would damage the traditional religion beyond repair. Yet the Court turned away their argument noting that it could not order the government to protect a religion of this kind. The majority decision compared it to a sudden rush of religious feeling by someone who had gazed upon the Lincoln Memorial, a dreadful and perhaps deliberate misunderstanding of the religious principles involved.

Education itself is a barrier to a permanent revival of tribal religions. Young people on reservations have available an increasingly complicated educational system. Perhaps like conservative Christians, older Indians see the educational system as basically godless and tending to destroy communities rather than create them. As more Indians fight their way through the education system in search of job skills, their education will increasingly concentrate on the tangible and technical aspects of contemporary society and away from the sense of wonder and mystery that has traditionally characterized religious experiences. In almost the same way that young whites have rejected religion once they have made strides in education, young Indians who have received solid educations have rejected traditional religious experiences. Education and religion apparently do not mix.

Tribal religions thus face the task of entrenching themselves in a contemporary Indian society that is becoming increasingly accustomed to the life-style of contemporary America. While traditional Indians speak of a reverence for the earth, Indian reservations continue to pile up junk cars and beer cans at an alarming rate. While traditional Indians speak of sharing the structure of jobs, insurance, and tribal politics, education prohibits a realistic sharing. To survive, people must in effect feed off one another, not share with each other.

In the old days leadership depended on the personal prestige of the people whom the community chose as its leaders. Their generosity, service to the community, integrity, and honesty had to be above question. Today tribal constitutions define who shall represent the tribe in its relationships with the outside world. No quality is needed to assume leadership except the ability to win elections. Consequently tribal elections have become one of the dirtiest forms of human activity in existence. Corruption runs rampant during tribal elections, and people deliberately vote in scoundrels over honest people for the personal benefits they can receive. Much of the formal resistance to federal programs for increasing tribal independence comes from the Indian people's mistrust of their own leadership, present and future. Many tribes want the tribal lands and assets so restricted that no one can use them to the tribe's detriment—or benefit.

One of the greatest hindrances to the reestablishment of tribal religions is the failure of Indian people to understand their own history. The period of cultural oppression in its severest form (1887–1934) served to create a collective amnesia in contemporary people. Too many Indians look backward to the treaties, neglecting the many laws and executive orders that have come to define their lives in the period since their first relationship with the United States was formed. Tribal people are in the unenviable position of dealing with problems the origins of which remain obscured to them.

The disruptions of tribal religions for a period of fifty years have resulted in the loss of a well-accepted recent tradition of ceremonies, religious leaders, and other ongoing developments characterizing a living religion. Contemporary efforts to reestablish tribal religions have come at too rapid a rate to be absorbed on many reservations. In some instances ceremonials are considered part of the tribal social identity rather than religious events. This attitude undercuts the original function of the ceremony and prevents people from reintegrating community life on a religious basis.

Most tribal religions, as we have seen, have not felt that history is an important aspect of religious life. Today as changes continue to occur in tribal peoples, the immediate past history of the group is vitally important in maintaining the nature of the ceremonies. The necessary shift in emphasis to a more historical approach can be seen in the various Indian studies programs that have attempted to fill in the missing tribal history. Indian tribal religions thus find themselves in the position of earlier Christian communities that were forced to derive historical interpretations to account for unfulfilled prophecies.

We may find the incongruous situation of many Indian people leaving Christianity to return to traditional religions, creating a tribal history to solve social problems, and falling into the historical trap that has plagued Christianity. It would seem that history itself is a deceremonial process that continues to strip away the mystery of human existence and replace it with intellectual propositions. As the mainstream of Christianity begins to face ecology and the problems inherent in its traditional doctrine of creation, tribal religions are running the risk of abandoning the traditional Indian concerns about the creation in favor of a more historical and intellectual religion.

Tribal religions in the old days did not create an external ethical system. Cultural considerations involving total tribal life enabled people to merge all societal functions into a unity from which all forms of behavior derived. With tribal members spread across the country today and the conditions on the reservations subject to radical shifting at every change of federal policy, there is not that continuity of experience or homogeneous community of people present that would enable Indian people to avoid creating ethical systems based on traditional values.

The closest parallel that we find in history to the present condition of Indians is the Diaspora of the Jews following the destruction of the temple. A surprising number of Indian activists have made this comparison without considering that the exile of the Jews was for a significant period of time and that the Jewish people almost immediately developed a strong scholarly tradition to preserve their ceremonies and beliefs in exile. The Indian exile is in a sense more drastic. The people often live less than 100 miles away from their traditional homelands; yet in the relative complexities of reservation and urban life, they might be two thousand or more years apart. It is not simply a spatial separation that has occurred but a temporal one as well.

Many traditional leaders have recognized this problem. In the 1970s an intertribal ecumenical council was formed to meet every summer to discuss ways of keeping the people focused on the nature of tribal religions and their meaning for the future of the tribes. The ecumenical council met most often on reserves in Canada because the Canadian Indians seemed more perceptive in defining the problem of reviewing the traditional way. In the summer of 1972 some five hundred people attended the sessions. The number of participants grew each year until it was apparent that the gatherings had deteriorated into pleasant sessions of reviewing the past because people were unwilling to forge into the future. Then the council ceased to exist.

One of the chief past functions of tribal religions was to perform healing ceremonies. This function was impaired by lack of any rights to train new people to perform the ceremonies and a general lessening of dependence on tribal medicine men because of the presence of Public Health Service hospitals on the larger reservations. Indian healers were generally considered as superstitious magicians by the missionaries and government officials, and healing arts were lost in many tribes.

Today healing remains one of the major strengths of tribal religions. Christian missionaries are unable to perform comparable healing ceremonies, and a great many still regard Indian healers as fakers and charlatans. This particular field is thus open for Indian religious figures who have received particular healing powers, and traditional healing ceremonies are being recognized by the Public Health Service as competent complementary healing practices. Some special grants have been given to train more healers and shamans and to have them work closely with doctors trained in internal medicine.

The modern world has lost a large number of healing medicines because of the arbitrary rejection of Indian religions. Some tribes had special roots and herbs that had amazing properties. Only a few have remained in use in some tribes while the vast majority have been lost for a number of reasons. Restriction of Indian people to the reservations has meant that long trips to particular places to gather specific kinds of roots and herbs have stopped. Gradually people have forgotten which plants were used for what purpose. As the older people have died off knowledge about a substantial number of medicinal plants has also been lost.

The great orgasm of dam building that hit the West following World War II also destroyed a number of Indian medicines. The
dams flooded the smaller creek and river bottom lands where many
plants grew, leaving only the higher reservation land above water.
Even those plants and herbs that had been remembered and used
regularly by the people were thus sometimes lost because the places
where they grew were under water. A comparable situation exists on
the land that has been reduced to farmland from its original state. Some
medicinal plants grew wild on certain parts of the prairie or in certain
places in the forests. The prairie in large part has now been reduced to
erosion-ridden wheat and corn fields, and in most places the forests
have given way to farmlands and cities.

When one remembers that a substantial number of people of
each tribe lives in urban areas away from the reservation, the problems
faced by Indian healers come into sharper focus. Only rather hopeless
cases or those presenting an extreme problem will reach traditional Indian
healers from people outside the reservation. The task of healing will thus
take on an Oral Roberts dimension in the future. People will indeed expect
miracles. Unless there is a determined effort to gather individual knowledge of healing plants, herbs, and earths as well as a general acceptance of
the necessity of rebuilding tribal use of healing people, the impact of
healing on Indian religions will continue to decline in spite of temporary
successes. Perhaps religious healing will lose validity as a ceremonial
experience in another generation.

A counterpart of the healing ceremonies are the rites performed by the religious practitioners that allow them to predict the
future in part or in whole, to give advice on courses of action, and to
give general advice and admonitions on a variety of subjects. Divination and foretelling the future were once major parts of religion; with
the coming of Christianity, they appear to have lost their respectability.
The result of this loss has been the survival of astrology, fortune-telling
through cards, and the use of the I Ching in recent years in Western
civilization. Discovering the future was once a major function of tribal
religious leaders. It remains today as one of the major strengths of
traditional religious people.

In the last two decades traditional healers have significantly
increased the scope and depth of their ability to foretell the future. The

impending earth catastrophes are appearing more and more in these rituals and this prospect had meant a great increase in the number of Indians returning to traditional ways. Unlike some Western efforts to predict specific personal fortunes, the information received by Indian religious leaders generally describes situations and conditions that are likely to come to pass, given existing circumstances. There is a sophisticated principle of probability here reminiscent of modern explanations of modern physics. So this aspect of tribal religion bears watching and reflection.

One can hardly speculate on either the problems or the changes this field will experience in the immediate future. The most important aspect that stands out is the insufficient number of people who can perform this special function. In many tribes it is a power given to people only after special ceremonies have been undertaken, and it is a power not always given. It would seem to be a gift most urgently needed by Indian people, as decisions of crucial importance are being forced on Indian people daily, particularly on tribal governments. Yet one can be forewarned and do nothing as Julius Caesar did. Learning the future will receive a great impetus if some of the present predictions do come to pass. The big danger is that this gift, which must remain a property of the Indian community, may become part of the popular New Age activities and the Indian religious leaders will lose this talent by secularizing it.

The rapid expansion of the New Age physic phenomena has been unusually detrimental to traditional religions. Non-Indians can pay very attractive fees to Indian shamans, and there has been a good deal of pressure on traditional healers to spend their time working with non-Indians and neglecting their own communities. Unfortunately there have also been an unusual number of Indian fakers who have invaded suburbia offering to perform ceremonies, primarily sweat lodges, for anyone with the money to pay. A regular circuit has been established that these people tour in search of gullible whites. It should be clear to non-Indians that if shamans really had significant powers, they would obtain these powers through constant ceremonial practice in their homeland, and they would not be out hustling the workshop circuits. But the hunger for some kind of religious experience is so great that whites shown no critical analysis when approaching alleged Indian religious figures.

A warning light should flash when the Indian practitioners say that their elders told them to go out into the world and teach the traditional ceremonies. If one were to gather the great number of Indians now alleging this divine commission and listen to their patter, it would be clear that they all spent their childhood in the wilderness with traditional people who had never seen whites and they learned secrets that had been hidden for thousands of years. It would be exceedingly interesting to compare this roster with tribal employment rolls of two decades ago because a good many of the names would be the same. Yet this alleged background is so irresistible to many whites that, even what blatant frauds are exposed, most of them cling to the belief that they have met a real, traditional Indian.

The situation, however, is far from hopeless. On the reservations we are seeing amazing resiliency in restoring the old ceremonies. A massive shift in allegiance is occurring in most tribes away from Christianity and secularism and back towards the traditional ways. A surprisingly high percentage of Native American clergy are also doing traditional ceremonies and urban area churches are often the scene of traditional healing ceremonies. The Native American clergy are to be congratulated for their efforts to bring the two religious traditions together, but it is clear that no synthesis will take place. In almost every instance the effect of merging the two traditions is to bring attention to traditional ways to the detriment of the particular Christian denomination. The result is that the semblance of a national Indian religion is being born that incorporates major Indian themes. As people are sensitized to this new religious milieu, being dissatisfied with the lack of specificity in this religious activity, they return to the more precise practices of their own tribes. Thus, it appears that traditional religions in some form will transcend the inroads that contemporary American culture has made.

Notes

1. Ernest Thompson Seton, *The Gospel of the Red Man* (New York: Doubleday Doran, 1936).
2. 6 Pet. 515 (1832)
3. 485 U.S. 439 (1988)

CHAPTER 15

THE ABORIGINAL WORLD AND CHRISTIAN HISTORY

Had the world been a three-story finite universe, the Christian doctrine of history might have maintained itself and been a valid consideration of modern people. The simple story of humankind growing out of the Garden of Eden and populating the world might have been sufficient for all people in their own times. The world did not remain as the early prophets conceived it. By 300 B.C. Alexander the Great had shown the Near Eastern peoples the wonders of India. Explorations by Europeans over a one-thousand-year period indicated that the globe was much larger than the writer of Genesis had figured. Columbus demonstrated that it was indeed a globe.

The trauma of discovery of the New World for the Christian theologians was immense. It had not yet been adequately understood by them. What were devout thinkers to make of the existence of millions of people living on lands larger than Europe? What was their status with respect to Christianity—the one true religion? Did God have a purpose for these people? Could Jesus return until all of these nations had been preached the gospel? What was the responsibility of God's chosen nations in the face of this revelation of the tremendous scope of humankind?

The reaction of the Christian nations to the discovery of the New World and its potential riches was one of unmitigated greed. Having been repulsed by the Muslims in their efforts to subjugate the Near East and nearly prostrated after the wars to establish the divine-right monarchies, the kings of Europe badly needed an inexhaustible source of income to maintain themselves. Visualizing a steady stream of wealth from the Indies, which would allow them to avoid giving political rights and economic benefits to the rising commercial classes in return for financial support to the crown, the heads of the European states saw in the New World the only hope of maintaining themselves.

The Christian church was also eager to exploit the new lands. Its political power beginning to wane with the rise of strong European political leaders, the Christian church saw a means of directing the invasion of the new lands by placing its imprimatur on exploitation, in effect taking a percentage of the loot in return for blessing the enterprise. In 1493 Pope Alexander VI issued his *Inter Caetera* bull, which laid down the basic Christian attitude toward the New World: "Among other works well pleasing to the Divine Majesty and cherished of our heart, this assuredly ranks highest, that in our times especially the Catholic faith and the Christian religion be exalted and everywhere increased and spread, that the health of souls be cared for and that barbarous nations be overthrown and brought to the faith itself."[1]

What this pious language meant in practical terms was that if confiscation of lands were couched in quasi-religious sentiments, the nations of Europe could proceed. In an immensely practical gesture the pope noted that he did thereby "give, grant, and assign forever to you and your heirs and successors, kings of Castile and Leon, all singular the aforesaid countries and islands ...hitherto discovered ... and to be discovered ...together with all their dominions, cities, camps, places, and villages, and all rights, jurisdictions, and appurtenances of the same."[2]

The lands and villages were not, of course, the pope's to give, unless the understanding of the universe, history, and the planet promulgated by Christianity were correct. If such were the case then it would have followed that, the entire planet being a franchise of the Holy Father, he could distribute it to whomever he found in need of rewarding. Regardless of the later totally secular exploitations of the native peoples conducted by the secular governments of Europe, this papal bull of 1493 marked the official attitude of Christianity toward peoples it had not previously thought to exist.

The controversy over the place of the newly discovered natives continued to rage, however, as more information on the New World was made available to the people of Europe. The Treaty of Tordesillas in the following year divided South America neatly between Spain and Portugal, allowing each primacy over portions of the continent that neither had explored or conquered. Plainly the pope was supervising not the divinely ordered division of the world's lands but national hunting licenses for rape and pillage.

The status of native peoples around the globe was firmly cemented by the intervention of Christianity into the political affairs of exploration and colonization. They were regarded as not having ownership of their lands, but as merely existing on them at the pleasure of the Christian God who had now given them to the nations of Europe. Upon encountering a tribe or nation of native peoples, the Spanish used to read their Requirement, which basically recited the Christian interpretation of history beginning with the Garden of Eden and ending with the pope enthroned in Rome. The natives were then asked to pledge their allegiance to the pope and the king of Spain. Failing to surrender to Christianity and the expanding Spanish empire meant that it was then legal and an act of religious piety for the Europeans to wage war to wrest the lands from the people.

Again the use of Christian doctrines served to justify the actions of the Christian nations. For centuries Christian theologians debated the conception of the nature of the "just war," in much the same manner as Protestant theologians used to debate the morality of killing people trying to get in your home bomb shelter during an atomic attack back in the days when America was paranoid over Russian missile attacks. The natives refusing to accept the gospel were thus made subjects of the just Christian war because they had refused to accept the truth that had been revealed some 1,500 years before.

As exploration and colonization continued, the debate expanded about the native peoples and their rights. The only available philosophical system purporting to explain the world of daily events was that of Aristotle, who had once divided mankind into men and slaves. The anti-Indian theologians relied heavily upon Aristotelian thinking to support their thesis that natives could be enslaved. Even pronative theologians admitted that the natives should be subjected to force until they were converted to the true faith.

In 1526 Francisco de Vitoria at Salamanca attacked the use of Aristotle to deny Indians of the New World their rights to property and liberty. Vitoria denied the right of the Christians to convert the natives forcibly because he was aware of the mistreatment that had been the lot of the natives resisting conversion. But he then justified conquest of the natives and their lands on the basis of Christian trade rights, finding that God had intended all nations to trade with one another. Any nation or group that prevented trade could then be conquered so that uninhibited trade might continue. Preventive conquest to protect commercial rights became the basis on which the Spanish and Portuguese made complete their mastery of the new lands and their peoples.

By 1550 two camps of theologians had developed, each with its own version of the legal and theological status of the peoples of the New World. Each theory, incidentally, led to justifying the exploitation and conquest. Father Bartolomé de Las Casas took the side of the natives, while Juan de Sepulveda took the opposing view and justified extinction and enslavement. Las Casas interpreted the Christian position and the 1493 papal bull as giving a right to Spain only to preach the Christian doctrine peaceably; the natives' existing property rights were to be recognized.

Sepulveda, a rigorous Aristotelian philosopher, simply classified the natives as among those who had been meant to be subjugated. Their opposition to Spanish enslavement was thus morally wrong because it violated the purpose for which God had intended the natives. For Sepulveda pure Christian chauvinism was the answer to the problems of the Old World meeting the New World. While he did not totally win the debate, his views were eagerly accepted by those Europeans going to the New World, thus winning his point in fact in what came after him.

By the time the other European nations got into the business of discovering lands and peoples in the Western Hemisphere, the struggle for recognition of native legal rights had for all practical purposes vanished. The European nations were more concerned with their wars for control of distant lands than acknowledging the rights of the peoples over whom they asserted control. The doctrine that the pope had been given total control over the planet by God was soon secularized into justification for European nations, definitively Christian, to conquer and subdue the peoples of the lands that they entered. Once the doctrine became secularized, it was impossible for anyone to question its validity; its impact was obvious and the results were satisfactory to European political heads of state.

Gradually, then, the colonizing European powers began to define their rights with respect to other nations of non-Christian peoples. The natives had rights to occupy the lands on which they had traditionally lived until such time as those lands were needed by the invading Europeans. At that time the European nation could extinguish the natives' title by purchase or conquest. With respect to each other, the European nations accepted the claims of the nation that first explored new lands and had sufficient military power to protect its claim. With respect to the natives who happened to occupy the lands, they were completely at the mercy of the acquisitive Christian nation.

The wars for control of the North American continent saw the claims of the various European nations dwindle as England consistently defeated the other nations and succeeded to their claims when each nation gave up its territory on the continent as part of the peace terms. While European wars raged among England, France, Spain, Holland, and other countries, the natives' legal rights were bounced back and forth as concessions were made in wars that had little to do with the people of the continent. England had no sooner achieved dominance in North America than the English colonists revolted against the mother country. Aided by France, which was still smarting over the defeat handed them by England a decade before, they succeeded in freeing themselves from English control.

Almost the first claim put forth by the new nation after the successful break with England was that the colonies had succeeded to the claims made by the mother country under the doctrine of Discovery. The United States was therefore under no obligation to deal justly with the continent's tribes. Rather it stood well within the tradition of Christian nations that had previously looted Central and South America and were then in the process of conquering India and Africa. The basic legal policy of the U.S. government became one of tentative recognition of the Indian interest in the land combined with the assertion that the lands could be taken from the people at any time they were needed by the federal government.

The first articulation of the Christian attitude toward the native peoples and their rights came in the Northwest Ordinance of 1787, in which the U.S. Congress proclaimed that it would never take the Indian lands except in just wars.[3] As it turned out, there were no just wars, and the lands were systematically taken. After a century of conflict and systematic oppression, the tribes were lucky to survive with a fragment of their former homelands as reservations for those who had not been killed.

The story is not simply that of the American Indians, however, because the history of Christian nations around the globe has been less than religious. England and France fought titanic struggles for control of the Indian subcontinent, for parts of Africa, and for trade rights in North Africa and Asia. As late as World War I nations were being given to dominant European nations as League of Nations "mandates" and "protectorates." Colonialism has still not vanished. It now shows itself as the American political crusade for a new world order or as the operational results of the giant supranational corporations of Western peoples. Western corporate imperialism so dominates the world scene it is easy to overlook Japan's taking sovereignty over a few islands.[4]

When Canada and Australia achieved independence from the British Crown, they allegedly stepped into the shoes of Queen Elizabeth II insofar as the natives of the lands were concerned. The queen had been the trustee for Indian lands in Canada, and a substantial portion of the Canadian lands had been held by the queen on behalf of the native Indian tribes. After the British North American Act, Canada refused to accept its responsibilities with respect to native land rights. Today the Canadian government still refuses to recognize the land titles of the Canadian Indian tribes. Thus, even the veneer of protection that aboriginal title has given to natives of the United States has been denied to Canadian Indians.

The aborigines of Australia are in worse shape. Because they are by definition without rights, they cannot enter the courts of that land to defend their rights to lands on which they have lived for thousands of years. Australia claims a legal right to the lands of the continent as derived from Great Britain, while denying the Australian aborigines the right to demand from the Australian government the protection in land occupancy such a derived title implies.

The South American countries make no bones about exterminating their Indians. Brazil has carried on systematic genocide against the interior native tribes for many years. The atrocities committed against these people have been well documented by numerous groups and promptly denied by Brazilian officials. Not the slightest pretense has been made that the natives could have any rights to land. They are simply moved or killed whenever land is needed by the Brazilian government. Almost all of the South American nations are predominantly Catholic and reflect the same attitude once promulgated by Sepulveda—some people are meant to be slaves and it is immoral for them to resist enslavement.

Even smaller nations that should have lands and rights protected have been denied any voice in the matter. Sweden moved into Lapland some centuries ago and now denies that the Lapps may have any rights in their own land. In a situation similar to Canada, changes in Swedish national law and status have erased any mention of the rights and property that the Lapps may have had. At present the Swedish government is busy finishing the cultural genocide of the Lapp or Same people through the travesty of court procedures that have already been arranged to divest the Lapps or any rights to their lands and national status.

The final arena of degradation is what is now known as the Trust Territories of the Pacific. During the period before World War II, Japan fortified those islands received as protectorates following World War I. As World War II got under way, the American forces invaded many of the islands Japan had occupied and many Japan had not occupied. As the war progressed a substantial number of peaceful islands got in the way of the two superpowers and were taken by one side or the other. The peaceful Pacific was soon divided between the United States and Japan.

After the Japanese surrender all the islands came under what may be euphemistically called a U.S. trust. That is to say, the

United States now holds the islands and will continue to do so until it feels like disposing of them. Little effort has been made to give the islands political freedom, and they are now being prepared for large excursions of affluent American tourists. The peaceful Pacific will shortly be America's vacationland, and its people will be servants to rich vacationing Americans. They will never receive even the degree of independence they enjoyed prior to World War II. Even worse, their lives are administered by the Department of the Interior, a bureaucracy hopelessly inept and unconcerned.

The responsibility of Christianity for this state of affairs must certainly be heavy. Without the initial Christian doctrines giving Europeans free reign over the rest of the world, much of the exploitation would not have occurred. It was only when people were able to combine Western greed with religious fanaticism that the type and extent of exploitation that history has recorded was made possible. Even today the Christian missionaries search the jungles of the Amazon looking for Indian tribes to convert. In their wake come the professional killers to exterminate the tribes, and following them the government bureaucracies, road builders, and land developers to subdue the lands of the interior for world commerce.

In almost every generation trade and conversion for religious purposes have gone hand in hand to destroy nations of the world on behalf of Western commercial interests and Christianity. Where the cross goes, there is never life more abundantly—only death, destruction, and ultimately betrayal. Among all the nations of the world the United States has created the best record in dealing with aboriginal peoples. The checks and balances of the American political system and the secular concern for justice have slowed the rate of exploitation of American Indians so that for many tribes at least a portion of legal status exists. The United States, for example, is the only nation to establish a claims commission to attempt to rectify treaty wrongs with the native inhabitants. Canada refuses to discuss such a commission; Australia loathes the suggestion.

Average Christians when hearing of the disasters wreaked on aboriginal peoples by their religion and its adherents are quick to state, "But the people who did this were not really Christians." In point of fact they really were Christians. In their day they enjoyed all the benefits and prestige Christendom could confer. They were cheered as heroes of the faith, enduring hardships that a Christian society might be built on the ruins of pagan villages. They were featured in Sunday school lessons as saints of the Christian church. Cities, rivers, mountains, and seas were named after them.

And if the exploiters of old were not Christians, why did not the true Christians rise up in defiance of the derogation of their religious heritage and faith? If the Prime Minister of Canada is today not Christian in his attitudes toward the Indians of Canada, where are the Christians in Canada who prophetically denounced his actions? If the leaders of the Brazilian government do not exercise Christian values, where are the Christians to disclaim their actions? If exploitation of the Amazon for commercial purposes by American investors results in the un-Christian activity of poisoning thousands of Indians, why are not the true Christians demanding the resignations of the heads of American corporations supporting Amazon development?

At this point in the clash between Western industrialism and the planet's aboriginal peoples we find little or no voice coming from the true Christians to prevent continued exploitation. Instead we find rhetorical assertions that the Christian God is controlling history and fulfilling His divine plan for all humankind. In the face of world events this assertion is fraudulent at best, an insult to the intelligence of humankind at worst. It is time to call a halt to the unchallenged assumptions of the Christian conception of history. This conception is even breaking apart in the national strongholds of Christianity.

The various tribal peoples of Europe that were bludgeoned into accepting supernationalism a century or more ago are flexing their muscles in resistance to continued oppression. The Irish, Welsh, and Celts are demanding freedom. In France the Bretons have a national movement, the Flemish are reviving their ancient customs, Italy is a virtual conglomerate rebelling at the continued supremacy of the national government. As we watched the Iron Curtain countries experience a general collapse of their economy and political institutions, the long-submerged ethnic minorities have begun to assert themselves once again. Even the horrific bloodshed in Serbia and Croatia testifies to the inability of the nation-state to deal realistically with ethnicity. Not only is Christian history at an end but quite possibly the end is in sight for its secular expansion—the manifest destiny of Europeans to rule the world.

The first step in this process of restitution should not be recitals by sincere followers of the Christian religion admitting their guilt for past wrongs. For example, we have already seen a multitude of tears fall over the demise of Dee Brown's Indians without a corresponding change in attitude or treatment of American Indians. Further confession of sins is useless and avoids the central question of history: why must men repeat past mistakes? Being guilty for remote sins is easy; accepting responsibilities for current and future sins is difficult. It is this contemporary attitude toward aboriginal peoples that must be changed rather than compensation for past wrongs.

Christians must disclaim the use of history as a weapon of conquest today. In doing so they must support the fight of the aboriginal peoples wherever it exists. They must demand a new status for native peoples around the planet. They must demand protection of natives and of their lands, cultures, and religions. They must honestly face the problems of the Western societies and consider what real alternatives now exist for those societies to survive in a world that is growing smaller—a world that must contain a great number of smaller groups whose existence is guaranteed and whose rights are not to be trampled underfoot.

The justification of past exploitations of native peoples has been that the gospel had to be preached to them and that a newer and better civilization had to rise from the native peoples' primitive hovels. Such a gospel of peace has been notoriously lacking as an element in Western civilization, and it is very questionable whether the present state of decay, corruption, and exploitation is better than what had existed before the coming of the Western Christian to the nations of the world. When ecologists find a predictable life-span of a generation separating us from total extinction, it would seem that we have a duty to search for another interpretation of humankind's life story instead of the traditional Christian view of the world and what it means. Unless we solve some of our problems, God will *have to intervene* to save any of us.

The present state of affairs cannot conceivably be justified. It cannot be justified at least religiously, and one must conclude that in

Christianity humankind has at best been deluded. While the religion appeared to give comfort and solace to people in all ages, its resultant impact on the world as a whole has been anything but comforting. It has been used by its followers to justify their most dastardly deeds, and it has focused our concern on the life hereafter so that we have refused to believe what our experiences tell us is true. We must now undertake to find a more profound explanation of ourselves and the planet on which we live.

Already in our secular society we are finding indications that, given a degree of concern for the land, people, and solving problems, changes can be made in our understanding of the world. We now recognize that the command of Genesis is not to be taken literally. We simply cannot continue to be fruitful and multiply without destroying everything. We need some relevant form of birth control. Two decades ago the legal status of abortion was changed and for a brief time we had some relief from the medieval conception of women as breeding stock. But the response of conservative Protestant and Roman Catholic Christians was anything but heartening. They promptly formed an aggressive and highly vocal political pressure group to seek reversal of the *Roe v. Wade* decision. With the recent appointment to the Supreme Court of determined antiabortion justices by Ronald Reagan and George Bush, this decision will soon be reversed. We will continue to see millions of children ushered into a life of starvation, sexual abuse, and meaninglessness. For some unknown reason, this branch of Christianity cherishes the unborn and hates the living person.

We have also seen the death penalty become a political controversy. First the Supreme Court declares it cruel and unusual punishment and then modifies its prohibition. We are now faced with the responsibility of acting as a mature society in relation to those who defy our laws. While a substantial number of Christians supported the abolition of the death penalty, an even greater number opposed abolition on biblical grounds. The fact that each justice of the Supreme Court has felt it necessary to outline his or her own position on the subject indicates that we are not far enough over the threshold of barbarity. No sooner had the first Supreme Court decision been announced than the nation's conservatives rose up to find ways to overcome the decision. In California a referendum was placed on the ballot in 1972 and was passed into law. It required the death penalty on a mandatory basis for a specific list of crimes, thereby circumventing the reasoning of the justices.

In recent years Congress has considered forms of compensation for victims of violent crimes. This development is a return to old Anglo-Saxon law and finds its natural roots in the beliefs of tribal religions. The reward for suffering in Christianity has always been in heaven, and the idea that a society has a responsibility to compensate those whom it failed to protect has not been a major value of Christian nations. Such a societal conception has always dominated Indian tribal groups. Beyond that, however, the idea of social compensation means that we have taken a major step in the conceptualization of America as a society with a potential for integrity. It is, perhaps, the most important aspect of the problem.

On almost every front, therefore, we find the old mythologies of Christianity being intellectually and often emotionally rejected by contemporary society. The rejection is not always for the better. Jumping from Christianity to devil worship can hardly be called an improvement. But the willingness to explore the unknown forces in our spiritual frontier can be called an improvement.

We cannot reject the Christian religion piecemeal. The importance of the decline of the specific doctrines of the Christian religion is that this decline means that the whole religion has been misdirected from its inception. It arose out of a Near Eastern milieu in which control of populations was the important value and in its institutions it had continually sought to exercise control over the beliefs, values, and behaviors of large masses of people. Merely canceling the belief in the Christian afterlife does not free us from the necessity of finding out the nature of that life if such exists. Rejecting the Christian interpretation of creation means a responsibility to find a better conception of a religion as it relates to creation. or creation as it testifies to religion or religious experiences.

Having changed and rejected Christian interpretations of many human experiences, we must in our generation reject the concept of history as an inevitable and controlled or controllable process. Our adventure in Vietnam should surely testify to the fact that we cannot control history and that what appears inevitable is only a projection of our wishes, not a future event. We need to take a new look at what the human experiences have been, and from our best conclusions begin to describe what we feel the whole nature of historical existence on the planet has meant.

Stabilizing societies so that further societal exploitation cannot exist is the first step in determining a new idea of history for humankind. The planet was not given to the pope, and his subsequent division of it to his favorite European sovereigns may have ultimately been illegal in the most fundamental sense of the term. Present unhampered exploitation of the lands and peoples of the world by post-Christian supranational corporations may have been the logical result of Western history, but that does not have to be its final result.

Christianity itself may find the strength to survive if it honestly faces the necessity to surrender its narrow interpretation of history and embark on a determined search for the true meaning of human life on this planet. Even surrendering a belief in a god who exercises supremacy over world events becomes possible if, in surrendering the belief, one comes to a greater understanding of the nature of religion and religious experiences. For a divinity, if indeed one exists, cannot even be bound in doctrines and beliefs in any ultimate sense. To restrict one's god then to a particular mode of operation and sequence of appearance would seem to be irreligious and the utmost folly.

Notes

1. Wilcomb E. Washburn, *Red Man's Land, White Man's Law: A Study of the Past and Present Status of the American Indian* (Garden City, N.Y.: Doubleday, 1971), 5.
2. Ibid, 5.
3. 1 Stat 50. This statute has always been regarded as the basic statement of Congressional policy with regard to American Indians.
4. The Kurile Islands were taken by Japan from the disintegrating Soviet Union. They had been taken by the Soviets after the defeat of Japan in World War II and taken originally by Japan from Russia in the Sino-Russian War.

CHAPTER 16

SACRED PLACES AND
MORAL RESPONSIBILITY

W hen the tribes were forced from their aboriginal homelands and confined to small reservations, many of the tribal religious
rituals were prohibited by the BIA in the 1870s and 1880s because of an
inordinately large number of Christian zealots as Indian agents. We
read in chapter 14 how traditional people had to adopt various subter-
fuges so that their religious life could be continued. Some tribes shifted
their ceremonial year to coincide with the whites' holidays and conducted their most important rituals on national holidays and Christian
feast days, explaining to curious whites that they were simply honor-
ing George Washington and celebrating Christmas and Easter. Many
shrines and holy places were located far away from the new reservation homelands, but because they were not being exploited economically or used by settlers, it was not difficult for small parties of people
to go into the mountains or to remote lakes and buttes and conduct
ceremonies without interference from non-Indians.

Since World War II, this situation has changed dramatically.
We have seen a greatly expanding national population, the introduction of corporate farming practices that have placed formerly submarginal lands under cultivation, more extensive mining and timber

industry activities, and a greatly expanded recreation industry—all of which have severely impacted the use of public lands in the United States. Few rural areas now enjoy the isolation of half a century ago, and as multiple use of lands increased, many of the sacred sites that were on public lands were threatened by visitors and subjected to new uses. Tribal religious leaders were often able to work out informal arrangements with federal and state agencies to allow them access to these places for religious purposes. But as the personnel changed in state and federal agencies, a new generation of bureaucrats, catering to developers, recreation interest, and the well-established economic groups who have always used public lands for a pittance, began to restrict Indian access to sacred sites by establishing increasingly narrow rules and regulations for managing public lands.

In 1978, in a symbolic effort to clarify the status of traditional religious practices and practitioners, Congress passed a Joint Resolution entitled the American Indian Religious Freedom Act. This act declared that it was the policy of Congress to protect and preserve the inherent right of American Indians to believe, express, and practice their traditional religions. The resolution identified the problem as one of a "lack of knowledge or the insensitive and inflexible enforcement of Federal policies and regulations." Section 2 of the resolution directed the president to require the various federal departments to evaluate their policies and procedures, report back to Congress on the results of their survey, and make recommendations for legislative actions.[1]

Many people assumed that this resolution clarified the federal attitude toward traditional religions, and it began to be cited in litigation involving the construction of dams, roads, and the management of federal lands. Almost unanimously, however, the federal courts have since ruled that the resolution did not protect or preserve the right of Indians to practice their religion and conduct ceremonies at sacred sites on public lands.[2] Some courts even hinted darkly that any formal recognition of the existence of tribal practices would be tantamount to establishing a state religion,[3] an interpretation that, upon analysis, is a dreadful misreading of American history and the Constitution and may have been an effort to inflame anti-Indian feelings.

A good example for making this claim was the 1988 Supreme Court decision in the *Lyng v. Northwest Indian Cemetery Protec-*

tive Association case that involved protecting the visitation rights of the traditional religious leaders of three tribes to sacred sites in the Chimney Rock area of the Six Rivers National Forest in Northern California. The Forest Service proposed to build a 6-mile paved road that would have opened part of the area to commercial logging. This area, known by three Indian tribes as the "High Country," was the center of their religious and ceremonial life. The lower federal courts prohibited the construction of the road on the grounds that it would have made religious ceremonial use of the are impossible. Before the Supreme Court could hear the appeal, Congress passed the California Wilderness Act that made the question of constructing the road moot for all practical purposes. But the Supreme Court insisted on hearing the appeal of the Forest Service and deciding the religious issues. It turned the tribes down flat, ruling that the Free Exercise clause did not prevent the government from using its property in any way it saw fit and in effect rolling back the religious use of the area completely.

Most troubling about the Supreme Court's decision was the insistence on analyzing tribal religions within the same conceptual framework as western organized religions. Justice O'Connor observed,

A broad range of government activities—from social welfare programs to foreign aid to conservation projects—will always be considered essential to the spiritual well-being of some citizens, often on the basis of sincerely held religious beliefs. Others will find the very same activity deeply offensive, and perhaps incompatible with their own search for spiritual fulfillment and with the tenets of their religion.[4]

Thus, ceremonies and rituals that had been performed for thousands of years were treated as if they were popular fads or simply matters of personal preference based upon the erroneous assumption that religion was only a matter of individual aesthetic choice.

Justice Brennan's dissent vigorously attacked this spurious line of reasoning, outlining with some precision the communal aspect of the tribal religions and their relationship to the mountains. But his argument failed to gather support within the Court. Most observers of the Supreme Court were simply confounded at the majority's conclusion that suggested that destroying a religion "did not unduly burden it" and that no constitutional protections were available to the Indians.[5]

When informed of the meaning of this decision, most people have shown great sympathy for the traditional religious people. At the same time, they have had great difficulty understanding why it is so important that these ceremonies be held, that they be conducted only at certain locations, and that they be held in secrecy and privacy. This lack of understanding highlights the great gulf that exists between traditional Western thinking about religion and the Indian perspective. It is the difference between individual conscience and commitment (Western) and communal tradition (Indian), these views can only be reconciled by examining them in a much broader historical and geographical context.

Justice Brennan attempted to make this difference clear when he observed, "Although few tribal members actually made medicine at the most powerful sites, the entire tribe's welfare hinges on the success of individual practitioner."[6] More than that, however, the "world renewal" ceremonies conducted by the tribes were done on behalf of the earth and all forms of life. To describe these ceremonies as if they were comparable to Oral Roberts seeking funds or Jimmy Swaggart begging forgiveness for his continuing sexual misconduct or Justice O'Connor's matters of community aesthetic preference is to miss the point entirely. In effect, the Court declared that Indians cannot pray for the planet or for other people and other forms of life in the manner required by their religion.

Two contradictory responses seem to characterize the non-Indian attitudes toward traditional tribal religions. Some people want the traditional healers to share their religious beliefs in the same manner that priests, rabbis, and ministers expound publicly the tenets of their denominations. Other people feel that Indian ceremonials are simply remnants of primitive life and should be abandoned. Neither perspective understands that Indian tribes are communities in ways that are fundamentally different than other American communities and organizations. Tribal communities are wholly defined by the family relationships; the non-Indian communities are defined primarily by residence, by an arbitrary establishment of political jurisdiction, or by agreement with generally applicable sets of intellectual beliefs.

Ceremonial and ritual knowledge is possessed by everyone in the Indian community, although only a few people may actually be chosen to perform these acts. Authorization to perform ceremonies comes from higher spiritual powers and not by certification through an institution or any formal organization.

A belief in the sacredness of lands in the non-Indian context may become the preferred belief of an individual or group of people based on their experiences or on an intensive study of preselected evidence. But this belief becomes the subject of intense criticism and does not, except under unusual circumstances, become an operative principle in the life and behavior of the non-Indian group. The same belief, when seen in the Indian context, is an integral part of the experiences of the people—past, present, and future. The idea does not become a bone of contention among the people for even if someone does not have the experience or belief in the sacredness of lands, he or she accords tradition the respect that it deserves. Indians who have never visited certain sacred sites nevertheless know of these places from the community knowledge, and they intuit this knowing to be an essential part of their being.

Justice Brennan, in countering the arguments aised by Justice O'Connor that any recognition of the sacredness of certain sites would allow traditional Indian religions to define the use of all public lands, suggested that the burden of proof be placed on the traditional people to demonstrate why some sites are central to their practice and other sites, while invoking a sense of reverence, are not as important. This requirement is not unreasonable, but it requires a willingness on the part of non-Indians and the courts to entertain different ideas about the nature of religion—ideas which until the present have not been a part of their experience or understanding.

If we were to subject the topic of the sacredness of lands to a Western rational analysis, fully recognizing the such an analysis is merely for our convenience in discussion and does not represent the nature of reality, we would probably find four major categories of description. Some of these categories are overlapping because some groups might not agree with the description of certain sites in the categories in which other Indians would place them. Nevertheless, it is the principle of respect for the sacred that is important.

The first and most familiar kind of sacred lands are places to which we attribute sanctity because the location is a site where, within our own history, something of great importance has taken place. Unfortunately, many of these places are related to instances of human violence. Gettysburg National Cemetery is a good example of this kind of sacred land. Abraham Lincoln properly noted that we cannot hallow the Gettysburg battlefield because others, the men who fought there, had already consecrated it by giving "that last full measure of devotion." We generally hold these places sacred because people did there what we might one day be required to do—give our lives in a cause we hold dear. Wounded Knee, South Dakota, has become such a place for many Indians where a band of Sioux Indians were massacred. On the whole, however, the idea of regarding a battlefield as sacred was entirely foreign to most tribes because they did not see war as a holy enterprise. The Lincoln Memorial in Washington, D.C., might be an example of a nonmartial location, and, although Justice O'Connor felt that recognizing the sacredness of land and location might inspire an individual to have a special fondness for this memorial, it is important to recognize that we should have some sense of reverence in these places.

Every society needs these kinds of sacred places because they help to instill a sense of social cohesion in the people and remind them of the passage of generations that have brought them to the present. A society that cannot remember and honor its past is in peril of losing its soul. Indians, because of our considerably longer tenure on this continent, have many more sacred places than do non-Indians. Many different ceremonies can be and have been held at these locations; there is both an exclusivity and an inclusiveness, depending upon the occasion and the ceremony. In this classification the site is all important, but it is sanctified each time ceremonies are held and prayers offered.

A second category of sacred lands has a deeper, more profound sense of the sacred. It can be illustrated in Old Testament stories that have become the foundation of three world religions. After the death of Moses, Joshua led the Hebrews across the River Jordan into the Holy Land. On approaching the river with the Ark of the Covenant, the waters of the Jordan "rose up" or parted and the people, led by the Ark, crossed over on "dry ground," which is to say they crossed without difficulty. After crossing, Joshua selected one man from each of the Twelve Tribes and told him to find a large stone. The twelve stones were then placed together in a monument to mark the spot where the people had camped after having crossed the river successfully. When asked about this strange behavior, Joshua then replied, "That this may be a sign among you, that when your children ask their fathers in time to come, saying 'What mean ye by these stones?' Then you shall answer them: That the waters of Jordan were cut off before the Ark of the Covenant of the Lord, when it passed over Jordan."[7]

In comparing this site with Gettysburg, we must understand a fundamental difference. Gettysburg is made sacred by the actions of men. It can be described as exquisitely dear to us, but it is not a location where we have perceived that something specifically other than ourselves is present, something mysteriously religious in the proper meaning of those words has happened or been made manifest. In the crossing of the River Jordan, the sacred or higher powers have appeared in the lives of human beings. Indians would say something holy has appeared in an otherwise secular situation. No matter how we might attempt to explain this event in later historical, political, or economic terms, the essence of the event is that the sacred has become a part of our experience.

Some of the sites that traditional religious leaders visit are of this nature. Buffalo Gap at the southeastern edge of the Black Hills of South Dakota marks the location where the buffalo emerged each spring to begin the ceremonial year of the Plains Indians, and it has this aspect of sacred/secular status. It may indeed be the starting point of the Great Race that determined the primacy between two-legged and four-legged creatures at the beginning of the world. Several mountains in New Mexico and Arizona mark places where the Pueblo, Hopi, and Navajo peoples completed their migrations, were told to settle, or where they first established their spiritual relationships with bear, deer, eagle, and other peoples who participate in the ceremonials.

Every identifiable region has sacred places peculiar to its geography and as we extend the circle geographically from any point in North America, we begin to include an ever-increasing number of sacred sites. Beginning in the American Southwest we must include the Apache, Ute, Comanche, Kiowa, and other tribes as we move away from the Pueblo and Navajo lands. These lands would be sacred to some tribes but secular to the Pueblo, Hopi, and Navajo. The difference would be in the manner of revelation and what the people experienced. There is immense particularity in the sacred and it is not a blanket category to be applied indiscriminately. Even east of the Mississippi, though many places have been nearly obliterated, people retain knowledge of these sacred sites. Their sacredness does not depend on human occupancy but on the stories that describe the revelation that enabled human beings to experience the holiness there.

In the religious world of most tribes, birds, animals, and plants compose the "other peoples" of creation. Depending on the ceremony, various of these "peoples" participate in human activities. If Jews and Christians see the action of a deity at sacred places in the Holy Land and in churches and synagogues, traditional Indian people experience spiritual activity as the whole of creation becomes active participants in ceremonial life. Because the relationship with the "other peoples" is so fundamental to the human community, most traditional practitioners are reluctant to articulate the specific elements of either the ceremony or the locations. Because some rituals involve the continued prosperity of the "other peoples," discussing the nature of the ceremony would violate the integrity of these relationships. Thus, traditional people explain that these ceremonies are being held for "all our relatives" but are reluctant to offer any further explanations. It is these ceremonies in particular that are now to be denied protection under the Supreme Court rulings.

It is not likely that non-Indians have had many of these kinds of religious experiences, particularly because most churches and synagogues have special rituals that are designed to cleanse the buildings so that their services can be held there untainted by the natural world. Non-Indians have simply not been on this continent very long; their families have rarely settled in one place for any period of time so that no profound relationship with the environment has been possible. Additionally, non-Indians have engaged in the senseless killing of wildlife and utter destruction of plant life. It is unlikely that they would have understood efforts by other forms of life to communicate with humans. Although, some non-Indian families who have lived continuously in isolated rural areas tell stories about birds and animals similar to the traditions of many tribes indicating that lands and the "other peoples" do seek intimacy with our species.

The third kind of sacred lands are places of overwhelming holiness where the Higher Powers, on their own initiative, have revealed Themselves to human beings. Again, we can illustrate this in the Old Testament narrative. Prior to his journey to Egypt, Moses spent his time herding his father-in-law's sheep on or near Mount Horeb. One day he took the flock to the far side of the mountain and to his amazement saw a bush burning with fire but not being consumed by it. Approaching this spot with the usual curiosity of a person accustomed to the outdoor life, Moses was startled when the Lord spoke to him from the bush, warning, "Draw not hither; put off thy shoes from thy feet, for the place where on thou standest is holy ground."[8]

This tradition tells us that there are places of unquestionable, inherent sacredness on this earth, sites that are holy in and of themselves. Human societies come and go on this earth and any prolonged occupation of a geographical region will produce shrines and sacred sites discerned by the occupying people, but there will always be a few sites at which the highest spirits dwell. The stories that explain the sacred nature of these locations will frequently provide startling parallels to the account about the burning bush. One need only look at the shrines of present-day Europe. Long before Catholic or Protestant churches were built in certain places, other religions had established shrines and temples of that spot. These holy places are locations where people have always gone to communicate and commune with higher spiritual powers.

This phenomenon is worldwide and all religions find that these places regenerate people and fill them with spiritual powers. In the Western Hemisphere these places, with few exceptions, are known only by American Indians. Bear Butte, Blue Lake, and the High Places in the *Lyng* case are all well known locations that are sacred in and of themselves. People have been commanded to perform ceremonies at these holy places so that the earth and all its forms of life might survive and prosper. Evidence of this moral responsibility that sacred places command has come through the testimony of traditional people when they have tried to explain to non-Indians at various times in this century—in court, in conferences, and in conversations—that they must perform certain ceremonies at specific times and places in order that the sun may continue to shine, the earth prosper, and the stars remain in the heavens. Tragically, this attitude is interpreted by non-Indians as indicative of the traditional leader's personal code or philosophy and is not seen as a simple admission of a moral duty.

Skeptical non-Indians, and representatives of other religions seeking to discredit tribal religions, have sometimes deliberately violated some of these holy places with no ill effects. They have then come to believe that they have demonstrated the false nature of Indian beliefs. These violations reveal a strange non-Indian belief in a form of mechanical magic that is touchingly adolescent, a belief that an impious act would, or could trigger an immediate response from the higher spiritual powers. Surely these impious acts suggest a deity who jealously guards his or her prerogatives and wreaks immediate vengeance for minor transgressions—much as some Protestant sects have envisioned God and much as an ancient astronaut (see chapter 9) wanting to control lesser beings might act.

It would be impossible for the thoughtless or impious acts of one species to have an immediate drastic effort on the earth. The cumulative effect of continuous secularity, however, poses a different kind of danger. Long-standing prophecies tell us of the impious people who would come here, defy the creator, and cause the massive destruction of the planet. Many traditional people believe that we are now quite near that time. The cumulative evidence of global warming, acid rain, the disappearance of amphibians, overpopulation, and other products of civilized life certainly testify to the possibility of these prophecies being correct.

Of all the traditional ceremonies extant and actively practiced at the time of contact with non-Indians, ceremonies derived from or related to these holy places have the highest retention rate because of their extraordinary planetary importance. Ironically, traditional people have been forced to hold these ceremonies under various forms of subterfuge and have been abused and imprisoned for doing them. Yet the ceremonies have very little to do with individual or tribal prosperity. Their underlying theme is one of gratitude expressed by human beings on behalf of all forms of life. They act to complete and renew the entire and complete cycle of life, ultimately including the whole cosmos present in its specific realizations, so that in the last analysis one might describe ceremonials as the cosmos becoming thankfully aware of itself.

Having used Old Testament examples to show the objective presence of the holy places, we can draw additional conclusions about the nature of these holy places from the story of the Exodus. Moses did not demand that the particular location of the burning bush become a place of worship for his people, although there was every reason to suppose that he could have done so. Lacking information, we must conclude that the holiness of this place precluded its use as a shrine. If Moses had been told to perform annual ceremonies at that location during specific days or times of the year, world history would have been entirely different.

Each holy site contains its own revelation. This knowledge is not the ultimate in the sense that Near Eastern religions like to claim the universality of their ideas. Traditional religious leaders tell us that in many of the ceremonies new messages are communicated to them. The ceremonies enable humans to have continuing relationships with higher spiritual powers so that each bit of information is specific to the time, place, and circumstances of the people. No revelation can be regarded as universal because times and conditions change.

The second and third kinds of sacred lands result from two distinctly different forms of sacred revelations where the sacred is actively involved in secular human activities and where the sacred takes the initiative to chart out a new historical course for humans. Because there are higher spiritual powers who can communicate with people, there has to be a fourth category of sacred lands. People must always be ready to experience new revelations at new locations. If this possibility did not exist, all deities and spirits would be dead. Consequently, we always look forward to the revelation of new sacred places and ceremonies. Unfortunately, some federal courts irrationally and arbitrarily circumscribe this universal aspect of religion by insisting that traditional religious practitioners restrict their identification of sacred locations to places that were historically visited by Indians, implying that at least for the federal courts, God is dead.

In denying the possibility of the continuing revelation of the sacred in our lives, federal courts, scholars, and state and federal agencies refuse to accord credibility to the testimony of religious leaders. They demand evidence that a ceremony or location has *always* been central to the beliefs and practices of an Indian tribe and impose exceedingly rigorous standards of proof on Indians who appear before them. This practice allows the Supreme Court to command what should not to be done, it lets secular institutions rule on the substance of religious belief and practice. Thus, courts will protect a religion that shows every symptom of being dead but will create formidable barriers if it appears to be alive. Justice Scalia made this posture perfectly clear when he announced in *Smith*, that it would be unconstitutional to ban the casting of "statues that are used for worship purposes" or to prohibit bowing down before a golden calf.

We live in time and space and receive most of our signals about proper behavior from each other and the environment around us. Under these circumstances, the individual and the group *must* both have some kind of sanctity if we are to have a social order at all. By recognizing the various aspects of the sacredness of lands as we have described, we place ourselves in a realistic context in which the individual and the group can cultivate and enhance the sacred experience. Recognizing the sacredness of lands on which previous generations have lived and died is the foundation of all other sentiment. Instead of denying this dimension of our emotional lives, we should be setting aside additional places that have transcendent meaning. Sacred sites that higher spiritual powers have chosen for manifestation enable us to focus our concerns on the specific form of our lives. These places remind us of our unique relationship with the spiritual forces that govern the universe and call us to fulfill our religious vocations. These kinds of religious experiences have shown us something of the nature of the universe by an affirmative manifestation of themselves and this knowledge illuminates everything else that we know.

The nature of tribal religion brings contemporary America a new kind of legal problem. Religious freedom has existed as a matter of course in America *only* when religion has been conceived as a set of objective beliefs. This condition is actually not freedom at all because it would be exceedingly difficult to read minds and determine what ideas were being entertained at the time. So far in American history religious freedom has not involved the consecration and setting aside

of lands for religious purposes or allowing sincere but highly divergent behavior by individuals and groups. The issue of sacred lands, as
we have seen was successfully raised in the case of the Taos Pueblo
people. Nevertheless, a great deal more remains to be done to guarantee Indian people the right to practice their own religion.

A number of other tribes have sacred sanctuaries in lands
that have been taken by the government for purposes other than
religion. These lands must be returned to the respective Indian tribes
for their ceremonial purposes. The greatest number of Indian shrines
are located in New Mexico and here the tribal religions have remained
comparatively strong. Cochiti Pueblo needs some 24,000 acres of land
for access to and use of religious shrines in what is now Bandelier
National Monument. The people also have shrines in the Tetilla Peak
area. San Juan Pueblo has also been trying to get lands returned for
religious purposes. Santa Clara Pueblo requested the Indian
Claims Commission to set aside 30,000 acres of the lands that have
religious and ceremonial importance to its people but are presently
in the hands of the National Forest Service and Atomic Energy
Commission.

In Arizona the Hopi people have a number of shrines that
are of vital importance to their religion. Traditionals regard the Black
Mesa area as sacred, but it is being leased to Peabody Coal by the more
assimilative tribal council. The San Francisco Peaks within the Coconino
National Forest are sacred because they are believed to be the homes
of the Kachinas who play a major part in the Hopi ceremonial system.
The Navajo have a number of sacred mountains now under federal
ownership. Mount Taylor in the Cibola National Forest, Blanca Peak in
southern Colorado, Hesperus Peak in the San Juan National Forest,
Huerfano Mountain on public domain lands, and Oak Creek canyon in
the Coconino National Forest are all sites integral to the Navajo
tradition. Part of the Navajo religion involves the "mountain chant"
that describes the seven sacred mountains and a sacred lake located
within these mountains. The Navajo believe their ancestors arose from
this region at the creation. Last, but certainly not least, is the valiant
struggle now being waged by the Apache people to prevent the
University of Arizona from building several telescopes on Mount
Graham in southern Arizona.

In other states several sacred sites are under threat of exploitation. The Forest Service is proposing to construct a major parking lot
and observation platform at the Medicine Wheel site near Powell,
Wyoming, that is sacred to many tribes from Montana, the Dakotas,
and Wyoming. Because the only value of this location is its relationship
to traditional Indian religions that need isolation and privacy, it seems
ludicrous to pretend that making it accessible to more tourists and
subject to increasing environmental degradation is enhancing it. The
Badger Two Medicine area of Montana, where oil drilling has been
proposed, is a sacred area for traditional Blackfeet who live in the
vicinity. The Pipestone Quarry in southwestern Minnesota was confis-
cated from the Yankton Sioux in the closing decades of the last century
when some missionaries pressure the federal government to eliminate
Indian access to this important spot.

Finally, there is the continuing struggle over the Black Hills
of South Dakota. Many Americans are now aware of this state thanks
to the success of the movie *Dances with Wolves* that not only depicted the
culture of the Sioux Indians but also filled the screen with the magnificent landscape of the northern Great Plains. Nineteen ninety-one was
a year of great schizophrenia and strange anomalies in South Dakota.
Local whites shamelessly capitalized on the success of the movie at the
same time they were frothing at the mouth over the continuing efforts
of the Sioux people to get the federal lands in the Black Hills returned
to them. Governor George Mickelson announced a "Year of Reconciliation" that simply became twelve months of symbolic maneuvering
for publicity and renewal of political images. When some of the Sioux
elders suggested that the return of Bear Butte near Sturgis would be a
concrete step toward reconciliation, non-Indians were furious that
reconciliation might require them to make good-faith effort to heal the
wounds from a century of conflict.

The question that must be addressed in the issue of sacred
lands is the extent to which the tribal religions can be maintained if
sacred lands are restored. Would restoration of the sacred Pipestone
Quarry result in more people seeking to follow the traditional religious
life or would it result in continued use of the stone for tourism and
commercial purposes? A small group of Sioux people have made a
living during this century from making ashtrays and decorative carv-

ings from this sacred rock; they refuse to stop their exploitation. A major shift in focus is needed by traditional Sioux people to prepare to reconsecrate the quarry and return to the old ways of reverence.

A very difficult task lies ahead for the people who continue to believe in the old tribal religions. In the past, these traditions have been ridiculed by disbelievers, primarily missionaries and social scientists. Today injuries nearly as grievous are visited on traditional religions by the multitude of non-Indians who seek entrance and participation in ceremonies and rituals. Many of these non-Indians blatantly steal symbols, prayers and teaching by laying claim to alleged offices in tribal religions. Most non-Indians see in tribal religions the experiences and revernce that are missing in their own heritage. No matter how hard they try, they always reduce the teachings and ceremonies to a complicated word game and ineffectual gestures. Lacking communities and extended families, they are unable to put the religion into practice.

Some major efforts must be made by the Indians of this generation to demonstrate the view of the world that their tradition teaches has an integrity of its own and represents a sensible and respectable perspective of the world and a valid means of interpreting experiences. There are many new studies that seem to confirm certain tribal practices as reasonable and sometimes even as sophisticated techniques for handling certain kinds of problems. It might be sufficient to show that these patterns of behavior are indicative of a consistent attitude toward the world and includes the knowledge that everything is alive and related.

Sacred places are the foundation of all other beliefs and practices because they represent the presence of the sacred in our lives. They properly inform us that we are not larger than nature and that we have responsibilities to the rest of the natural world that transcend our own personal desires and wishes. This lesson must be learned by each generation; unfortunately the technology of industrial society always leads us in the other direction. Yet it is certain that as we permanently foul our planetary nest, we shall have to learn a most bitter lesson. There probably is not sufficient time for the non-Indian population to understand the meaning of sacred lands and incorporate the idea into their lives and practices. We can but hope that some protection can be afforded these sacred places before the world becomes wholly secular and is destroyed.

Notes

1. 92 Stat 469, 42 U.S.C. §1996.

2. See *Wilson v. Block*, 708 F 2d. 735 (D.C. Cir 1983). Hopi and Navajo sacred sites and shrines on San Francisco peak were destroyed by the U.S. Forest Service to make room for a new ski lift. In *Fools Crow v. Gullet*, 706 F. 2d 856 (8th Cir 1983) the court upheld intrusions by the U.S. Park Service on Sioux vision quest use of Bear Butte. In *Badoni v. Higginson*, 638 F. 2d. 172 (10th Cir 1980) the court allowed the destruction of a Navajo sacred site at Rainbow Bridge in the Grand Canyon area.

3. The majority decision in *Lyng* even suggested that to recognize traditional Indian religious freedom would make it seem as if the Indians owned the federal lands.

No disrespect for these practices is implied when one notes that such beliefs could easily require de facto beneficial ownership of some rather spacious tracts of public property. Even without anticipating future cases, the diminution of the government's propety rights, and the concomitant subsidy of the Indian religion, would in this case be far from trivial .... 108 S. Ct 1319, 1327 (1988)

4. At 1327

5. Justice Brennan's dissent makes this point specifically,

The Court today, however, ignores *Roy's* emphasis on the internal nature of the government practice at issue there, and instead construes that case as further support for the proposition that governmental action that does not coerce conduct inconsistent with religious faith simply does not implicate the concerns of the Free Exercise Clause. That such a reading is wholly untenable, however, is demonstrated by the cruelly surreal result it produces here: *governmental action that will virtually destroy a religion is nevertheless deemed not to 'burden' that religion.* (at 1337) (Emphasis added.)

6. At 1332

7. Joshua 4:6-7

8. Exodus 3:5

CHAPTER 17

RELIGION
TODAY

In preceding chapters we have made tentative comparisons between Christian doctrines and beliefs and some of the beliefs of Indian tribal groups, which appear to stand in direct opposition. The opposition is more than conceptual; it colors the manner in which non-Indians view the world and the people they deal with in that world, particularly Indians. While many Christian doctrines have now passed into the sphere of Western civilization's general beliefs, others continue to form the basis of Christian belief and determine in large measure the manner in which Christians understand the world and form their responses to its events.

Opposing tribal concepts to Christian concepts does not mean that tribal conceptions are necessarily correct because Christianity is wrong. That Christianity is unable to speak to certain problems without facing internal collapse of its doctrinal structure means that of the possible alternative answers, one starting point must certainly be the ideas found in American Indian tribal religions. Balanced against the tribal religions, however, is that, for the most part, these religions provided for a meaningful existence for a people facing a world far different than the one presently experienced. Whether the old tribal religions can survive prolonged exposure to modern conditions is yet to be demonstrated.

In our present situation, we therefore face a most difficult question of meaning. Ecologists project a world crisis of severe intensity within our lifetime, whereas religious mythologies project the end of our present existence and the eventual salvation of the chosen people and the creation of another world. It is becoming increasingly apparent that we shall not have the benefits of this world for much longer. The imminent and expected destruction of the life cycle of world ecology can be prevented by a radical shift in outlook from our present naive conception of this world as a testing ground of abstract morality to a more mature view of the universe as a comprehensive matrix of life forms. Making this shift in viewpoint is essentially religious, not economic or political.

The problem of contemporary people, whatever their ethnic or cultural background, lies in finding the means by which they can once again pierce the veil of unreality to grasp the essential meaning of their existence. For people from a Western European background or deeply imbued with Christian beliefs, the task is virtually impossible. The interpretation of religion has always been regarded as the exclusive property of Westerners, and the explanatory categories used in studying religious phenomena have been derived from the doctrines of the Christian religion. The minds and eyes of Western people have thus been permanently closed to understanding or observing religious experiences. Religion has become a comfortable ethic and a comforting aesthetic for Westerners, not a force of undetermined intensity and unsuspected origin that may break in on them.

Many thoughtful and useful systems of belief of ancient peoples have been simply rejected a priori by Western religious thinkers. This attitude has intruded into Western science and then emerged as the intellectual criteria by which the world of our experience is judged, condemned, and too often sentenced to death. Many people, for example, have developed astrological systems by which they have charted the nature of relationships between the lives of people and the movement of the planets and stars. Given that modern science now views the universe as an extremely sophisticated electromagnetic complex, the contentions of astrologers as to the influence of the heavens on individual propensities to behave in certain ways may not be as superstitious as it would at first appear. Yet astrology is rejected out of hand by many followers of Western religious thinking because it conflicts with the philosophical problem of free will.

For centuries the Chinese have used and practiced acupuncture as a regular part of their religious and cultural beliefs. The idea that there might be centers of feeling within the human body that can block off pain and sensation if properly understood was virtually an anathema to many Westerners. The same situation exists today with respect to the conception of Chakras, as defined by some of the Eastern religions. Apparently such conceptions collide with Western beliefs about the human being composed of body, mind, and spirit—the neo-Greek beliefs about the "soul" of man that have intruded into Christianity or the Western conceptions of psychology and psychological problems.

A number of religions have concentrated on the development of beliefs covering the spirits of places; the relationship of people to animal, bird, and reptile forms of life; and the nature of religious healing. Again these beliefs have been rejected on dogmatic grounds, not because they were not suitable for the communities that held them as beliefs. The usual answer given to questions about the nature of religion is highly unsatisfactory. Other religions have been given credibility to the extent to which they conformed or paralleled certain Christian doctrines. To the extent to which they varied or were in direct opposition to Christian doctrines, they have been regarded as false and sometimes as deliberate attempts on the part of the Christian devil to mislead people.

All of these things have been excluded from our consideration. We have been taught to consider problems using logic and concepts that ignore certain facets of existence. Religious experiences are not nearly as important to Westerners as their creeds, theologies, and speculations—all products of the intellect and not necessarily based on experiences. Regardless of the experience of a multitude of gods, monotheism has come to be regarded as the highest form of religious knowledge. Yet religions that have achieved a monotheistic doctrine are often rapidly intruded upon by a development of lesser spiritual beings forming a pantheon. It is interesting to note that

Nathan Soderblum determined that monotheism was almost always a product of the political arrangement of a society and not the natural product of religious activities or experiences. When a religion is based in experience whether it be theological or popular, it seems to be of a polytheistic or pantheon-oriented nature.

We cannot be absolutely certain that we are dealing with only one god. The fact that monotheism is logically pleasing does not mean that it is an accurate description of reality. The universe, being somewhat discontinuous in other respects, may also conceivably be discontinuous with respect to divinity. Wotan appears to have amazing resiliency; Yahweh's rainbow still shines in the sky; ghosts prowl the British Isles; the picture of Jesus is appearing more frequently in unexpected places—and the Hopi have rain.

A more basic question about people's psychological processes must be resolved before we begin to understand the breadth of the nature of religious questions. What are religious experiences? Are they of such a nature that they can only be described in terms of the Western peoples, or do they properly belong in non-Western categories? It is a fact that many societies have had definable and satisfactory relationships with some form of divinity almost from the beginning of humankind's journey on the planet. Traditional Western thought, and more specifically traditional Christian thought, has been based on the assumption that these religions have often been cruel delusions perpetrated against primitive societies by religious leaders, shamans, and medicine people seeking personal gain or additional powers, or people forced into trickery to preserve their place in society.

We cannot conclude that other peoples spent centuries in a state of delusion simply because their experiences of God were radically different from those of Western peoples. That their experiences could not be either described accurately by Westerners or understood in Western categories of thought does not make them false. The least we can do is to understand that it is in the nature of religion to exert a profound influence within societies and groups and sustain the community or national group over a period of time. Having retreated even that much, the Western world must be prepared to analyze religion as a phenomenon that does not necessarily explain the unanswered questions posed by the philosophical mind but that may, in itself, cause such questions to occur to all manner of people in a great variety of situations.

As we find religion in the societies, there are a number of factors that appear generally to be present as preconditions to religious experiences. While religious experiences may be individual in specific events, the impact of them is generally quickly felt by respective groups so that the individualistic nature of religion is not that emphasized in Christianity but that given credence in tribal religions. That is to say, whatever else a particular experience may be, religion itself exists in specific groups and is probably more a national or tribal affair than either an individual or universal affair. Universal ethics, however, generally do arise during the course of a religion's growth, and rules for conduct of lives and general theories of salvation seem to appear as religions become more mature. The religions that grow in these ways also lose those aspects that give religion its special importance to a society—healing and divination powers.

Many Christians will vehemently argue that the places at which religious experiences take place are of no consequence. God, they maintain, was released from the bounds of time and space with the revelation of Christianity. Thus, God is everywhere at all times, and to define divinity according to sacred or holy places is to limit His powers beyond reason, reducing Him to a facade of power and intelligence. The impact of Christianity on the questions of time and space, however, was to transfer our real human and environmental problems to "another world" thus sidestepping the question. The final result of this emphasis was to banish God from any possibility of relating to time and space, thus in effect precluding Him from interference with this world.

The major step to be taken to understand religion today is to understand the nature of religion as it occurs in specific places. There is a reason why shrines exist over and above the piety of the uneducated religious person who has visions while tending sheep. Mount Sinai, for example, has been a holy mountain for a considerable length of time, thus indicating that it has a religious existence over and above any temporary belief held by particular people. If this concept is true, then economics cannot and should not be the sole determinant of land use. Unless the sacred places are discovered and protected and used as religious places, there is no possibility of a nation ever coming to grips with the land itself. Without this basic relationship, national psychic stability is impossible.

A corollary of this concept is the possibility that each land projects a particular religious spirit, which largely determines what types of religious beliefs will arise on it. Judaism, Islam, and Christianity do not radically differ about the nature of creation and the final days, when even nature is to be renewed. Arising as they did from the desert of the Near East, it may be that concern with a renewal of that particular land has preformed their religious conceptions. The fact that Druidism is once again rising in parts of Europe may indicate that those lands, in largely determining the shape and beliefs of religious experiences, are Druid lands.

The effort to shift religious thinking so as to examine this theory appeared ludicrous to Westerners when first proposed. We do not have any exact knowledge of what Druid religious beliefs and practices were. Whether present practitioners are precisely following ancient religious practices is less important than the fact that religion has contemporary followers who are attempting to make the proper connections with what has gone before. That religions change is a foregone conclusion. To go from Jesus on the hillside advocating the message of the Beatitudes to a Cotton Bowl filled with Jesus freaks chanting "Two bits, four bits, six bits, a dollar, all those for Jesus stand up and holler!" indicates that anything can occur in a religious tradition.

Nearly as important may be the fact that lands can apparently be consecrated by a particular religious group wishing to place its roots in the land. The persistence of some religions on originally foreign lands would appear to testify to the fact that peoples and lands can relate to each other in a very powerful manner to develop a spiritual unity. It may be this possibility that will prove the salvation of Christianity in the modern world. Once having developed roots as did the Five Nations at the Great Tree of Peace at Onondaga, the land and the religion apparently become as one. The Hopi also established themselves on a land.

Rather than attempt to graft contemporary ecological concern onto basic Christian doctrines and avoid blame for the current planetary disaster, Christians would be well advised to surrender many of their doctrines and come to grips with the lands now occupied. To admit that certain lands will create divergent beliefs and practices and to change to accommodate to those realities is certainly preferable to extinction. The problem of relating to a place's spirit or alternatively bringing a spiritual reality to a particular place is yet to be understood in the sphere of religious thought. That a fundamental element of religion is an intimate relationship with the land on which the religion is practiced should be a major premise of future theological concern.

Given a specific land on which a religion can grow, the problem then shifts to the nature of the people adhering to that religion. Is religion necessarily a universal condition for all, or is it a phenomenon that can manifest itself to different societies in different ways? The very conception of a Chosen People implies a lost religious ethnicity. Most likely religions do not in fact cross national and ethnic lines without losing their power and identity. It is probably more in the nature of things to have different groups with different religions. The traditional objection to this concept is that it would create religious wars. If the number of important religious experiences occurring in a specific community were supported by homogeneous cultural and political factors, the religion would probably have more impact, and religious wars would not occur. At present we have wars fought with religious justification as well as religious wars. The past history of the West is eloquent testimony to the fact that a universal religion crossing ethnic lines does not lessen wars; it tends to increase them until one particular ethnic group comes to dominate the religious beliefs of the whole group with its own cultural values.

Besides the importance of land in religion, the existence of a specific religion among a distinct group of people is probably a fundamental element of human experience. Once religion becomes specific to a group, its nature also appears to change, being directed to the internal mechanics of the group, not to grandiose schemes of world conquest or the afterlife. What a religion does to a group of people on a distinct land is thus a vital question for future analysis. The phenomenon that is most clearly seen among the non-Western religions is the element of healing ceremonies. It is this fact of religious life, Oral Roberts excepted, that appears to dominate land-based religions of particular peoples.

One cannot separate the spiritual problems of people from their religion; particularly the tribal religions treat healing as a major part of religious life. Inherent in ceremonial healing practices are powers given to religious people in their visions and religious experiences. The tribal religions look at healing in an entirely different manner than do Christian religious healers. The predictable Christian religious healers build their audience to a fever pitch, hoping that supreme acts of willpower will release individuals from their infirmities. No consideration is given to the people's cultural practices or the particular spirit of the lands on which they live. In a very real way healing is an abstract process, dependent as much on the self-motivation of the infirm as it is on the healer's powers.

Tribal religions do not place as much emphasis on the infirm's rigorous willpower. Rather, specific ceremonies and healing songs and practices are used to cure specific types of sicknesses. Many Indian religious healers can tell at a glance if they can heal a particular illness. No pretense is made if it appears that the medicine cannot be used for a particular illness. And the healers do not pretend to be able to cure any sickness. The individual healer has specific powers—his or her own gifts received through his or her experiences. The counterpart of healing is a recognition of his healing powers' limitations.

Almost all of the healing disciplines came originally from religious beliefs and the religious leader's practices. The severance of medicine and psychology from religion has only been a recent event in the histories of religious people. In the West it has taken extreme forms, and the rising number of psychoanalysts coupled with the declining number of professional clergy testifies to the fact that the religious crisis of Western civilization is taking extreme forms of alienation within itself. The phenomenon of a substantial number of clergy suffering psychological problems indicates that religious and mental difficulties have not been solved by Christianity in any of its denominational expressions.

Again in the field of healing, relationships already seen as crucial to tribal religions are prerequisites for receiving healing powers. Healing may indeed be a means of determining the extent to which a religion is weak or strong, declining or growing. In none of the three areas—land, ethnicity, or healing—is any set of beliefs required in the traditional sense that Western thinkers have defined beliefs. The transition from traditional Western/Christian categories to tribal and non-Western categories of religious experience is not then a matter of learning new facts about life, the world, human history, or adopting new symbols and garments. It is primarily a matter of participation in terms of the real factors of existence—living on the land, living within a specific community, and having religious people with special powers within that community.

It is the nonphilosophical quality of tribal religions that makes them important for this day and age. Modern society has now reached the stage at which any particular proposition is viewed as partially or relatively true but most probably not ultimately true Truth, in the Western scientific sense, is what can be verified. In tribal religions no effort is made to define religion as a system of doctrinal truths about the nature of the world. It cannot, therefore, be verified, and only in a certain sense can it be experienced by a specific community. Over a long period of time, however, the cumulative experiences of the community become a truth that has been manifested for the people.

The analytical error of contemporary society is that they have not understood, in religious terms, the meaning of what they have already accomplished scientifically by revealing the world of sensory perceptions. In seeking an ultimate answer to the meaning of existence, that is, in reading God's mind as early scientists described their work, modern society has foreclosed the possibility of experiencing life in favor of explaining it. Even in explaining the world, however, Western people have misunderstood it.

We stand today at a series of crossroads. Rather than revolutionary movements we may have possibly lapsed into a prolonged period of respectable boredom from which we will never recover. Clearly the current tendency is to attempt to reclaim the nineteenth-century roots of social existence that can give us a sense of permanency in a world of increasing change. But the stability of that era was at best a mythological memory of a golden age. Our very refusal to acknowledge the failures of both American and world history and our patriotic effort to make it into a golden age show how pathetic and inadequate our tools for confronting change really are.

Within the traditions, beliefs, and customs of the American Indian people are the guidelines for society's future. It is this spirit of the continent, of all continents, that shines through the Indian anthologies and glimmers in the Indian communities in grotesque and tortured forms. The vision of stability of the community is found by non-Indians who venture into the reservations, and yet in viewing the remnants of Indian religion they understand neither Indians nor themselves. White America and Western industrial societies have not heard the call of either the lands or the aboriginal peoples. In the appalling indices of social disorder of the tribal peoples Westerners see only continued disruption and, being unaccustomed to viewing life as a totality, cannot understand the persistence of the tribal peoples in preserving their communities, lands, and religions.

The lands of the planet call to humankind for redemption. But it is a redemption of sanity, not a supernatural reclamation project at the end of history. The planet itself calls to the other living species for elief. Religion cannot be kept within the bounds of sermons and scriptures It is a force in and of itself and it calls for the integration of lands and peoples in harmonious unity. The lands wait for those who can discern their rhythms. The peculiar genius of each continent—each river valley, the rugged mountains, the placid lakes—all call for relief from the constant burden of exploitation.

Who will find peace with the lands? The future of humankind lies waiting for those who will come to understand their lives and take up their responsibilities to all living things. Who will listen to the trees, the animals and birds, the voices of the places of the land? As the long-forgotten peoples of the respective continents rise and begin to reclaim their ancient heritage, they will discover the meaning of the lands of their ancestors. That is when the invaders of the North American continent will finally discover that for this land, God is red.

Appendix I

Sierra Club vs. Morton involved federal approval of the extensive ski development in the Mineral King Valley in the Sequoia National Forest. In this suit Justice William O. Douglas dissented from the majority and wrote what may come to be regarded in later years as the first major effort in the history of American jurisprudence to incorporate a contemporary understanding of nature into law. Douglas' effort to redefine man's relationship with nature by recognizing the standing of a particular feature of nature to sue is a fascinating review of the many nonhuman entities that have been recognized in law for commercial and criminal purposes. It would have, or at least should have, according to Justice Douglas, been a natural step to come full circle and vest in the lands and rivers themselves a legal power to be represented in the courts of the land. Douglas' opinion is reproduced in full below:

MR. JUSTICE DOUGLAS, dissenting.
     I share the views of my Brother Blackmun and would reverse the judgment below.
     The critical question of "standing" would be simplified and also put neatly in focus if we fashioned a federal rule that allowed environmental issues to be litigated before federal agencies or federal courts in the name of the inanimate object about to be despoiled, defaced, or invaded by roads and bulldozers and where injury is the subject of public outrage. Contemporary public concern for protecting nature's ecological equilibrium should lead to the conferral of standing

upon environmental objects to sue for their own preservation. See Stone, "Should Trees Have Standing?" 45 Southern California Law Revision 450 (1972). This suit would therefore be fore properly labeled as *Mineral King vs. Morton.*

Inanimate objects are sometimes parties in litigation. A ship has a legal personality, a fiction found useful by maritime purposes. The corporation soul—a creature of ecclesiastical law—is an acceptable adversary and large fortunes ride on its cases. The ordinary corporation is a "person" for purposes of the adjudicatory process, whether it represents proprietary, spiritual, esthetic, or charitable causes.

So it should be as respects valleys, alpine meadows, rivers, lakes, estuaries, beaches, ridges, groves of trees, swampland, or even air that feels the destructive pressures of modern technology and modern life. The river, for example, is the living symbol of all the life it sustains or nourishes—fish, aquatic insects, water ouzels, otter, fisher, deer, elk, bear, and all other animals, including man, who are dependent on it or who enjoy it for its sight, its sound, or its life. The river as plaintiff speaks for the ecological unit of life that is part of it. Those people who have a meaningful relation to that body of water—whether it be a fisherman, a canoeist, a zoologist, or a logger—must be able to speak for the values which the river represents and which are threatened with destruction.

I do not know Mineral King. I have never seen it nor travelled it, though I have seen articles describing its proposed "development," notably Hano, "Protectionists *vs.* Recreationists—The Battle of Mineral King," *New York Times Magazine,* Aug. 17, 1969, and Browning, "Mickey Mouse in the Mountains," *Harper's,* March 1972, p. 65. The Sierra Club in its complaint alleges that, "One of the principal purposes of the Sierra Club is to protect and conserve the national resources of the Sierra Nevada Mountains." The District Court held that this uncontested allegation made the Sierra Club "sufficiently aggrieved" to have "standing" to sue on behalf of Mineral King.

Mineral King is doubtless like other wonders of the Sierra Nevada such as Tuolumne Meadows and the John Muir Trail. Those who hike it, fish it, hunt it, camp in it, or frequent it, or visit it merely to sit in solitude and wonderment are legitimate spokesmen for it, whether they may be a few or many. Those who have that intimate relation with the inanimate object about to be injured, polluted, or otherwise despoiled are its legitimate spokesmen.

The Solicitor General, whose views on this subject are in the Appendix to this opinion, takes a wholly different approach. He considers the problem in terms of "government by the Judiciary." With all respect, the problem is to make certain that the inanimate objects, which are the very core of America's beauty, have spokesmen before they are destroyed. It is, of course, true that most of them are under the control of a federal or state agency. The standards given those agencies are usually expressed in terms of the "public interest." Yet, "public interest" has so many differing shades of meaning as to be quite meaningless on the environmental front. Congress accordingly has adopted ecological standards in the National Environmental Policy Act of 1969, Pub. L. 91–90, 83 Stat. 852, 42

U.S.C. s 4321, et seq., and guidelines for agency action have been provided by the Council on Environmental Quality of which Russell E. Train is Chairman. See 36 Fed Reg. 7724.

Yet the pressures on agencies for favorable action one way or the other are enormous. The suggestion that Congress is too remote to give meaningful direction, and its machinery is too ponderous to use very often. The federal agencies of which I speak are not venal or corrupt. But they are notoriously under the control of powerful interests who manipulate them through advisory committees, or friendly working relations, or who have that natural affinity with the agency which in time develops between the regulator and the regulated. As early as 1894, Attorney General Olney predicted that regulatory agencies might become "industry-minded," as illustrated by his forecast concerning the Interstate Commerce Commission:

The Commission is or can be made of great use to the railroads. It satisfies the public clamor for supervision of the railroads, at the same time that supervision is almost entirely nominal. Moreover, the older the Commission gets to be, the more likely it is to take a business and railroad view of things. (M. Josephson, *The Politicos* 526 (1938).)

Years later a court of appeals observed, "The recurring question which has plagued public regulation of industry (is) whether the regulatory agency is unduly oriented toward the interests of the industry. It is designed to regulate, rather than the public interest it is supposed to protect."

The Forest Service—one of the federal agencies behind the scheme to despoil Mineral King—has been notorious for its alignment with lumber companies, although its mandate from Congress directs it to consider the various aspects of multiple use in its supervision of the national forests.

The voice of the inanimate object, therefore, should not be stilled. That does not mean that the judiciary takes over the managerial functions from the federal agency. It merely means that before these priceless bits of Americana (such as a valley, an alpine meadow, a river, or a lake) are forever lost or are so transformed as to be reduced to the eventual rubble of our urban environment, the voice of the existing beneficiaries of these environmental wonders should be heard.

Perhaps they will not win. Perhaps the bulldozers of "progress" will plow under all the esthetic wonders of this beautiful land. That is not the present question. The sole question is, who has standing to be heard?

Those who hike the Appalachian Trail into Sunfish Pond, New Jersey, and camp or sleep there, or run the Allagash in Maine, or climb the Guadalupes in West Texas, or who canoe and portage the Quetico Superior in Minnesota, certainly should have standing to defend those natural wonders before courts or agencies, though they live 3,000 miles away. Those who merely are caught up in environmental news or propaganda and flock to defend these waters or areas may be treated differently. That is why these environmental issues should be tended by the inanimate object itself. Then there will be assurances that all of the forms of life which it represents will stand before the court—the pileated woodpecker as well as the coyote and bear, the lemmings as well as the rout in the streams. Those inarticulate members of the ecological group cannot speak. But those people who have so frequented the place as to know its values and wonders will be able to speak for the entire ecological community.

Ecology reflects the land ethic; and Aldo Leopold wrote in *A Sand County Almanac* 204 (1949), "The land ethic simply enlarges the boundaries of the community to include soils, waters, plants, and animals, or collectively, the land."

That, as I see it, is the issue of "standing" in the present case and controversy.

APPENDIX II

The tribe was known to the white man as:	The people called themselves:	The name meant:
Abnaki (Maine)	Alnanbai	men or people
Iroquois (New York)	Ongwanosionmi	we are of the extended lodge
Delaware (New Jersey)	Lenni Lenape	true men
Biloxi (Mississippi)	taneks aya	first people
Tunica (Mississippi)	Yoron	those who are people
Cherokee (Georgia)	ani yun wiya	real people
Illinois (Illinois)	Illinois	men or people
Winnebago (Wisconsin)	Hotcangara	people of the real speech
Chippewa (Minnesota)	anish insubag	spontaneous men
Arikara (North Dakota)	Tanish	the people
Mandan (North Dakota)	Numakaki	people
Sioux (South Dakota)	Lakota	the allies
Pawnee (Nebraska)	Chahiksichahiks	men of men
Kiowa (Oklahoma)	Kiowa	principal people
Wichita (Oklahoma)	wits	man
Comanche (Oklahoma)	nemene	people
Navajo (Arizona)	Dine	the people
Zuni (New Mexico)	a shiwi	the flesh

The tribe was known to the white man as:	*The people called themselves:*	*The name meant:*
Hopi (Arizona)	hopitu	the peaceful ones
Maricopa (Arizona)	Pipatsje	people
Pima (Arizona)	a atam	people
Yavapai (Arizona)	enyaeva	sun people
Washo (Nevada)	washui	person
Arapaho (Wyoming)	Inuna-ina	our people
Nez Percé (Idaho)	Nimipu	the people
Clallam (Washington)	Nu-sklaim	strong people
Skagit (Washington)	Hum-a-luh	the people

BIBLIOGRAPHY

Alexander, Hartley Burr. *The World's Rim*. Omaha: Bison Books, University of Nebraska Press, 1953.

Andrews, Lynn V. *Medicine Woman*. San Francisco: Harper & Row, 1981.

Andrist, Ralph K. *The Long Death*. New York: Macmillan, 1964.

Armstrong, Virginia. *I Have Spoken*. Chicago: Swallow Press, 1971.

Augustine, Saint. *The Confessions*. London: Burns & Oates, 1954.

Berger, Thomas. *Little Big Man*. New York: Delacorte Press, 1979.

Black Hawk. *Autobiography of Ma-ka-tai-me-she-lia-kiak*. St. Louis, Mo.: Press of Continental Printing, 1882.

Borland, Hal. *When the Legends Die*. Philadelphia: Lippincott, 1963.

Brown, Dee. *Bury My Heart at Wounded Knee*. New York: Holt Winston & Rinehart, 1971.

Brown, Joseph Epes. *The Sacred Pipe: Black Elk's Account of the Seven Rites of the Oglala Sioux*. Norman: University of Oklahoma Press, 1953.

Burnette, Robert. *The Tortured Americans*. Englewood Cliffs, N.J.: Prentice-Hall, 1971.

Camus, Albert. *The Rebel*. New York: Vintage Books, 1956.

Cardinal, Harold. *The Unjust Society: The Tragedy of Canadian Indians*. Edmonton, Canada: H.G. Hurtig, 1969.

Carter, Forrest. *The Education of Little Tree*. New York: Delacorte Press/E. Friede, 1976.

Castaneda, Carlos. *A Separate Reality: Further Conversations with Don Juan* New York: Simon & Schuster, 1971.

————. *The Teachings of Don Juan: A Yaqui Way of Knowledge.* Berkeley: University of California Press, 1968.

Collingwood, R. G. *The Idea of Nature.* New York: Dover, 1962.

Corlett, William Thomas. *The Medicine-Man of the American Indians and His Cultural Background.* Baltimore, Md.: C. C. Thomas, 1935.

Cox, Harvey Gallagher. *The Secular City: Secularization and Urbanization in Theological Perspectives.* New York: Macmillan, 1966.

Cullman, Oscar. *Immortality of the Soul or Resurrection of the Dead?* New York: Macmillan, 1958.

Cushman, Dan. *Stay Away, Joe.* Great Falls, Mont.: Stay Away, Joe Publishers, 1953.

de Grazia, Alfred. *The Velikovsky Affair: The Warfare of Science and Scientism.* New Hyde Park, N.Y.: University Books, 1966.

Deloria, Vine, Jr. *Custer Died for Your Sins.* New York: Macmillan, 1969.

Dupre, Louis K. *The Other Dimension.* Garden City, N.Y.: Doubleday, 1972.

Eastman, Charles. *The Soul of the Indian.* Boston: Houghton Mifflin, 1911.

Erdoes, Richard. *Crying for a Dream: The World through Native American Eyes.* Santa Fe, N.M.: Bear & Co., 1990.

————. *The Rain Dance People: The Pueblo Indians, Their Past and Present.* New York: Knopf, 1976.

Fairservis, Walter. *The Ancient Kingdoms of the Nile.* New York: Thomas Y. Crowell, 1962.

Farb, Peter. *Man's Rise to Civilization As Shown by the Indians of North America from Primeval Times to the Coming of the Industrial State.* New York: Dutton, 1968.

Fire, John (Lame Deer), and Richard Erdoes. *Lame Deer, Seeker of Visions.* New York: Simon & Schuster, 1972.

Gaster, Theodor Herzl. *Passover: Its History and Traditions.* New York: Henry Schuman, 1949.

Gordon, Cyrus. *Before Columbus: Links between the Old World and Ancient America.* New York: Crown, 1971.

Heim, Karl. *Christian Faith and Natural Science.* New York: Harper Torchbooks, 1957.

Heine, Heinrich. *Religion and Philsophy in Germany: A Fragment.* Boston: Beacon Press, 1959.

Hill, Ruth Beebe. *Hanta Yo.* Garden City, N.Y.: Doubleday, 1979.

Hodge, Frederick Webb. *Handbook of American Indians North of Mexico,* vol. II. Lanham, Md.: Rowman & Littlefield, 1965.

Houseman, A. E. *A Shropshire Lad.* New York: Grosset & Dunlop, 1932.

Jeans, James. *Physics and Philosophy.* Ann Arbor Papers. Ann Arbor: University of Michigan Press, 1958.

Johnson, A. H. *Whitehead's Theory of Reality.* New York: Dover Publications, 1962.

Josephy, Alvin. *The Indian Heritage of America.* New York: Knopf, 1968.

Jung, Carl. "Wotan," in *Civilization in Transition, Collected Works,* edited by Herbert Read, Michael Fordham, and Gerhard Adler, vol. 10. New York: Pantheon Books, 1953–1979.

Kramer, Samuel Noah. *History Begins at Sumer*. Garden City, N.Y.: Doubleday, 1959.

Kroeber, Theodora. *Ishi in Two Worlds: A Bibliography of the last Wild Indian in North America*. Berkeley: University of California Press, 1976.

Left Handed. *Son of Old Man Hat*. New York: Harcourt, Brace, 1938.

Levitan, Sar A., and Barbara Hetrick. *Big Brother's Indian Programs; with Reservations*. New York: McGraw-Hill, 1971.

Mails, Thomas E. *Sundancing at Rosebud and Pine Ridge*. Sioux Falls, S.D.: Center for Western Studies, 1978.

Matthiessen, Peter. *In the Spirit of Crazy Horse*. New York: Viking Press, 1983.

McLaughlin, James. *My Friend the Indian*. A Salisbury Press Book. Seattle, Wash.: Superior Publishing, 1970.

McLuhan, T. C. *Touch the Earth: A Self-Portrait of Indian Existence*. New York: Outerbridge & Dienstfrey, 1971.

Michener, James. *A Quality of Life*. Philadelphia: Lippincott, 1970.

Momaday, N. Scott. *House Made of Dawn*. New York: Harper & Row, 1968.

Munitz, Milton K. ed. *Theories of the Universe*. Glencoe, Ill.: The Free Press, 1957.

Neihardt, John. *Black Elk Speaks: Being the Life Story of a Holy Man of the Oglala Sioux*. Lincoln: University of Nebraska Press, 1979.

Packard, Vance Oakley. *A Nation of Strangers*. New York: McKay, 1972.

Pedersen, Johannes. *Israel: Its Life and Culture*, vols. III–IV. Translated by Geoffrey Cumberledge. London: Oxford University Press, 1959.

Powell, Peter J. *Sweet Medicine: The Continuing Role of the Sacred Arrows, the Sun Dance, and the Sacred Buffalo Hat in Northern Cheyenne History*. Norman: University of Oklahoma Press, 1979.

Red Fox, Chief. *The Memories of Chief Red Fox*. Introduction by Cash Asher. New York: McGraw-Hill, 1971.

Reich, Charles. *The Greening of America: How the Youth Revolution Is Trying to Make America Livable*. New York: Random House, 1970.

Seton, Ernest Thompson. *The Gospel of the Red Man*. New York: Doubleday Doran, 1936.

Sitchin, Zecharia. *Genesis Revisited: Is Modern Science Catching Up with Ancient Knowledge?* New York: Avon Books, 1990.

———. *The Stairway to Heaven*. New York: St. Martin's Press, 1980.

———. *The Twelfth Planet*. New York: Avon Books, 1978.

———. *The Wars of Gods and Men*. New York: Avon Books, 1985.

Sorkin, Alan. *American Indians and Federal Aid*. Washington, D.C.: Brookings Institute, 1971.

Spicer, Edward Holland. *A Short History of the Indians of the United States*. New York: Van Nostrand Reinhold, 1969.

Standing Bear, Luther. *Land of the Spotted Eagle*. Lincoln: University of Nebraska Press, 1978.

Steiner, Stan. *The New Indians*. New York: Harper & Row, 1967.

Storm, Hyemeyohsts. *Seven Arrows*. New York: Random House, 1970.

Talayesva, Don C. *Sun Chief*. New Haven, Conn.: Yale University Press, 1942

Tillich, Paul. *Systematic Theology*, vol. II. Chicago: University of Chicago Press, 1957.

Toffler, Alvin. *Future Shock*. New York: Random House, 1970.

Tompkins, Peter. *Secrets of the Great Pyramid*. New York: Harper & Row, 1971.

Tooker, Elisabeth. *The Iroquois Ceremonial of Midwinter*. Syracuse, N.Y.: Syracuse University Press, 1970.

Uncommon Controversy. A report prepared for the American Friends Service Committee. Seattle: University of Washington Press, 1970.

Underhill, Ruth. *Red Man's Religion: Beliefs and Practices of the Indians North of Mexico*. Chicago: University of Chicago Press, 1965.

Velikovsky, Immanuel. *Earth in Upheaval*. From His Ages in Chaos Series. Garden City, N.Y.: Doubleday, 1955.

———. *Oedipus and Akhnaton*. Garden City, N.Y.: Doubleday, 1960.

Wallace, Anthony F.C. *The Death and Rebirth of the Seneca*. New York: Knopf, 1970.

Washburn, Wilcomb. *The Indian and the White Man*. Garden City, N.Y.: Doubleday, 1964.

———. *Red Man's Land, White Man's Law: A Study of the Past and Present Status of the American Indian*. Garden City, N.Y.: Doubleday, 1971.

Waters, Frank, and Oswald White Bear Fredericks. *Book of the Hopi*. New York: Viking Press, 1963.

Wills, Garry. *Bare Ruined Choirs: Doubt, Prophecy, and Radical Religions*. Garden City, N.Y.: Doubleday, 1972.

———. *Nixon Agonistes: The Crisis of the Self-Made Man*. Boston: Houghton Mifflin, 1970.

Wise, Jennings. *Red Man in the New World*. Edited by Vine Deloria, Jr. New York: Macmillan, 1971.

INDEX